The RSC Shakespeare

WILLIAM SHAKESPEARE

HENRY V

Edited by
Jonathan Bate and Eric Rasmussen

Introduced by Jonathan Bate

Macmillan

Published 2010 by
MACMILLAN PUBLISHERS LTD
registered in England, company number 785998, of Houndmills, Basingstoke, Hampshire RG21 6XS.
Companies and representatives throughout the world

ISBN-13 978–0–230–24382–8 paperback

This book is printed on paper suitable for recycling and made from fully managed and sustained forest sources. Logging, pulping and manufacturing processes are expected to conform to the environmental regulations of the country of origin.

A catalogue record for this book is available from the British Library.

10   9   8   7   6   5   4   3   2   1
19   18   17   16   15   14   13   12   11   10

Printed in China

CONTENTS

INTRODUCTION

THE THEATRE OF WAR

Henry V has become synonymous with English patriotism. A dashing young king achieves a stunning military victory against all odds, stirring his men to impossible valour through sheer rhetorical force. The phrases have become legendary: 'Once more unto the breach, dear friends, once more'; 'Cry "God for Harry, England, and Saint George!"'; 'We few, we happy few, we band of brothers'. Whereas all Shakespeare's other history plays of the 1590s portray an England riven by faction and anxiety over rightful succession to the throne, here the nation seems united and all-conquering.

Perhaps no other Shakespeare play has such a simple plot: King Harry makes his claim for France, sees off a small conspiracy, sets sail, takes Harfleur, wins the battle of Agincourt and marries the defeated king's daughter. The cast consists almost entirely of his loyal army and his French enemies, among whom the dauphin in particular is a parodic reprise of the fiery Hotspur of *Henry IV Part I*. Yet, as so often with Shakespeare, a wealth of reservations are held within that 'almost'. *Henry IV Part II* had ended with an epilogue promising a continuation of the story with Sir John Falstaff in it: the fat knight's absence casts a shadow across the king's triumphs. (We do not know why Shakespeare failed to fulfil his promise: it might have been because he didn't want Falstaff's presence to overshadow the military glory, or it might have been because the comic actor for whom the part may have been written, Will Kempe, had suddenly left the company.)

The play does not begin with a ceremonial entrance and a large-scale royal court scene. First the Chorus appears alone on the bare stage. The audience are invited to reflect upon the fact that what they are about to witness is performance, not reality, and that their imaginary forces will be necessary in order to transform stage and playing company into battlefield and army. The play is intended to work upon us as King Harry works upon his followers: the dazzling power of words creates the triumph out of extremely limited resources.

Between each act the Chorus returns to remind us that it is all a theatrical trick: we only suppose that we have been transported to France and that the little band of players and extras constitute a great army on the march or fighting to the death in hand-to-hand combat. Players, as Macbeth and Prospero will remind later Shakespearean audiences, are but shadows. After two or three turns of the hourglass, the revels end and the action vanishes like a dream. So too with Harry's triumph: the closing chorus, an artfully turned sonnet, compares the imaginative work of the author ('In little room confining mighty men') with the brevity of the victorious king's reign ('Small time, but in that small most greatly lived/This star of England'). Could it then be that the secret of Harry's success is linguistic might rather than the right of his cause?

The action proper commences with the representatives of the church confirming the 'reformation' of the king, his conversion to piety from the 'wildness' of the *Henry IV* plays, in which he had been seen as a wayward youth in the company of lowlife characters in London's East End. Now he has transformed himself into a master of divinity, political affairs and the theory of war. The dialogue of the bishops also introduces another theme, familiar from the historical reformation of the sixteenth century: the sequestration of ecclesiastical assets by the state. This precipitates a political deal: the archbishop will provide legal justification for the king's proposed invasion of France and in return the crown will take the side of the church in their financial dispute with parliament. The whole apparatus of justification by precedent, descent and debate over the applicability of the Salic law, elaborated in the archbishop's interminable speech in the following scene, is a charade acted out for politic ends. The king has a one-line question – 'May I with right and conscience make this claim?' – and he gets the answer he wants to hear: yes. He is not interested in the small print.

By starting the action with the scheming bishops, Shakespeare suggests that the motivation for war is more a matter of political pragmatism than high principle. King Harry is anxious about a possible Scottish incursion and he is aware that his own hold on the throne is insecure – hence the need to reveal the iron fist in his velvet glove by dispatching the traitors Cambridge, Scroop and Grey. Their unmasking is achieved by means of a piece of theatre that shows Harry's capacity for both mercy and stern justice. For all the talk of ancient rights to France and the need to bounce back the insult of the tennis balls, one cannot help suspecting that the real driving force behind the war is that recommended by the king's father on his death-bed:

> ... Therefore, my Harry,
> Be it thy course to busy giddy minds
> With foreign quarrels, that action, hence borne out,
> May waste the memory of the former days.
>
> *(Henry IV Part II*, Act 4 scene 2)

There is nothing like an overseas military adventure to unite a divided nation.

Prince Hal's riotous behaviour in the *Henry IV* plays is now revealed to have been an elaborate game, a piece of play-acting. He continues to play games once he is king: his handling of the traitors in the second act and the business of the glove in the cap after Agincourt are theatrical devices designed to demonstrate his quasi-magical power of seeing into his subjects' souls. The manner in which an actor plays the part of King Harry will be largely determined by the extent to which he plays up the character's actorliness. The wooing of Katherine is a crux in this regard: how much of a *performance* is the combination of charm, wit, boyish embarrassment and delight in power ('in loving me, you should love the friend of France, for I love France so well that I will not part with a village of it')? Or is Harry genuinely smitten with Kate?

The king's mastery comes above all from what the archbishop calls 'his sweet and honeyed sentences'. Rhetorical force is his greatest gift: he can debate, cajole, command, inspire. Shakespeare gives him more than three times as many words as any other character in the play. Only Hamlet can match Harry in the ease with which he moves between highly-wrought verse and conversational prose. Many a modern general has reached for the Crispin's day oration in preparing his men to go into battle: Laurence Olivier's 1944 film, dedicated to the British, American and other Allied troops who were liberating Europe from the Nazis, is only the most renowned of the frequent military appropriations of the play (it was reputedly at Winston Churchill's insistence that Olivier cut the scene with the three traitors – at such a critical historical moment, there had to be unity in the Allied ranks). Even hardened cynics find themselves becoming patriotic when the king addresses his band of brothers, especially in film when the words are further pumped up by sweeping camera action and rousing music.

But the words are not just a form of music. There is sharp political intelligence at work. So, for instance, 'Once more unto the breach, dear friends, once more' is carefully modulated in three parts. The 'dear friends' with which it begins are the king's immediate kinsmen and closest followers. They set the lead example. Attention then turns to the aristocracy and gentry, the 'noblest English', whose role is to 'Be copy now to men of grosser [i.e. less high-class] blood / And teach them how to war'. Then come the 'yeomen' and finally 'the mean and base'. All will be of 'noble lustre' if they surge forward into the breach in Harfleur's wall. The speech thus enacts the chain of command down the ranks. It offers a textbook image of the officer class leading from the front by example. Even lowly Corporal Bardolph is momentarily inspired. But Nym, Pistol and Falstaff's boy are not. They stop in their tracks and have to be physically beaten to the breach by loyal Captain Fluellen. The power of the king's rhetoric is thus called into question.

Fluellen believes in fighting war by the book. His modern equivalent would be a liberal-minded army officer intent upon fighting according to the rules of the Geneva convention. But his very mode of thinking exposes cracks in the king's moral armour. King Harry of Monmouth is compared to Alexander the Great of Macedon, not only because they are both great warriors (who both come from places beginning with 'M', each of which has a river running through it, 'and there is salmons in both'), but also because 'as Alexander killed his friend Cleitus, being in his ales and his cups, so also Harry Monmouth, being in his right wits and his good judgements, turned away the fat knight with the great belly-doublet'. The audience is thus reminded that the price of Harry's greatness is the killing of Falstaff's heart.

There is also the matter of the killing of the French prisoners, strikingly omitted not only from Olivier's wartime film but also from Kenneth Branagh's generally more hard-edged portrayal of Agin-court in his 1989 movie. For Fluellen, the French army's killing of the boys and the baggage-handlers is 'expressly against the law of arms'. Gower replies that, since the French have broken the rules, the English have been forced to do so as well: 'wherefore the king, most worthily, hath caused every soldier to cut his prisoner's throat. O, 'tis a gallant king!' But the text is quite explicit that King Harry gives the order to kill the prisoners before he hears of the attack on the camp followers. The reason for their summary slaughter is that every last soldier is needed to cope with the arrival of French reinforcements. It is a pragmatic decision, not a gallant or a worthy one. So too at Harfleur earlier: though a threat rather than an action, the idea of raping the maidens and massacring the innocents of the city does not immediately conjure up the terms 'gallant' or 'worthily'.

'THOU IDLE CEREMONY'

Most searching of all is the debate between the disguised Harry 'le Roi' and the common soldiers, John Bates and Michael Williams, on the night before the battle. In the sixteenth century there was a heated debate about whether the law took primacy over the monarch or whether the monarch was the embodiment of the law. Was it ever justifiable to depose a monarch? If a king was unjust, then he could be described as a 'tyrant'. In that case, it was sometimes argued, the people, or at least the magistrates, had the right to remove him. Both biblical and classical precedents could be found for such a belief, and debates regarding it swirled in the political treatises of the sixteenth century, not least because John Calvin's Protestant theology had broken the chain of association between God, Pope and king. Shakespeare's history plays and tragedies are full of usurpers. They are usually ambitious and self-serving disciples of the much-maligned Machiavelli. But this does not make Shakespeare an uncritical apologist for the divine right of kings: when a Richard II or a Henry VI fails to fulfil the responsibilities of sovereignty, the state totters.

As the son of a usurper, Henry V is acutely conscious of the fragility of his own claim to the throne. Since he cannot rely on the theory of divine right – that belonged to Richard II, not Henry IV – he has to fall back on rational argument and what was known as 'natural law' (as there is an order and a hierarchy in nature, so must there be in human society). His debate with Williams and Bates throws up some awkward questions. 'Methinks I could not die anywhere so contented as in the king's company, his cause being just and his quarrel honourable' says the disguised 'Harry le Roi'. 'That's more than we know', replies Williams: only God can ultimately judge whether the cause is just. Bates says that it is enough to 'know we are the king's subjects'. This has the advantage for the commoner that 'If his cause be wrong, our obedience to the king wipes the crime of it out of us'. Williams will not let the point go:

> But if the cause be not good, the king himself hath a heavy reckoning to make, when all those legs and arms and heads, chopped off in a battle, shall join together at the latter day and cry all, 'We died at such a place' — some swearing, some crying for a surgeon, some upon their wives left poor behind them, some upon the debts they owe, some upon their children rawly left. I am afeard there are few die well that die in a battle, for how can they charitably dispose of anything, when blood is their argument? Now, if these men do not die well, it will be a black matter for the king that led them to it — who to disobey were against all proportion of subjection.

Henry replies with a series of analogies seeking to prove that 'Every subject's duty is the king's, but every subject's soul is his own'. He is, however, shaken by the debate, and in soliloquy after the common soldiers have left he confronts the possibility that the whole edifice of sovereignty is nothing more than a quasi-theatrical performance:

> And what have kings, that privates have not too,
> Save ceremony, save general ceremony?
> And what art thou, thou idle ceremony?
> What kind of god art thou, that suffer'st more
> Of mortal griefs than do thy worshippers?
> What are thy rents? What are thy comings in?
> O ceremony, show me but thy worth.
> What? Is thy soul of adoration?
> Art thou aught else but place, degree and form,
> Creating awe and fear in other men?
> Wherein thou art less happy being feared
> Than they in fearing.
> What drink'st thou oft, instead of homage sweet,
> But poisoned flattery? O, be sick, great greatness,
> And bid thy ceremony give thee cure!

What would a king be without 'ceremony' – without coronations and state funerals, investitures and rituals of obligation? What would be the basis of sovereignty if ceremony were seen as an idle waste of time or even, by punning implication, as an 'idol', a false God worshipped in place of the true God before whom all men and women should show equal humility? The notion that the 'ceremony' on which kingship depends may be a device for the creation of 'awe and fear in other men' is deeply machiavellian. It is a sign of Shakespeare's deep political cunning that he should have put this thought into the mouth of his most heroic king, not that of one of his machiavellian schemers or usurpers (let alone the mouth of Machiavelli himself, as Christopher Marlowe had done in the prologue to his hugely successful *Jew of Malta*).

After the battle, the king succeeds in embarrassing, and, with typical double-handedness, then offering to reward, Williams. But he never finds a full answer to the point: every subject's duty is the king's while every subject's soul is his own, but the fact remains that bloody battle is not a place for 'dying well' in the sense of drawing up one's spiritual accounts and making peace with God.

The complex scene on the eve of Agincourt reveals that for Shakespeare politics was a matter for serious debate. And debate is premised on the notion of opposing points of view, each having an element of validity. Shakespeare does not impose his own political views. He leaves a space for the audience to make up their own minds, and that is inherently a way of giving the power of free thought to the people.

The dangers of open debate were all too apparent in an England fractured by religious dissension. Queen Elizabeth, her council and her magistrates were all too aware of the uncertainty of their hold upon power. They could not rely on divine right theory alone. After all, Mary Queen of Scots had been expelled by her Protestant subjects and Elizabeth had (eventually, reluctantly) countenanced her execution. In the Netherlands, meanwhile, the English had taken the side of the people as they rose against their king, Philip II of Spain. Insurrection was always a dangerous matter.

'THE GENERAL OF OUR GRACIOUS EMPRESS'

The 1580s was a decade of war in Flanders, where the English fought with the Dutchmen against the might of Catholic Spain. The 1590s was a decade of war in Ireland, where the Earl of Essex struggled in vain to quell the rebellion of the irrepressible Hugh O'Neill, Earl of Tyrone. For the first half of his career, all through the last years of old Queen Elizabeth's reign, Shakespeare was a war poet. He had an obsessive interest in military life. Richard III, Titus Andronicus and all his sons, Othello, Iago and Cassio, Macbeth and the other Thanes, Hamlet's armoured father and young Fortinbras, King Lear, Julius Caesar, Brutus and Cassius, Mark Antony and Octavius Caesar, Coriolanus and Aufidius, Alcibiades, Henry IV and Sir John Falstaff, dozens of dukes, earls and knights in the ranks of the history plays, Benedick and his colleagues in *Much Ado about Nothing*, Bertram and Parolles in *All's Well that Ends Well*: all are soldiers; some by profession and others by force of circumstance. All are defined to a greater or lesser degree by the hunger to fill the vacuum left by battle and by war as the defining male action (which is not to say that Shakespeare failed to create a good line in female soldiers – Queen Margaret in the *Henry VI* plays, Tamora Queen of Goths, Joan of Arc, Cordelia and her sisters, Cleopatra). But the most famous of all his soldiers was King Henry V.

At the beginning of the fifth act of King Harry's play, the Chorus describes his triumphal procession through the streets of London upon his return to England after his astonishing victory on the field of Agincourt. At Blackheath, the audience is told, the king's lords urged him to have 'His bruisèd helmet and his bended sword' borne before him through the city. Harry forbids it,

> Being free from vainness and self-glorious pride;
> Giving full trophy, signal and ostent
> Quite from himself to God . . . .

This accords with his attribution of the victory to God on hearing news of the disproportionate numbers of the French and English dead ('And not to us, but to thy arm alone, / Ascribe we all'). And it accords with historical reality: in 1415 Henry V made solemn progress to the shrine in Westminster Abbey that contained the bones of Edward the Confessor. Despite the loudly cheering citizens, triumphal arches, and fountains flowing with wine, not once during the five-hour procession across London did Henry smile. All glory should go to God and Saint George, he said, and no thanks should be given to him.

Shakespeare accordingly declined the opportunity to present a spectacular victory procession on stage. Instead, he devoted the fifth act to the humbler and messier matter of the quarrel between Fluellen and Pistol, then the carving up of the victor's spoils in France. Fluellen and Pistol are effectively surrogates for King Henry and his old companion Sir John Falstaff (Fluellen is a soldier and a Welshman, utterly loyal to the king who was once Prince Harry of Monmouth, while Pistol is a braggart, a coward and a drinker, bearing the memory of riotous Prince Hal of Eastcheap). The 'Welsh correction' of the 'English condition' is the final episode in what might be called the battle for the soul of the king between the spirit of Hal and that of Harry, an inner and outer struggle that goes right back to the beginning of *Henry IV Part I*. Pistol's ignominious exit replays the rejection of Falstaff in a sour minor key, even as the focus on the common soldiers returning from the war remains in keeping with the play's refusal to see only from the point of view of kings and earls and those who have power.

The play ends with an epilogue in which the Chorus reminds the audience that King Harry's life was all too short and that he was succeeded by the child king, Henry VI, whose state was mangled and mismanaged by so many rival lords 'That they lost France and made his England bleed, / Which oft our stage hath shown'. The latter line is a jokey reference to the fact that Shakespeare had made his theatrical name with the *Henry VI* plays. There is a strong possibility that Shakespeare played the part of the Chorus himself: such lines as 'Thus far, with rough and all-unable pen, / Our bending author hath pursued the story' would come well and wittily from his lips. Whether or not he spoke the lines, in writing them Shakespeare gives the sense of coming full circle, bringing his long cycle of English history plays to a close. When his fellow-actors collected his plays in the First Folio after his death, they arranged the English history plays in sequence not of composition but of the chronology of events. Readers of the Folio would have turned the page from this mention of Henry V's 'small time' of life and found *Henry VI Part I* beginning with his funeral procession. In all probability the wooden coffin in that procession would have been adorned with 'His bruisèd helmet and his bended sword' in order to evoke his military greatness. These would of course have been stage props, but their design could easily have been based on their historical originals.

Whenever Shakespeare or a member of his acting company or his audience went into Westminster Abbey (as many of them, Shakespeare included, may well have done early in 1599 for the funeral of the national poet, Edmund Spenser), they would have seen Henry V's saddle, helm and shield. These objects, his so-called 'funeral achievements', were displayed on the wooden beam above the chantry where he was laid. Katherine of Valois, his queen, the real-life original of the charming Kate who is wooed in the final scene of the play, lay nearby in an open coffin of loose boards beside him (a generation after Shakespeare, the diarist Samuel Pepys saw her mummified remains and was allowed to kiss her lips).

The prominence of the relics in the Abbey is a reminder that the story of Henry V was very much alive and significant in 1599. Shakespeare boldly stressed the contemporaneity of the figure of conquering Harry in some other lines in the chorus at the beginning of the final act, lines that allude both back to ancient Rome and forward to the moment when the play was first performed. By so doing, they constitute the most explicit and striking topical allusion anywhere in his works:

> ... But now behold,
> In the quick forge and working-house of thought,
> How London doth pour out her citizens.
> The mayor and all his brethren in best sort,
> Like to the senators of th'antique Rome,
> With the plebeians swarming at their heels,
> Go forth and fetch their conqu'ring Caesar in:
> As by a lower but by loving likelihood,
> Were now the general of our gracious empress,
> As in good time he may, from Ireland coming,
> Bringing rebellion broachèd on his sword,
> How many would the peaceful city quit,
> To welcome him? Much more, and much more cause,
> Did they this Harry ....

Few audience members could have had any doubt what the Chorus was talking about. The 'gracious empress' is Queen Elizabeth and 'the general' is the Earl of Essex – the queen's sometime favourite, embodiment of the martial code of chivalry and honour, leader of the war party in the longstanding debate at court over how to proceed in relation to Spain. The reference to Essex's Irish campaign against the 'rebellion' of Tyrone is unmistakable.

Shakespeare does not let go of his habitual political caution. It is a 'likelihood', not a certainty, that Essex will return from Ireland bringing rebellion broached on his sword (in fact, he returned in ignominious failure a few months after the premiere of the play). In the mind's eye of Shakespeare's Chorus it is an open question how many people will turn out to cheer Essex. In Elizabethan punctuation a question mark served the function of both exclamation and interrogation: Shakespeare's political slipperiness becomes visible if we think about the difference in tone between the equally legitimate modernizations of punctuation, 'How many ... To welcome him!' and 'How many ... To welcome him?'

But, for all the hedging, there is still a boldness in the comparison. When 'conquering Caesar' crossed the Rubicon and returned to Rome, there was talk of him seizing an imperial crown and Brutus and his friends had to take drastic action to save the republic. Shakespeare dramatized that story in the other historical drama he brought to the London stage in 1599, *Julius Caesar*. Conversely, there were moments in late Elizabethan court politics when exasperation with the old, childless queen's refusal to name an heir led some to wonder whether there might not be a future for England in some form of Roman-style republican government, with the Privy Council serving as its Senate and a strong man such as Essex in the role of Consul.

Essex was widely perceived as a heroic figure, a no-nonsense military man. He was greeted with acclaim whenever he rode through the streets of London, as he did before heading off on his French campaign in 1591. Intriguingly, Shakespeare had previously created an image of Henry V's father, Henry IV, formerly Henry Bullingbrook, that was highly evocative of this aspect of Essex. At the climax of *Richard II*, he describes Bullingbrook in London:

> ... the duke, great Bullingbrook,
> Mounted upon a hot and fiery steed
> Which his aspiring rider seemed to know,
> With slow but stately pace kept on his course,
> While all tongues cried 'God save thee, Bullingbrook!'

There was no precedent in Shakespeare's chronicle source for this striking image of Bullingbrook's popularity. It has been invented in order to establish a contrast with the deposed Richard II, who follows in after with no man crying 'God save him' as dust and rubbish are thrown out of the windows on his head.

In the *Henry IV* plays, however, Shakespeare conspicuously dropped the image of Bullingbrook, now king, as a popular figure. Far from showing himself among his people and exemplifying strong government, Henry IV skulks in his palace as his kingdom disintegrates around him, the penalty for his usurpation of his throne. The horseman and populist is his son Hal, who goes on to become Henry V, leading his men to triumph in battle. The language of the fifth act Chorus' description of his return to London after the victory at Agincourt echoes that of the speech about his father at the corresponding moment in *Richard II*. As so often in Shakespeare, the wheel of history comes full circle. But, unusually for Shakespeare, it also comes directly into the present. Regardless of Shakespeare's semi-concealed political intentions in making the allusion – one gets the sense that he is only somewhere a little over halfway to being, as his sometime patron the Earl of Southampton certainly was, a supporter of the Earl of Essex – it is easy to see how the two remarkably similar passages in *Richard II* and *Henry V* could have been perceived as pro-Essex and therefore why the Essex faction turned to the Chamberlain's Men and asked them to stage a Shakespeare play on the day in February 1601 that turned out to be the eve of the abortive rebellion against Queen Elizabeth that cost Essex his life on the scaffold.

As Nicholas Hytner suggests in his interview about his 2003 National Theatre production of the play, Shakespeare's allusion to Essex implicitly licenses producers and directors of *Henry V* to establish resonances with the wars of their own time. Though there is a long history of patriotic productions, a close examination of the text provides ample justification for readings and performances that are sceptical and anxious about the values of war.

'WHAT ISH MY NATION?'

Where *Henry IV* began with rebellion coming from Scotland (the Douglas) and Wales (Owen Glendower), *Henry V* brings the whole of the British Isles together in the fight against France. Included in King Henry's army is a quartet representing England (Gower), Wales (Fluellen), Scotland (Jamy) and Ireland (MacMorris). But we cannot say for sure that the play is celebrating the unification of the four nations into one, for during the campaign against France, King

Harry's army is not without its tensions. The Irish MacMorris, in particular, is an odd man out, not even at peace with the affable Fluellen:

> FLUELLEN Captain MacMorris, I think, look you, under your correction, there is not many of your nation—
>
> MACMORRIS Of my nation? What ish my nation? Ish a villain and a bastard and a knave and a rascal? What ish my nation? Who talks of my nation?

In the chorus to the fifth act, the Earl of Essex is seemingly celebrated because as the audience is watching the play in London in 1599 he is broaching the Irish on his sword. Yet here in the body of the third act, Shakespeare gives a voice to Ireland. Or rather, he questions England's – for the Welsh Fluellen in his loyalty to Harry of Monmouth, once Prince of Wales and now king of England, speaks for England – he questions England's right to speak for Ireland. What Englishman or anglicized Welshman dare talk of MacMorris's nation? What kind of a nation can Ireland be when the Irish are construed by the English as villains and bastards and knaves and rascals? And that is how the dominant voice of Elizabethan England's national poet, Edmund Spenser, did construe them in his dialogue of the mid-1590s, *A View of the Present State of Ireland*. But even Spenser had his counter-voices. *A View* is written in the form of a dialogue and it is more sharply critical of the 'Old English' settlers in Ireland than the Irish themselves, while in *The Faerie Queene* there is a Savage Nation resembling Ireland, but also a Savage Man who is the noblest man.

As for Shakespeare, he is all counter-voice. When MacMorris says 'What ish my nation?' Ireland in its anguish is allowed to speak, just as in *The Tempest* Shakespeare's most beautiful poetry is put into the mouth of a 'savage and deformed slave' whose name evokes Caribbean and Cannibal. Because Shakespeare's own allegiances are so elusive, because every one of his voices has its counter-voice – Fluellen his MacMorris, King Harry his Michael Williams, Prospero his Caliban – he has become the voice of many positions, whether political, ethnic or ethical.

Perhaps surprisingly, given the amount of space that is given to the king's stirring speeches and the archbishop's convoluted history lesson, *Henry V* has almost as a high proportion of prose as the two parts of *Henry IV*. And it is the prose scenes that are the most emotionally engaging: Hostess Quickly's simultaneously comic and moving account of Falstaff's death, the moment of tenderness as the women say farewell to their men going off to war, the figure of Fluellen (portrayed with great affection for his loyalty and professionalism, yet simultaneously teased for his pedantry in the history and theory of warfare), the utterly authentic combination of fear, common sense and bloody-mindedness shown by the common soldiers in their debate with the disguised king on the night before the battle.

Falstaff is dead, but his spirit is reanimated in his friends who follow the wars to France. Throughout the *Henry IV/V* trilogy, there is an under-commentary cutting away at Prince Hal's growth into the role of warrior-king and patriot: a confused but vibrant prose voice is counterpointed against the polished verse of law, order and military glory. It is a voice summed up most concisely in the words of Falstaff's sometime page. In response to the king's cry that battle is the opportunity to achieve immortal fame, the boy says 'Would I were in an ale-house in London. I would give all my fame for a pot of ale and safety'. This is not just the sentiment of a pint-sized Falstaff out from under Arthur's bosom: it is the voice of the foot-soldier in every age. After Agincourt, the king thanks God for the miracle whereby fewer than thirty English have been killed in the battle. In his listing of the dead, he does not mention Falstaff's proxies, yet they are the ones whom the audience mourns most: Bardolph and Nym, hanged; the boy, killed with the luggage; Quickly or Doll,[*] dead in the spital of a malady of France. They have died not for Harry's but for Falstaff's England; they have fought not for a palace or parliament in Westminster but for an ale-house in Eastcheap.

---

[*] Pistol is married to Nell Quickly, but says in Act 5 that 'my Doll is dead i'th'spital/Of malady of France': this is one of the numerous cruxes where Shakespeare or the printer may have muddled a name or where there may be purposeful dramatic play. The sense of loss suggests that he is talking about his wife but death by way of sexually transmitted disease (the French malady) is much likelier for the whore Doll Tearsheet than the hostess Quickly, and has already been prepared for by Pistol's lines in Act 2 scene 1 about Doll in 'the powdering-tub of infamy'. Either way, the point is to make Pistol into the last survivor of the Eastcheap cronies.

ABOUT THE TEXT

Shakespeare endures through history. He illuminates later times as well as his own. He helps us to understand the human condition. But he cannot do this without a good text of the plays. Without editions there would be no Shakespeare. That is why every twenty years or so throughout the last three centuries there has been a major new edition of his complete works. One aspect of editing is the process of keeping the texts up to date – modernizing the spelling, punctuation and typography (though not, of course, the actual words), providing explanatory notes in the light of changing educational practices (a generation ago, most of Shakespeare's classical and biblical allusions could be assumed to be generally understood, but now they can't).

But because Shakespeare did not personally oversee the publication of his plays, editors also have to make decisions about the relative authority of the early printed editions. Half of the sum of his plays only appeared posthumously, in the elaborately produced First Folio text of 1623, the original 'Complete Works' prepared for the press by Shakespeare's fellow-actors, the people who knew the plays better than anyone else. The other half had appeared in print in his lifetime, in the more compact and cheaper form of 'Quarto' editions, some of which reproduced good quality texts, others of which were to a greater or lesser degree garbled and error-strewn. In the case of a few plays there are hundreds of differences between the Quarto and Folio editions, some of them far from trivial.

If you look at printers' handbooks from the age of Shakespeare, you quickly discover that one of the first rules was that, whenever possible, compositors were recommended to set their type from existing printed books rather than manuscripts. This was the age before mechanical typesetting, where each individual letter had to be picked out by hand from the compositor's case and placed on a stick (upside down and back to front) before being laid on the press. It was an age of murky rush-light and of manuscripts written in a secretary hand that had dozens of different, hard-to-decipher forms. Printers' lives were a lot easier when they were reprinting existing books rather than struggling with handwritten copy. Easily the quickest way to have created the First Folio would have been simply to reprint those eighteen plays that had already appeared in Quarto and only work from manuscript on the other eighteen.

But that is not what happened. Whenever Quartos were used, playhouse 'promptbooks' were also consulted and stage directions copied in from them. And in the case of several major plays where a reasonably well-printed Quarto was available, the Folio printers were instructed to work from an alternative, playhouse-derived manuscript. This meant that the whole process of producing the first complete Shakespeare took months, even years, longer than it might have done. But for the men overseeing the project, John Hemings and Henry Condell, friends and fellow-actors who had been remembered in Shakespeare's will, the additional labour and cost were worth the effort for the sake of producing an edition that was close to the practice of the theatre. They wanted all the plays in print so that people could, as they wrote in their prefatory address to the reader, 'read him and again and again', but they also wanted 'the great variety of readers' to work from texts that were close to the theatre-life for which Shakespeare originally intended them. For this reason, the *RSC Shakespeare*, in both *Complete Works* and individual volumes, uses the Folio as base text wherever possible. Significant Quarto variants are, however, noted in the Textual Notes.

Henry V is one of those plays that was first published in a Quarto text of uncertain status. Some scholars call it a 'bad' text, others a 'short' one. It seems to have been 'unauthorized' and has been seen as a 'memorial reconstruction' as opposed to a text based on the playwright's script. The Quarto offers invaluable, if inscrutable, testimony as to the early stage history of the play, but all modern editors begin with the Folio text.

The following notes highlight various aspects of the editorial process and indicate conventions used in the text of this edition:

Lists of Parts are supplied in the First Folio for only six plays, not including *Henry V*, so the list here is editorially supplied. Capitals indicate that part of the name which is used for speech headings in the script (thus 'Duke of EXETER, the king's uncle').

Locations are provided by the Folio for only two plays. Eighteenth-century editors, working in an age of elaborately realistic stage sets, were the first to provide detailed locations. Given that Shakespeare wrote for a bare stage and often an imprecise sense of place, we have relegated locations to the explanatory notes at the foot of the page, where they are given at the beginning of each scene where the imaginary location is different from the one before.

Act and Scene Divisions were provided in the Folio in a much more thoroughgoing way than in the Quartos. Sometimes, however, they were erroneous or omitted; corrections and additions supplied by editorial tradition are indicated by square brackets. Five-act division is based on a classical model, and act breaks provided the opportunity to replace the candles in the indoor Blackfriars playhouse which the King's Men used after 1608, but Shakespeare did not necessarily think in terms of a five-part structure of dramatic composition. The Folio convention is that a scene ends when the stage is empty. Nowadays, partly under the influence of film, we tend to consider a scene to be a dramatic unit that ends with either a change of imaginary location or a significant passage of time within the narrative. Shakespeare's fluidity of composition accords well with this convention, so in addition to act and scene numbers we provide a *running scene* count in the right margin at the beginning of each new scene, in the typeface used for editorial directions. Where there is a scene break caused by a momentary bare stage, but the location does not change and extra time does not pass, we use the convention *running scene continues*. There is inevitably a degree of editorial judgment in making such calls, but the system is very valuable in suggesting the pace of the plays.

Speakers' Names are often inconsistent in Folio. We have regularized speech headings, but retained an element of deliberate inconsistency in entry directions, in order to give the flavour of Folio.

Verse is indicated by lines that do not run to the right margin and by capitalization of each line. The Folio printers sometimes set verse as prose, and vice versa (either out of misunderstanding or for reasons of space). We have silently corrected in such cases, although in some instances there is ambiguity, in which case we have leaned towards the preservation of Folio layout. Folio sometimes uses contraction ('turnd' rather than 'turned') to indicate whether or not the final '-ed' of a past participle is sounded, an area where there is variation for the sake of the five-beat iambic pentameter rhythm. We use the convention of a grave accent to indicate sounding (thus 'turnèd' would be two syllables), but would urge actors not to overstress. In cases where one speaker ends with a verse half-line and the next begins with the other half of the pentameter, editors since the late eighteenth century have indented the second line. We have abandoned this convention, since the Folio does not use it, and nor did actors' cues in the Shakespearean theatre. An exception is made when the second speaker actively interrupts or completes the first speaker's sentence.

Spelling is modernized, but older forms are occasionally maintained where necessary for rhythm or aural effect.

Punctuation in Shakespeare's time was as much rhetorical as grammatical. 'Colon' was originally a term for a unit of thought in an argument. The semi-colon was a new unit of punctuation (some of the Quartos lack them altogether). We have modernized punctuation throughout, but have given more weight to Folio punctuation than many editors, since, though not Shakespearean, it reflects the usage of his period. In particular, we have used the colon far more than many editors: it is exceptionally useful as a way of indicating how many Shakespearean speeches unfold clause by clause in a developing argument that gives the illusion of enacting the process of thinking in the moment. We have also kept in mind the origin of punctuation in classical times as a way of assisting the actor and orator: the comma suggests the briefest of pauses for breath, the colon a middling one and a full stop or period a longer pause. Semi-colons, by contrast, belong to an era of punctuation that was only just coming in during Shakespeare's time and that is coming to an end now: we have accordingly only used them where they occur in our copy-texts (and not always then). Dashes are sometimes used for parenthetical interjections where the Folio has brackets. They are also used for interruptions and changes in train of thought. Where a change of addressee occurs within a speech, we have used a dash preceded by a full stop (or occasionally another form of punctuation). Often the identity of the respective addressees is obvious from the context. When it is not, this has been indicated in a marginal stage direction.

Entrances and Exits are fairly thorough in Folio, which has accordingly been followed as faithfully as possible. Where characters are omitted or corrections are necessary, this is indicated by square brackets (e.g. '[*and Attendants*]'). *Exit* is sometimes silently normalized to *Exeunt* and *Manet* anglicized to 'remains'. We trust Folio positioning of entrances and exits to a greater degree than most editors.

Editorial Stage Directions such as stage business, asides, indications of addressee and of characters' position on the gallery stage are only used sparingly in Folio. Other editions mingle directions of this kind with original Folio and Quarto directions, sometimes marking them by means of square brackets. We have sought to distinguish what could be described as *directorial* interventions of this kind from Folio-style directions (either original or supplied) by placing them in the right margin in a different typeface. There is a degree of subjectivity about which directions are of which kind, but the procedure is intended as a reminder to the reader and the actor that Shakespearean stage directions are often dependent upon editorial inference alone and are not set in stone. We also depart from editorial tradition in sometimes admitting uncertainty and thus printing permissive stage directions, such as an

Aside? (often a line may be equally effective as an aside or a direct address – it is for each production or reading to make its own decision) or a *may exit* or a piece of business placed between arrows to indicate that it may occur at various different moments within a scene.

Line Numbers in the left margin are editorial, for reference and to key the explanatory and textual notes.

Explanatory Notes at the foot of each page explain allusions and gloss obsolete and difficult words, confusing phraseology, occasional major textual cruces, and so on. Particular attention is given to non-standard usage, bawdy innuendo and technical terms (e.g. legal and military language). Where more than one sense is given, commas indicate shades of related meaning, slashes alternative or double meanings.

Textual Notes at the end of the play indicate major departures from the Folio. They take the following form: the reading of our text is given in bold and its source given after an equals sign, with 'Q' indicating that it derives from the First Quarto of 1600, 'F' from the First Folio of 1623, 'F2' a correction introduced in the Second Folio of 1632, 'F4' a correction introduced in the Fourth Folio of 1685 and 'Ed' one that derives from the subsequent editorial tradition. The rejected Folio ('F') reading is then given. Thus, for example, '**2.1.22 mare** = Q. F = name' indicates that at Act 2 scene 1 line 22, we have preferred the Quarto reading, 'though patience be a tired mare, yet she will plod' which makes better sense of the line: it is hard to imagine Folio's 'name' as anything other than a printer's error.

KEY FACTS

MAJOR PARTS: *(with percentage of lines/number of speeches/scenes on stage)* King Henry V (32%/147/11), Fluellen (9%/68/6), Chorus (7%/6/6), Archbishop of Canterbury (7%/18/2), Pistol (5%/62/7), Duke of Exeter (4%/22/8), Constable of France (4%/40/5), Lewis the Dauphin (4%/31/5), French King (3%/19/3), Boy (2%/16/4), Williams (2%/28/3), Duke of Burgundy (2%/8/1), Gower (2%/5/1), Katherine (2%/33/2), Montjoy (2%/11/3), Nym (1%/20/3), Hostess (1%/11/2), Duke of Orléans (1%/29/3).

LINGUISTIC MEDIUM: 60% verse, 40% prose.

DATE: 1599. Must have been written soon after *2 Henry IV*; not mentioned by Meres in 1598; published 1600. It is nearly always assumed that 'the general ... from Ireland coming' (Act 5 Chorus) refers to the Earl of Essex's Irish expedition, which lasted from March to September 1599. A small minority of commentators suppose that 'the general' is Lord Mountjoy, who was Master-General of the Ordnance and Lord Deputy of Ireland from February 1600 onwards, which would date the play, or at least the choruses, rather later, but the allusion implies public fame much more fitting with Essex than Mountjoy. Self-conscious theatrical references ('this wooden O') suggest that the play may have been written as a showpiece for the newly-built Globe theatre, which opened some time between February and September 1599, but it could have opened at the Curtain.

SOURCES: Based primarily on the 1587 edition of Holinshed's Chronicles; some probable use of Holinshed's main source, Edward Halle's *Union of the Two Noble and Illustre Families of Lancaster and York* (1548). Like the Henry IV plays, also draws on the anonymous play, *The Famous Victories of Henry the Fifth: containing the Honourable*

Battell of Agin-court (published 1598, but in the repertoire for up to a decade before this). The old play includes such details as Canterbury's justification of the claim to France, the tennis balls and the courtship of Princess Katherine. The rival acting company of Philip Henslowe also had a *Henry V* play, but it is lost, so its influence on Shakespeare cannot be determined. The sequence on the night before Agincourt is influenced by a 1590s dramatic tradition of scenes in which a ruler goes in disguise among his people.

TEXT: A Quarto was published in 1600 (*The Chronicle History of Henry the fift, With his battell fought at Agin Court in France. Together with Auntient Pistoll. As it hath bene sundry times playd by the Right honorable the Lord Chamberlaine his servants*). Less than half the length of the later Folio text, with many errors and inconsistencies, and some notable differences from the Folio (e.g. no Chorus whatsoever; Bourbon instead of the dauphin on the French side in the Agincourt scenes), it is some kind of reconstruction, perhaps from memory, of a version of the play as performed on stage. This Quarto was reprinted in 1602 and 1619 (the latter with a false date of 1608). The Folio text is much fuller and better printed; it is almost certainly derived from Shakespeare's manuscript or a scribal copy of it. There are, however, some occasions when the Quarto can be used to correct errors. It is possible that the Folio editor occasionally consulted a copy of the Third Quarto. The most awkward speeches for modern editors are those written in French: a combination of Shakespeare's imperfect French, incomprehension on the part of the printers and the differences between sixteenth-century and modern French means that the creation of a usable text requires more than usual editorial licence in correcting and modernizing.

THE LIFE OF HENRY THE FIFTH

CHORUS

The English side

KING HENRY V

Duke of **BEDFORD**, his younger brother

Humphrey, Duke of **GLOUCESTER**, another younger brother

Duke of **EXETER**, the king's uncle

Duke of **YORK**, the king's cousin

Earl of **WESTMORLAND**

Earl of **WARWICK**

Earl of **SALISBURY**

Archbishop of **CANTERBURY**

Bishop of **ELY**

Richard Earl of **CAMBRIDGE**
Henry, Lord **SCROOP** of Masham } conspirators against the king
Sir Thomas **GREY**

Corporal **NYM**

Lieutenant **BARDOLPH**

Ancient **PISTOL**

HOSTESS QUICKLY, keeper of a tavern, married to Pistol

BOY, previously page to Falstaff

Sir Thomas **ERPINGHAM**
Captain **GOWER**, an Englishman } officers in the king's army
Captain **FLUELLEN**, a Welshman

Captain **JAMY**, a Scotsman
Captain **MACMORRIS**, an Irishman } officers in the king's army

John **BATES**
Alexander **COURT** } English soldiers
Michael **WILLIAMS**

HERALD

The French side

FRENCH KING, Charles VI

QUEEN ISABEL, his wife

Lewis the **DAUPHIN**, their son and heir

KATHERINE, their daughter

ALICE, Katherine's lady-in-waiting

CONSTABLE of France

Duke of **BURGUNDY**

MONTJOY, the French Herald

GOVERNOR of Harfleur

Duke of **BOURBON**

Duke of **ORLÉANS**

Duke of **BERRI**

Lord **RAMBURES**

Lord **GRANDPRÉ**

French **AMBASSADORS** to England

FRENCH LORDS

Soldiers, Messengers, Attendants

Prologue

Enter Prologue

CHORUS O, for a muse of fire, that would ascend
      The brightest heaven of invention,
      A kingdom for a stage, princes to act
      And monarchs to behold the swelling scene!
5   Then should the warlike Harry, like himself,
      Assume the port of Mars, and at his heels,
      Leashed in like hounds, should famine, sword and fire
      Crouch for employment. But pardon, gentles all,
      The flat unraisèd spirits that hath dared
10   On this unworthy scaffold to bring forth
      So great an object. Can this cockpit hold
      The vasty fields of France? Or may we cram
      Within this wooden O, the very casques
      That did affright the air at Agincourt?
15   O, pardon! Since a crooked figure may
      Attest in little place a million,
      And let us, ciphers to this great accompt,
      On your imaginary forces work.
      Suppose within the girdle of these walls
20   Are now confined two mighty monarchies,
      Whose high uprearèd and abutting fronts
      The perilous narrow ocean parts asunder.
      Piece out our imperfections with your thoughts:
      Into a thousand parts divide one man,
25   And make imaginary puissance.
      Think when we talk of horses, that you see them
      Printing their proud hoofs i'th'receiving earth,

---

1 muse source of inspiration (originally, one of nine classical goddesses inspiring learning and the arts)
2 invention imagination, creativity/rhetorical term for the discovery of topics   **4 swelling** growing/
magnificent   **5 warlike** skilled in warfare/like war (or **Mars**) itself   **like himself** in a manner befitting his
status as a kingly warrior   **6 port** bearing, stance   **Mars** Roman god of war   **8 gentles** ladies and
gentlemen   **9 flat unraisèd** dull, lifeless, dormant   **spirits** i.e. the actors and playwright (plays on the idea
of supernatural spirits that may be raised by incantation)   **10 scaffold** stage   **11 cockpit** circular arena
(literally, ring used for cockfighting – much smaller than a theatre)   **12 vasty** vast   **13 wooden O** i.e. the
circular, timber-built theatre (**wooden** plays on the sense of 'dull, lifeless')   **casques** helmets   **14 affright**
frighten   **Agincourt** English forces defeated the French at the battle of Agincourt (northern France) on 25
October 1415   **15 crooked ... million** i.e. a zero added to 100,000 increases the number to 1,000,000
crooked rounded; perhaps with connotations of 'deceptive, crafty'   **figure** may play on the sense of 'person,
actor'   **17 ciphers** zeros/non-entities/symbols, visual representations   **accompt** account, total/story
18 imaginary imaginative   **19 Suppose** imagine   **girdle** circumference   **20 monarchies** i.e. England
and France   **21 uprearèd** raised up, erected, reared up   **abutting** neighbouring, adjoining (perhaps with a
suggestion of fighting animals butting one another)   **fronts** cliffs of Dover and Calais/frontiers/foreheads
22 narrow ocean i.e. the English Channel   **23 Piece out** supplement   **25 puissance** power

For 'tis your thoughts that now must deck our kings,
Carry them here and there, jumping o'er times,
30 Turning th'accomplishment of many years
Into an hourglass: for the which supply,
Admit me chorus to this history;
Who prologue-like your humble patience pray,
Gently to hear, kindly to judge, our play.   *Exit*

Act 1 Scene 1   *running scene 1*

Enter the two Bishops of Canterbury and Ely

CANTERBURY My lord, I'll tell you: that self bill is urged,
Which in th'eleventh year of the last king's reign
Was like, and had indeed against us passed,
But that the scambling and unquiet time
5 Did push it out of further question.
ELY But how, my lord, shall we resist it now?
CANTERBURY It must be thought on: if it pass against us,
We lose the better half of our possession.
For all the temporal lands which men devout
10 By testament have given to the Church
Would they strip from us; being valued thus:
As much as would maintain, to the king's honour,
Full fifteen earls and fifteen hundred knights,
Six thousand and two hundred good esquires,
15 And, to relief of lazars and weak age
Of indigent faint souls past corporal toil,
A hundred almshouses right well supplied,
And to the coffers of the king beside,
A thousand pounds by th'year. Thus runs the bill.
20 **ELY** This would drink deep.
CANTERBURY 'Twould drink the cup and all.
ELY But what prevention?
CANTERBURY The king is full of grace and fair regard.
ELY And a true lover of the holy church.

---

28 **deck** adorn, equip   31 **for ... supply** for the purposes of which   **1.1** *Location: the royal court, London*   1 **self** same   **urged** put forward   2 **last king's** i.e. Henry IV's   3 **like** likely (to have been passed)   4 **scambling** quarrelsome, scuffling   5 **question** consideration   9 **temporal** secular, not belonging to the Church   10 **By testament** in their wills   12 **maintain** stand the cost of   14 **esquires** one ranking just below a knight   15 **lazars** lepers   16 **indigent** needy, poor   **corporal toil** physical work   18 **coffers** money chests, i.e. treasury   **beside** in addition   19 **bill** (proposed) parliamentary act/total owed   20 **drink deep** i.e. swallow much of their wealth   23 **grace** honour/virtue/divine grace/good will   **fair regard** consideration, respect/is well-respected

25 CANTERBURY The courses of his youth promised it not.
        The breath no sooner left his father's body,
        But that his wildness, mortified in him,
        Seemed to die too. Yea, at that very moment
        Consideration like an angel came
30   And whipped th'offending Adam out of him,
        Leaving his body as a paradise,
        T'envelop and contain celestial spirits.
        Never was such a sudden scholar made,
        Never came reformation in a flood,
35   With such a heady currance, scouring faults,
        Nor never Hydra-headed wilfulness
        So soon did lose his seat, and all at once,
        As in this king.
    ELY We are blessèd in the change.
40 CANTERBURY Hear him but reason in divinity,
        And, all-admiring, with an inward wish
        You would desire the king were made a prelate.
        Hear him debate of commonwealth affairs,
        You would say it hath been all in all his study.
45   List his discourse of war, and you shall hear
        A fearful battle rendered you in music.
        Turn him to any cause of policy,
        The Gordian knot of it he will unloose,
        Familiar as his garter, that, when he speaks,
50   The air, a chartered libertine, is still,
        And the mute wonder lurketh in men's ears
        To steal his sweet and honeyed sentences,
        So that the art and practic part of life
        Must be the mistress to this theoric:
55   Which is a wonder how his grace should glean it,
        Since his addiction was to courses vain,
        His companies unlettered, rude and shallow,

25 courses actions, behaviour   27 mortified killed/subdued by self-denial   29 Consideration meditation, self-reflection   30 th'offending Adam i.e. original sin, the result of the biblical Adam and Eve's disobedience to God   31 paradise i.e. place of innocence, like Eden before Adam and Eve sinned   32 spirits traits of character (perhaps plays on the sense of 'supernatural celestial beings')   35 heady currance strong current   scouring cleaning away   36 Hydra-headed in Greek mythology, the Hydra was a monster who grew two new heads for every one that was cut off   37 seat throne/position   44 all in all entirely, exclusively   45 List listen to   46 rendered...music i.e. described eloquently   47 cause of policy political issue, explanation of statecraft   48 Gordian knot proverbially too intricate to undo (a prophecy decreed that whoever could untie the knot would rule Asia; Alexander the Great cut it with his sword)   49 Familiar...garter as easily as his garter (band tied around leg to keep up hosiery)   50 chartered privileged, licensed   libertine free spirit   53 practic practical   54 Must...theoric must have taught him how to theorize   55 glean have learned   56 courses vain idle, worthless behaviour   57 companies companions   unlettered illiterate, ignorant   rude rough, coarse uncivilized

His hours filled up with riots, banquets, sports,
And never noted in him any study,
60 Any retirement, any sequestration
From open haunts and popularity.
ELY The strawberry grows underneath the nettle
And wholesome berries thrive and ripen best
Neighboured by fruit of baser quality.
65 And so the prince obscured his contemplation
Under the veil of wildness, which, no doubt,
Grew like the summer grass, fastest by night,
Unseen, yet crescive in his faculty.
CANTERBURY It must be so, for miracles are ceased.
70 And therefore we must needs admit the means
How things are perfected.
ELY But, my good lord,
How now for mitigation of this bill
Urged by the commons? Doth his majesty
75 Incline to it, or no?
CANTERBURY He seems indifferent,
Or rather swaying more upon our part
Than cherishing th'exhibitors against us,
For I have made an offer to his majesty,
80 Upon our spiritual convocation
And in regard of causes now in hand,
Which I have opened to his grace at large,
As touching France, to give a greater sum
Than ever at one time the clergy yet
85 Did to his predecessors part withal.
ELY How did this offer seem received, my lord?
CANTERBURY With good acceptance of his majesty,
Save that there was not time enough to hear,
As I perceived his grace would fain have done,
90 The severals and unhidden passages
Of his true titles to some certain dukedoms

58 **riots** debauched, disorderly behaviour, revelry   59 **noted** was seen   60 **sequestration** retreat into
privacy   61 **open** public   **popularity** associating with the public, low company   65 **obscured** disguised,
hid   **contemplation** meditation, thought   68 **crescive ... faculty** growing, in accordance with its natural
function   70 **needs** necessarily   **means** natural cause   73 **mitigation** reducing (the severity of)
74 **commons** the House of Commons, parliament   75 **Incline to** favour   77 **upon** towards
78 **th'exhibitors against us** i.e. those who are putting forward the bill   80 **Upon** on behalf of
convocation assembly, gathering   81 **causes** matters, legal issues   82 **opened** disclosed, explained
at large in full   83 **touching** concerning   84 **Than ... withal** than the clergy ever gave to any previous
monarch   **withal** with   89 **fain** gladly   90 **severals** particulars   **unhidden passages** clear, undisputed
lines of inheritance

And generally to the crown and seat of France,
Derived from Edward, his great-grandfather.
ELY What was th'impediment that broke this off?
95   CANTERBURY The French ambassador upon that instant
Craved audience; and the hour I think is come
To give him hearing. Is it four o'clock?
ELY It is.
CANTERBURY Then go we in to know his embassy,
100   Which I could with a ready guess declare,
Before the Frenchman speak a word of it.
ELY I'll wait upon you and I long to hear it.   *Exeunt*

[Act 1 Scene 2]   *running scene 1 continues*

Enter the King [Henry V], Humphrey [Duke of Gloucester],
Bedford, Clarence, Warwick, Westmorland, Exeter [and
Attendants]

KING HENRY V Where is my gracious lord of Canterbury?
EXETER Not here in presence.
KING HENRY V Send for him, good uncle.
WESTMORLAND Shall we call in th'ambassador, my liege?
5   KING HENRY V Not yet, my cousin: we would be resolved,
Before we hear him, of some things of weight
That task our thoughts, concerning us and France.
Enter [the] two Bishops
CANTERBURY God and his angels guard your sacred
throne
And make you long become it!
10   KING HENRY V Sure, we thank you.
My learnèd lord, we pray you to proceed
And justly and religiously unfold
Why the law Salic that they have in France
Or should, or should not, bar us in our claim.
15   And God forbid, my dear and faithful lord,
That you should fashion, wrest, or bow your reading,
Or nicely charge your understanding soul
With opening titles miscreate, whose right

---

93 **Edward** i.e. Edward III   99 **embassy** message   **1.2   1 gracious** holy, filled with divine grace
2 **presence** the royal presence   5 **cousin** term of address used by members of the nobility   **resolved**
satisfied, decided about   7 **task** occupy   9 **become** grace, honour   12 **justly** precisely/in a legal sense
unfold reveal, explain   13 **law Salic** a law preventing inheritance through the female line   14 **Or** either
bar prevent, obstruct   16 **fashion...bow** shape, twist or bend   **reading** interpretation   17 **nicely**
charge burden through ingenious subtlety   18 **opening titles miscreate** expounding false claims

Suits not in native colours with the truth,
20 For God doth know how many now in health
Shall drop their blood in approbation
Of what your reverence shall incite us to.
Therefore take heed how you impawn our person,
How you awake our sleeping sword of war;
25 We charge you, in the name of God, take heed,
For never two such kingdoms did contend
Without much fall of blood, whose guiltless drops
Are every one a woe, a sore complaint
Gainst him whose wrongs gives edge unto the swords
30 That make such waste in brief mortality.
Under this conjuration, speak, my lord,
For we will hear, note and believe in heart
That what you speak is in your conscience washed
As pure as sin with baptism.
35 CANTERBURY Then hear me, gracious sovereign, and
            you peers,
That owe yourselves, your lives and services
To this imperial throne. There is no bar
To make against your highness' claim to France
But this, which they produce from Pharamond,
40 '*In terram Salicam mulieres ne succedant*',
'No woman shall succeed in Salic land.'
Which Salic land the French unjustly gloss
To be the realm of France, and Pharamond
The founder of this law and female bar.
45 Yet their own authors faithfully affirm
That the land Salic is in Germany,
Between the floods of Sala and of Elbe,
Where Charles the Great, having subdued the
            Saxons,
There left behind and settled certain French,
50 Who, holding in disdain the German women
For some dishonest manners of their life,
Established then this law; to wit, no female
Should be inheritrix in Salic land —
Which Salic, as I said, 'twixt Elbe and Sala,

19 Suits . . . colours i.e. does not match   **21 drop their blood** i.e. be injured or die   **approbation** putting
to the test   **23 how . . . person** i.e. what you commit me to   **25 charge** command   **28 complaint**
lament   **29 wrongs** grievances/wrongdoings   **31 conjuration** solemn appeal   **32 note** pay attention
39 Pharamond legendary French king   **42 gloss** define   **47 floods** rivers   **Sala and of Elbe** rivers in
Germany (**Sala** is now Saale)   **48 Charles the Great** Charlemagne, Holy Roman Emperor and
eighth-century French king   **51 dishonest manners** unchaste behaviour   **52 to wit** that is to say
53 inheritrix heiress   **54 'twixt** between

55   Is at this day in Germany called Meisen.
      Then doth it well appear the Salic law
      Was not devisèd for the realm of France,
      Nor did the French possess the Salic land
      Until four hundred one-and-twenty years
60   After defunction of King Pharamond —
      Idly supposed the founder of this law —
      Who died within the year of our redemption
      Four hundred twenty-six, and Charles the Great
      Subdued the Saxons, and did seat the French
65   Beyond the river Sala, in the year
      Eight hundred five. Besides, their writers say,
      King Pepin, which deposèd Childeric,
      Did, as heir general, being descended
      Of Blithild, which was daughter to King Clothair,
70   Make claim and title to the crown of France.
      Hugh Capet also, who usurped the crown
      Of Charles the Duke of Lorraine, sole heir male
      Of the true line and stock of Charles the Great,
      To find his title with some shows of truth,
75   Though, in pure truth, it was corrupt and naught,
      Conveyed himself as th'heir to th'Lady Lingare,
      Daughter to Charlemagne, who was the son
      To Lewis the emperor, and Lewis the son
      Of Charles the Great. Also King Lewis the Tenth,
80   Who was sole heir to the usurper Capet,
      Could not keep quiet in his conscience,
      Wearing the crown of France, till satisfied
      That fair Queen Isabel, his grandmother,
      Was lineal of the Lady Ermengare,
85   Daughter to Charles the foresaid Duke of Lorraine:
      By the which marriage the line of Charles the Great
      Was reunited to the crown of France.
      So that, as clear as is the summer's sun,
      King Pepin's title and Hugh Capet's claim,
90   King Lewis his satisfaction, all appear
      To hold in right and title of the female:
      So do the kings of France unto this day,

---

60 defunction death   **61 Idly** foolishly   **62 within … redemption** i.e. AD   **64 seat** settle, establish
66 Besides in addition   **68 heir general** legitimate heir (claiming through male or female lines)
73 Charles the Great Charlemagne   **74 find** supply, refine   **76 Conveyed himself** pretended to be
77 Charlemagne Charles II, rather than the Charlemagne mentioned earlier   **79 King … Tenth** an error
for Louis IX, thirteenth-century King of France; the slip appears in Holinshed's *Chronicles*, Shakespeare's
source here   **81 quiet** peace of mind   **84 lineal** a direct descendant   **90 satisfaction** i.e. of his lineage
91 hold in rely on, derive from

Howbeit they would hold up this Salic law
To bar your highness claiming from the female,
95   And rather choose to hide them in a net
Than amply to imbar their crooked titles
Usurped from you and your progenitors.

KING HENRY V May I with right and conscience make
this claim?

CANTERBURY The sin upon my head, dread sovereign!
100   For in the book of Numbers is it writ,
When the man dies, let the inheritance
Descend unto the daughter. Gracious lord,
Stand for your own, unwind your bloody flag,
Look back into your mighty ancestors:
105   Go, my dread lord, to your great-grandsire's tomb,
From whom you claim; invoke his warlike spirit,
And your great-uncle's, Edward the Black Prince,
Who on the French ground played a tragedy,
Making defeat on the full power of France,
110   Whiles his most mighty father on a hill
Stood smiling to behold his lion's whelp
Forage in blood of French nobility.
O, noble English, that could entertain
With half their forces the full pride of France
115   And let another half stand laughing by,
All out of work and cold for action!

ELY Awake remembrance of these valiant dead
And with your puissant arm renew their feats;
You are their heir, you sit upon their throne:
120   The blood and courage that renownèd them
Runs in your veins, and my thrice-puissant liege
Is in the very May-morn of his youth,
Ripe for exploits and mighty enterprises.

93 Howbeit however   **would** wish to   **95 net** i.e. tangle of contradictory legalities/network of lineal justifications (rather than a direct line)/possibly refers to the proverbial 'you dance in a net and think nobody sees you' – i.e. try to conceal what is obvious   **96 amply** openly   **imbar** bar claim to/make bare, reveal   **crooked** false/indirect   **97 progenitors** ancestors   **99 The . . . head** i.e. if the claim is false, the moral blame will lie with Canterbury   **dread** revered   **100 book . . . daughter** a reference to Numbers 27:8   **103 Stand for** defend/uphold   **105 great-grandsire's** i.e. Edward III's   **106 From . . . claim** i.e. as whose ancestor you make this claim; Edward was descended through his mother from the French King Philip IV   **107 Edward . . . France** the English defeated France at the battle of Crécy, 1346; Edward III had given command of his armies to his eldest son, **the Black Prince**   **111 lion's whelp** cub   **112 Forage** plunder/eat greedily   **113 entertain** engage, meet with   **116 for** through lack of   **117 valiant dead** i.e. Henry's ancestors   **118 puissant** powerful   **120 renownèd** made famous

EXETER Your brother kings and monarchs of the earth

125   Do all expect that you should rouse yourself,
       As did the former lions of your blood.

WESTMORLAND They know your grace hath cause and
           means and might;
       So hath your highness. Never King of England
       Had nobles richer and more loyal subjects,

130   Whose hearts have left their bodies here in England
       And lie pavilioned in the fields of France.

CANTERBURY O, let their bodies follow, my dear liege,
       With bloods and sword and fire to win your right.
       In aid whereof we of the spiritualty

135   Will raise your highness such a mighty sum
       As never did the clergy at one time
       Bring in to any of your ancestors.

KING HENRY V We must not only arm t'invade the
           French,
       But lay down our proportions to defend

140   Against the Scot, who will make road upon us
       With all advantages.

CANTERBURY They of those marches, gracious
           sovereign,
       Shall be a wall sufficient to defend
       Our inland from the pilfering borderers.

145   **KING HENRY V** We do not mean the coursing snatchers
           only,
       But fear the main intendment of the Scot,
       Who hath been still a giddy neighbour to us.
       For you shall read that my great-grandfather
       Never went with his forces into France

150   But that the Scot on his unfurnished kingdom
       Came pouring like the tide into a breach,
       With ample and brim fullness of his force,
       Galling the gleanèd land with hot assays,
       Girding with grievous siege castles and towns,

---

126 **former . . . blood** i.e. kingly ancestors; the lion is the symbol of kingship, and appears on the royal coat of arms   130 **Whose . . . England** i.e. who are already imagining themselves in France   131 **pavilioned** in military tents   133 **right** i.e. rightful claim to the French throne   134 **spiritualty** clergy   139 **lay . . . proportions** allocate troops   140 **make road** invade   141 **advantages** opportunities   142 **marches** northern border regions   144 **borderers** i.e. the Scottish   145 **coursing snatchers** swift-riding raiders (from hare-coursing with greyhounds; the 'snatch' was the act of capture)   146 **intendment** intention   147 **giddy** wild, unstable   150 **unfurnished** unprotected   151 **breach** hole, gap (in this instance in a sea wall)   152 **brim** i.e. total   153 **Galling** vexing, wounding   **gleanèd** stripped (of defenders)   **hot** fast/hot-tempered   **assays** attacks   154 **Girding** surrounding

155   That England, being empty of defence,
          Hath shook and trembled at th'ill neighbourhood.
          CANTERBURY She hath been then more feared than
              harmed, my liege,
          For hear her but exampled by herself:
          When all her chivalry hath been in France
160   And she a mourning widow of her nobles,
          She hath herself not only well defended
          But taken and impounded as a stray
          The king of Scots, whom she did send to France,
          To fill King Edward's fame with prisoner kings
165   And make their chronicle as rich with praise
          As is the ooze and bottom of the sea
          With sunken wreck and sumless treasuries.
          ELY But there's a saying very old and true,
          'If that you will France win,
170   Then with Scotland first begin.'
          For once the eagle England being in prey,
          To her unguarded nest the weasel Scot
          Comes sneaking and so sucks her princely eggs,
          Playing the mouse in absence of the cat,
175   To 'tame and havoc more than she can eat.
          EXETER It follows then the cat must stay at home,
          Yet that is but a crushed necessity,
          Since we have locks to safeguard necessaries
          And pretty traps to catch the petty thieves.
180   While that the armèd hand doth fight abroad,
          Th'advisèd head defends itself at home,
          For government, though high and low and lower,
          Put into parts, doth keep in one consent,
          Congreeing in a full and natural close,
185   Like music.
          CANTERBURY Therefore doth heaven divide
          The state of man in divers functions,
          Setting endeavour in continual motion,

---

156 th'ill neighbourhood poor neighbourliness, hostility **157 She** i.e. England **158 hear … herself** i.e. listen to instructive examples from the past **159 chivalry** knights, protectors **162 stray** stray dog **163 king … France** David II of Scotland was captured and imprisoned by English forces in 1346; Edward III was in France at the time but David was not, in fact, sent there **164 fame** reputation **165 their** i.e. Edward and England's **chronicle** historical account **166 ooze** mud **168 ELY** spoken by Ely in Folio, but many editors reassign to WESTMORLAND, who speaks the corresponding lines in Shakespeare's chronicle sources (would the Bishop contradict his superior, the archbishop?) **171 in prey** out hunting **175 'tame** attame, i.e. break into **havoc** destroy **177 crushed** forced, distorted **179 pretty** clever **181 Th'advisèd** the sensible, prudent **182 high … parts** divided into melodies of differing pitches **high … lower** i.e. of three different social groups **183 consent** harmony **184 Congreeing** coming together, agreeing **close** cadence **187 divers** various, different

To which is fixèd, as an aim or butt,
190   Obedience, for so work the honeybees,
Creatures that by a rule in nature teach
The act of order to a peopled kingdom.
They have a king and officers of sorts,
Where some, like magistrates, correct at home,
195   Others, like merchants, venture trade abroad:
Others, like soldiers, armèd in their stings,
Make boot upon the summer's velvet buds,
Which pillage they with merry march bring home
To the tent-royal of their emperor,
200   Who, busied in his majesty, surveys
The singing masons building roofs of gold,
The civil citizens kneading up the honey,
The poor mechanic porters crowding in
Their heavy burdens at his narrow gate,
205   The sad-eyed justice, with his surly hum,
Delivering o'er to executors pale
The lazy yawning drone. I this infer,
That many things, having full reference
To one consent, may work contrariously.
210   As many arrows, loosèd several ways,
Come to one mark, as many ways meet in one town,
As many fresh streams meet in one salt sea,
As many lines close in the dial's centre,
So may a thousand actions, once afoot
215   End in one purpose, and be all well borne
Without defeat. Therefore to France, my liege.
Divide your happy England into four,
Whereof take you one quarter into France,
And you withal shall make all Gallia shake.
220   If we with thrice such powers left at home
Cannot defend our own doors from the dog,
Let us be worried and our nation lose
The name of hardiness and policy.

---

189 aim target   **butt** archery target   **193 king** Aristotle's belief that the queen bee was male remained influential   **194 correct** enforce order   **196 stings** bee stings/staffs used as weapons   **197 Make boot upon** plunder   **198 pillage** spoils, booty   **200 majesty** royal responsibilities   **201 masons** stonemasons, builders   **202 civil** civilized, orderly   **203 mechanic** engaged in manual labour   **205 sad-eyed justice** solemn judge   **surly** stern   **hum** 'hmm' – noise signifying displeasure or deliberation/noise made by a bee   **206 executors** executioners   **207 drone** male bee whose sole function was to impregnate the queen; they died after mating or were cast out of the hive to die   **208 having . . . consent** working together for an agreed cause   **209 contrariously** in opposed ways   **211 mark** target   **ways** roads   **213 close** converge, meet   **dial's** sundial's   **215 borne** carried out   **217 happy** fortunate   **219 withal** with it   **Gallia** Gaul, i.e. France   **222 worried** anxious, concerned/shaken in the jaws of a dog   **223 policy** statesmanship, strategy

KING HENRY V Call in the messengers sent from the
    dauphin.   [*Exeunt some*]
225   Now are we well resolved, and, by God's help
    And yours, the noble sinews of our power,
    France being ours, we'll bend it to our awe,
    Or break it all to pieces. Or there we'll sit,
    Ruling in large and ample empery
230   O'er France and all her almost kingly dukedoms,
    Or lay these bones in an unworthy urn,
    Tombless, with no remembrance over them:
    Either our history shall with full mouth
    Speak freely of our acts, or else our grave,
235   Like Turkish mute, shall have a tongueless mouth,
    Not worshipped with a waxen epitaph.
Enter Ambassadors of France
    Now are we well prepared to know the pleasure
    Of our fair cousin dauphin, for we hear
    Your greeting is from him, not from the king.
240 **FIRST AMBASSADOR** May't please your majesty to give
    us leave
    Freely to render what we have in charge,
    Or shall we sparingly show you far off
    The dauphin's meaning and our embassy?
    KING HENRY V We are no tyrant, but a Christian king,
245   Unto whose grace our passion is as subject
    As are our wretches fettered in our prisons:
    Therefore with frank and with uncurbèd plainness
    Tell us the dauphin's mind.
    FIRST AMBASSADOR Thus, then, in few:
250   Your highness, lately sending into France,
    Did claim some certain dukedoms, in the right
    Of your great predecessor, King Edward the Third.
    In answer of which claim, the prince our master
    Says that you savour too much of your youth,
255   And bids you be advised there's naught in France
    That can be with a nimble galliard won.

---

224 dauphin title of the heir to the French throne   **225 well resolved** free from doubt/determined
227 bend . . . awe make it revere us   **228 Or** either   **229 large** great/generous/unrestrained   **empery**
sovereignty   **233 with full mouth** loudly, with mouth wide open   **235 Turkish mute** a Turkish slave,
perhaps a castrated harem guard, who has had his tongue cut out to ensure secrecy   **236 waxen** i.e.
quickly worn away and forgotten   **237 pleasure** wish, intention   **241 render** deliver   **in charge** been
ordered (to say)   **242 sparingly** with restraint and delicacy   **far off** indirectly, more generally
245 Unto . . . subject i.e. his temper is ruled by his Christian goodness   **246 fettered** chained   **249 in few**
in brief   **250 sending into** i.e. sending an ambassador with his claims   **254 savour** smell, have a
flavour   **255 advised** warned/informed   **256 galliard** lively dance

You cannot revel into dukedoms there:
He therefore sends you, meeter for your spirit,
This tun of treasure; and in lieu of this,   *Presents a box*
260 Desires you let the dukedoms that you claim
Hear no more of you. This the dauphin speaks.
KING HENRY V What treasure, uncle?
EXETER Tennis balls, my liege.   *Looks in the box*
KING HENRY V We are glad the dauphin is so pleasant
        with us.
265 His present and your pains we thank you for:
When we have matched our rackets to these balls,
We will in France, by God's grace, play a set
Shall strike his father's crown into the hazard.
Tell him he hath made a match with such a wrangler
270 That all the courts of France will be disturbed
With chaces. And we understand him well,
How he comes o'er us with our wilder days,
Not measuring what use we made of them.
We never valued this poor seat of England,
275 And therefore, living hence, did give ourself
To barbarous licence, as 'tis ever common
That men are merriest when they are from home.
But tell the dauphin I will keep my state,
Be like a king and show my sail of greatness
280 When I do rouse me in my throne of France.
For that I have laid by my majesty
And plodded like a man for working days,
But I will rise there with so full a glory
That I will dazzle all the eyes of France,
285 Yea, strike the dauphin blind to look on us.
And tell the pleasant prince this mock of his
Hath turned his balls to gun-stones, and his soul
Shall stand sore chargèd for the wasteful vengeance
That shall fly with them, for many a thousand
        widows

---

258 meeter more suitable   **259 tun** box, chest   **264 pleasant** merry, jocular   **266 rackets** tennis rackets/noisy assaults of war   **268 crown** royal crown/coin staked on a game of tennis, which gave its name to the final point scored in the game   **hazard** danger/opening in the wall of a tennis court; a ball that entered it became unplayable so no point could be scored   **269 wrangler** quarrelsome opponent   **270 courts** tennis courts/royal court   **271 chaces** double bounces of the ball in tennis before it is returned, hence no points/hunts, pursuits   **272 comes o'er us** assumes superiority, taunts us   **273 measuring** judging   **274 seat** throne   **275 hence** i.e. away from the court   **276 licence** wild freedoms   **278 state** throne/dignity, kingship   **279 sail of greatness** fully unfurled power   **280 rouse me** raise or rear up   **281 For that** with that ultimate glory in mind   **282 like … days** i.e. like a common man   **286 mock** act of mockery   **287 balls** tennis balls (may also play on the sense of 'testicles')   **gun-stones** cannon balls   **288 chargèd** burdened (plays on the sense of 'loaded with ammunition')   **wasteful** damaging

290 Shall this his mock mock out of their dear husbands;
Mock mothers from their sons, mock castles down,
And some are yet ungotten and unborn
That shall have cause to curse the dauphin's scorn.
But this lies all within the will of God,
295 To whom I do appeal, and in whose name
Tell you the dauphin I am coming on
To venge me as I may and to put forth
My rightful hand in a well-hallowed cause.
So get you hence in peace, and tell the dauphin
300 His jest will savour but of shallow wit,
When thousands weep more than did laugh at it.
Convey them with safe conduct. Fare you well.
                                    Exeunt Ambassadors
EXETER This was a merry message.
KING HENRY V We hope to make the sender blush at it:
305 Therefore, my lords, omit no happy hour
That may give furth'rance to our expedition,
For we have now no thought in us but France,
Save those to God, that run before our business.
Therefore let our proportions for these wars
310 Be soon collected and all things thought upon
That may with reasonable swiftness add
More feathers to our wings, for, God before,
We'll chide this dauphin at his father's door.
Therefore let every man now task his thought,
315 That this fair action may on foot be brought.
                                    Flourish.   Exeunt

[Act 2]

Enter Chorus

CHORUS Now all the youth of England are on fire,
And silken dalliance in the wardrobe lies:
Now thrive the armourers, and honour's thought
Reigns solely in the breast of every man.
5 They sell the pasture now to buy the horse,
Following the mirror of all Christian kings,

---

292 **ungotten** not yet conceived   297 **venge me** revenge myself   298 **well-hallowed** holy, much blessed   305 **omit...hour** do not neglect any favourable opportunity   306 **furth'rance** help   308 **to** for   309 **proportions** military resources   312 **God before** with God on our side   313 **chide** rebuke, punish   314 **task** employ   315 **fair** honourable/favoured/lawful   **on...brought** get underway   *Flourish* trumpet fanfare accompanying a person in authority   2   1 **on fire** i.e. burning to fight   2 **silken dalliance** fine clothes/idle pastimes   6 **mirror** i.e. model, example

With wingèd heels, as English Mercuries.
For now sits expectation in the air,
And hides a sword from hilts unto the point
10   With crowns imperial, crowns and coronets,
Promised to Harry and his followers.
The French, advised by good intelligence
Of this most dreadful preparation,
Shake in their fear and with pale policy
15   Seek to divert the English purposes.
O England! Model to thy inward greatness,
Like little body with a mighty heart,
What mightst thou do, that honour would thee do,
Were all thy children kind and natural?
20   But see, thy fault France hath in thee found out,
A nest of hollow bosoms, which he fills
With treacherous crowns, and three corrupted men:
One, Richard Earl of Cambridge, and the second,
Henry Lord Scroop of Masham, and the third,
25   Sir Thomas Grey, knight, of Northumberland,
Have, for the gilt of France — O guilt indeed! —
Confirmed conspiracy with fearful France,
And by their hands this grace of kings must die,
If hell and treason hold their promises,
30   Ere he take ship for France, and in Southampton.
Linger your patience on, and we'll digest
Th'abuse of distance; force a play.
The sum is paid, the traitors are agreed,
The king is set from London, and the scene
35   Is now transported, gentles, to Southampton.
There is the playhouse now, there must you sit,
And thence to France shall we convey you safe,
And bring you back, charming the narrow seas
To give you gentle pass, for if we may,
40   We'll not offend one stomach with our play.

---

7 wingèd...Mercuries i.e. swiftly, like Mercury, messenger of the Roman god, Jove; he wore winged sandals   **9 hilts** crosspiece by the handle   **10 coronets** small crowns, worn by some members of the nobility   **12 intelligence** information obtained by spying   **13 preparation** equipped military force
14 pale fearful, cowardly, ineffective   **policy** stratagems, intrigue   **16 Model to** replica of   **18 What** i.e. what great things   **would** i.e. would have   **19 thy children** i.e. Englishmen   **kind** honourable/full of natural family affection   **21 hollow** empty/false   **bosoms** hearts/clothing covering the breast, in which a purse could be concealed   **22 crowns** gold coins   **26 gilt** gold   **27 fearful** frightened   **28 this...kings** i.e. Henry V   **30 Ere** before   **Southampton** port on the south coast of England   **31 digest** break down/set in order   **32 Th'abuse of distance** i.e. the violation of the theatrical unity of place as the action moves to Southampton   **force** cram full   **38 charming** casting a spell over   **39 pass** passage   **40 offend one stomach** offend good taste/make anyone seasick

But, till the king come forth, and not till then,
Unto Southampton do we shift our scene.   *Exit*

[Act 2 Scene 1]

Enter Corporal Nym and Lieutenant Bardolph

BARDOLPH Well met, Corporal Nym.

NYM Good morrow, Lieutenant Bardolph.

BARDOLPH What, are Ancient Pistol and you friends yet?

NYM For my part, I care not: I say little, but when time
5   shall serve, there shall be smiles — but that shall be
as it may. I dare not fight, but I will wink and hold
out mine iron: it is a simple one, but what though? It
will toast cheese, and it will endure cold as another
man's sword will, and there's an end.

10   **BARDOLPH** I will bestow a breakfast to make you friends,
and we'll be all three sworn brothers to France. Let't
be so, good Corporal Nym.

NYM Faith, I will live so long as I may, that's the certain
of it. And when I cannot live any longer, I will do as I
15   may. That is my rest, that is the rendezvous of it.

BARDOLPH It is certain, corporal, that he is married to
Nell Quickly, and certainly she did you wrong, for
you were troth-plight to her.

NYM I cannot tell. Things must be as they may: men may
20   sleep, and they may have their throats about them at
that time, and some say knives have edges. It must be
as it may: though patience be a tired mare, yet she
will plod. There must be conclusions. Well, I cannot
tell.

Enter Pistol and [Hostess] Quickly

25   **BARDOLPH** Here comes Ancient Pistol and his wife. Good
corporal, be patient here.— How now, mine host
Pistol?

---

41 till ... then i.e. this accounts for the fact that the following scene takes place in London   **2.1** *Location: in London, but unspecified, probably a street*   **Nym** means 'thief' or 'to thieve'   **2 morrow** morning
3 Ancient ensign, i.e. soldier responsible for carrying military banners   **Pistol** pronounced 'pizzle', generating a pun on the sense of 'penis'   **4 part** possible sexual quibble on the sense of 'penis'
time ... serve i.e. opportunity arises   **6 wink** close both eyes   **7 iron** sword (perhaps with phallic connotations)   **what though** what of it   **9 there's an end** i.e. that's that (**end** may play on the sense of 'penis')   **10 bestow** give   **11 sworn brothers** avowedly loyal brothers-in-arms   **13 certain** certainty, fact   **15 rest** last resolve (term from card-playing referring to the final, reserved stake)   **rendezvous** last resort, refuge   **18 troth-plight** engaged, betrothed (a much more binding contract than it is now)
19 cannot tell do not know   **22 though ... plod** plod on, wait her turn; Nym may hint at eventual revenge on Pistol   **26 host** innkeeper (Pistol picks up on the sense of 'pimp')

PISTOL Base tike, call'st thou me host? Now, by this
     hand,

     I swear, I scorn the term, nor shall my Nell keep
     lodgers.

30 HOSTESS QUICKLY No, by my troth, not long, for we
     cannot lodge and board a dozen or fourteen
     gentlewomen that live honestly by the prick of
     their needles, but it will be thought we keep a bawdy
     house straight. O, well-a-day, lady. If he be not   *Nym and*
35 drawn now, we shall see wilful adultery and murder   *Pistol draw*
     committed.

     BARDOLPH Good lieutenant, good corporal, offer nothing
     here.

     NYM Pish!

40 PISTOL Pish for thee, Iceland dog! Thou prick-eared cur
     of Iceland!

     HOSTESS QUICKLY Good Corporal Nym, show thy valour
     and put up your sword.   *They sheathe their*

     NYM Will you shog off? I would have you solus.   *swords*

     PISTOL 'Solus', egregious dog? O viper vile!
45 The 'solus' in thy most marvellous face,
     The 'solus' in thy teeth and in thy throat
     And in thy hateful lungs, yea, in thy maw, perdy,
     And, which is worse, within thy nasty mouth!
     I do retort the 'solus' in thy bowels,
50 For I can take, and Pistol's cock is up,
     And flashing fire will follow.

     NYM I am not Barbason. You cannot conjure me. I have
     an humour to knock you indifferently well. If you

---

28 tike dog, mongrel   **29 keep lodgers** rent out rooms/run a brothel   **30 troth** faith   **32 live ...**
needles make a respectable living from taking in sewing (but **prick** plays on the senses of 'penis/sexual
penetration' and **needles** on 'vaginas')   **33 bawdy house** brothel   **34 straight** straight away   **well-a-day**
exclamation of dismay   **lady** i.e. by Our Lady (the Virgin Mary)   *draw* i.e. draw their swords   **35 drawn**
refers to his sword being out/his penis being erect   **37 offer** start, attempt   **39 Pish!** exclamation of
contempt, disgust   **40 Iceland dog** species of lap dog with an abundance of long, rough hair (being a lap
dog may generate sexual connotations: one that burrows into ladies' laps)   **prick-eared** pointy-eared/with
an eagerly erect penis/having cuckold's horns (men with unfaithful wives were popularly supposed to grow
horns)   **cur** dog   **41 valour** honour/courage   **42 put up** sheathe, put away   **43 shog off** go
away   **solus** alone   **44 egregious** outrageous   **47 maw** throat/stomach   **perdy** i.e. *par dieu*, French for
'by God'   **49 retort** return   **bowels** intestines, guts   **50 take** catch fire/have sex   **cock is up** pistol is
cocked, ready to fire/penis is erect   **51 fire** the retort of the gun/the burning effects of venereal
disease   **52 Barbason** name of a demon   **conjure** summon/control   **53 humour** inclination, mood
(governed by one of the four 'humours', or bodily fluids believed to influence health and disposition)
indifferently fairly

grow foul with me, Pistol, I will scour you with my
55   rapier, as I may, in fair terms. If you would walk off, I
would prick your guts a little, in good terms, as I
may, and that's the humour of it.

PISTOL O braggart vile and damnèd furious wight!
The grave doth gape, and doting death is near:
60   Therefore exhale.   *They draw again*

BARDOLPH Hear me, hear me what I say: he that strikes   *Draws*
the first stroke, I'll run him up to the hilts, as I am a
soldier.   *They sheathe their swords*

PISTOL An oath of mickle might, and fury shall abate.—
65   Give me thy fist, thy fore-foot to me give.   *To Nym*
Thy spirits are most tall.

NYM I will cut thy throat, one time or other, in fair terms:
that is the humour of it.

PISTOL 'Couple a gorge!'
70   That is the word. I defy thee again.
O hound of Crete, think'st thou my spouse to get?
No, to the spital go,
And from the powd'ring tub of infamy
Fetch forth the lazar kite of Cressid's kind,
75   Doll Tearsheet she by name, and her espouse:
I have, and I will hold, the quondam Quickly
For the only she; and — *pauca*, there's enough.
Go to.

Enter the Boy

BOY Mine host Pistol, you must come to my master, and
80   you, hostess. He is very sick, and would to bed.—
Good Bardolph, put thy face between his sheets, and
do the office of a warming-pan. Faith, he's very ill.

BARDOLPH Away, you rogue!

---

54 foul insulting, foul-mouthed/dirty from firing/syphilitic ('the foul disease')   **scour** clean (a gun) with a scouring-rod/stab/have sex   **55 rapier** light sword used for fencing   **fair terms** plain language/justly, legitimately/terms that are not foul, like Pistol's   **56 prick** stab (with sexual connotations)   **58 braggart** boaster   **wight** person   **60 exhale** i.e. draw your sword   **62 run... hilts** i.e. plunge my sword all the way into him   **64 mickle** much   **65 fist** hand   **fore-foot** hand, paw   **66 tall** bold, valiant   **69 'Couple a gorge!'** i.e. *Couper la gorge!* – French for 'Cut the throat!'   **71 hound of Crete** hairy dog   **72 spital** hospital   **73 powd'ring tub** sweating tub for the treatment of venereal disease   **infamy** bad reputation   **74 lazar** leprous   **kite** bird of prey/prostitute   **Cressid's** in classical legend, Cressida was the unfaithful lover of Troilus; in Robert Henryson's *Testament of Cressid* she gets leprosy   **75 Doll Tearsheet** Doll was a common name for a prostitute; Tearsheet is similarly suggestive, evoking vigorous sexual activity sufficient to tear the bedsheets   **espouse** marry   **76 have... hold** familiar phrase from the marriage service   **quondam** former (her name has changed through marriage)   **77 only she** i.e. unequalled female   *pauca* 'few' (Latin), i.e. few words   **79 my master** i.e. Falstaff, companion of Henry's wild youth (see *1* and *2 Henry IV*)   **81 put... warming-pan** i.e. because his face is fiery red from drinking   **warming-pan** flat, closed dish used to hold hot coals for warming pan

HOSTESS QUICKLY By my troth, he'll yield the crow a
85   pudding one of these days. The king has killed his
heart. Good husband, come home presently.

Exeunt [Hostess and Boy]

BARDOLPH Come, shall I make you two friends? We
must to France together.

Why the devil should we keep knives to cut one
another's throats?

PISTOL Let floods o'erswell, and fiends for food howl on!
90   NYM You'll pay me the eight shillings I won of you at
betting?

PISTOL Base is the slave that pays.

NYM That now I will have: that's the humour of it.

PISTOL As manhood shall compound. Push home.

[They] draw

95   BARDOLPH By this sword, he that makes the first thrust,
I'll kill him. By this sword, I will.

PISTOL Sword is an oath, and oaths must have their   *Sheathes his*
course.   *sword*

BARDOLPH Corporal Nym, an thou wilt be friends, be
friends: an thou wilt not, why, then, be enemies with
100   me too. Prithee put up.

PISTOL A noble shalt thou have, and present pay,
And liquor likewise will I give to thee,
And friendship shall combine, and brotherhood.
I'll live by Nym, and Nym shall live by me.
105   Is not this just? For I shall sutler be
Unto the camp, and profits will accrue.
Give me thy hand.

NYM I shall have my noble?

PISTOL In cash most justly paid.

110   NYM Well, then, that's the humour of't.

Enter Hostess [Quickly]

HOSTESS QUICKLY As ever you come of women, come in
quickly to Sir John. Ah, poor heart! He is so shaked of

---

84 yield . . . pudding i.e. die (proverbial, referring to providing the crow with dead flesh to eat)
85 king . . . heart on coming to the throne, Henry rejected Falstaff and his former wild companions (see
2 Henry IV, Act 5 scene 5)   **86 presently** immediately/soon   **92 Base** poor, low (in spirit/in money)
94 manhood shall compound i.e. valour will decide (in a fight)   **97 Sword . . . oath** plays on ''s word' –
i.e. 'by God's word', a common **oath**   **98 an** if   **100 put up** sheathe (your sword)   **101 noble** gold coin
worth six shillings and eightpence   **104 Nym** may play on the meaning of the name: 'thieving'   **105 just**
honourable/true   **sutler** seller of provisions   **106 camp** military camp   **109 justly** exactly/fairly
111 come of were born of (may play on 'come off' – i.e. dismount after sex)

a burning quotidian tertian, that it is most
lamentable to behold. Sweet men, come to him. [*Exit*]

115 **NYM** The king hath run bad humours on the knight,
that's the even of it.

PISTOL Nym, thou hast spoke the right.
His heart is fracted and corroborate.

NYM The king is a good king, but it must be as it may, he

120 passes some humours and careers.

PISTOL Let us condole the knight, for, lambkins we will
live.   [*Exeunt*]

[Act 2 Scene 2]   *running scene 3*

Enter Exeter, Bedford and Westmorland

BEDFORD 'Fore God, his grace is bold to trust these
traitors.

EXETER They shall be apprehended by and by.

WESTMORLAND How smooth and even they do bear
themselves,
As if allegiance in their bosoms sat,

5 Crownèd with faith and constant loyalty.

BEDFORD The king hath note of all that they intend,
By interception which they dream not of.

EXETER Nay, but the man that was his bedfellow,
Whom he hath dulled and cloyed with gracious
favours,

10 That he should for a foreign purse so sell
His sovereign's life to death and treachery.
                                                    Sound trumpets

Enter the King, Scroop, Cambridge, Grey [and Attendants]

KING HENRY V Now sits the wind fair, and we will
aboard.—
My lord of Cambridge, and my kind lord of Masham,
And you, my gentle knight, give me your thoughts:

---

113 **quotidian tertian** types of fever, a quotidian afflicting the patient daily, a tertian every third day; illness that combined fevers was deemed almost certainly fatal   115 **run bad humours** i.e. vented his bad temper/ caused Falstaff's misery and illness   116 **even of it** i.e. the truth of the matter   118 **fracted** broken **corroborate** strengthened; Pistol presumably errs, meaning the opposite   120 **passes** lets pass, indulges in **humours** inclinations, whims   **careers** short gallops at full speed – i.e. sudden impulses
121 **condole** comfort, sympathize with   **live** i.e. outlive Falstaff   **2.2** *Location: Southampton (a port on the south coast of England)*   1 **bold** daring/overconfident   2 **apprehended** arrested   3 **smooth** in a pleasant, plausible manner   **even** steadily   **bear** present, conduct   6 **hath note** is informed aware
7 **interception** i.e. intercepting their messages   8 **bedfellow** i.e. close companion   9 **dulled** dulled the appetite of   **cloyed** overfilled and sickened   10 **a foreign purse** i.e. French money   14 **gentle** noble

15   Think you not that the powers we bear with us
        Will cut their passage through the force of France,
        Doing the execution and the act
        For which we have in head assembled them?
      SCROOP No doubt, my liege, if each man do his best.
20   KING HENRY V I doubt not that, since we are well
            persuaded
        We carry not a heart with us from hence
        That grows not in a fair consent with ours,
        Nor leave not one behind that doth not wish
        Success and conquest to attend on us.
25   CAMBRIDGE Never was monarch better feared and loved
        Than is your majesty: there's not, I think, a subject
        That sits in heart-grief and uneasiness
        Under the sweet shade of your government.
      GREY True: those that were your father's enemies
30   Have steeped their galls in honey and do serve you
        With hearts create of duty and of zeal.
      KING HENRY V We therefore have great cause of
            thankfulness,
        And shall forget the office of our hand,
        Sooner than quittance of desert and merit
35   According to the weight and worthiness.
      SCROOP So service shall with steelèd sinews toil,
        And labour shall refresh itself with hope,
        To do your grace incessant services.
      KING HENRY V We judge no less.— Uncle of Exeter,
40   Enlarge the man committed yesterday,
        That railed against our person: we consider
        It was excess of wine that set him on,
        And on his more advice we pardon him.
      SCROOP That's mercy, but too much security.
45   Let him be punished, sovereign, lest example
        Breed, by his sufferance, more of such a kind.
      KING HENRY V O, let us yet be merciful.
      CAMBRIDGE So may your highness, and yet punish too.

---

15 powers troops   17 execution action/killing   18 in head as an army   22 grows . . . consent is not in total agreement, sympathy   24 attend on wait upon   25 feared revered, viewed with awe   27 heart-grief discontent, unhappiness   30 steeped . . . honey soaked their bitterness in honey   31 create created 33 And . . . merit i.e. I am more likely to forget how to use my own hand than to forget to repay what is due to people   office use, proper function   35 quittance repayment   35 weight and worthiness due proportion and worth (of the deserving deeds)   36 steelèd hardened, steely   39 judge think   40 Enlarge release   committed imprisoned   41 railed ranted, spoke abusively   43 more advice thinking better of it (in sobriety)   44 security complacency, overconfidence   46 his sufferance i.e. your pardoning him

GREY Sir,
50   You show great mercy, if you give him life,
        After the taste of much correction.
KING HENRY V Alas, your too much love and care of me
        Are heavy orisons gainst this poor wretch!
        If little faults, proceeding on distemper
55   Shall not be winked at, how shall we stretch our eye
        When capital crimes, chewed, swallowed and
            digested,
        Appear before us? — We'll yet enlarge that man,
        Though Cambridge, Scroop and Grey, in their dear
            care
        And tender preservation of our person,
60   Would have him punished. — And now to our
            French causes:
        Who are the late commissioners?
CAMBRIDGE I one, my lord.
        Your highness bade me ask for it today.
SCROOP So did you me, my liege.
65 **GREY** And I, my royal sovereign.
KING HENRY V Then, Richard Earl of Cambridge, there is
            yours.—   *Gives each a paper*
        There yours, Lord Scroop of Masham.— And, sir
            knight,
        Grey of Northumberland, this same is yours.
        Read them, and know I know your worthiness.—
70   My lord of Westmorland, and uncle Exeter,
        We will aboard tonight.— Why, how now,
            gentlemen?
        What see you in those papers that you lose
        So much complexion?— Look ye, how they change:
        Their cheeks are paper.— Why, what read you there
75   That hath so cowarded and chased your blood
        Out of appearance?
CAMBRIDGE I do confess my fault,
        And do submit me to your highness' mercy.
GREY *and* **SCROOP**   To which we all appeal.

---

51 correction punishment   **53 orisons** pleas, prayers   **54 on distemper** from mental ill-health (in this case, drunkenness)   **55 winked at** i.e. ignored   **how . . . eye** how wide must we open our eyes   **56 capital** punishable by death   **chewed . . . digested** i.e. carefully planned and organized   **58 dear** worthy, tender (puns on the sense of 'dire, grievous')   **61 late commissioners** officials recently appointed to act for the king in his absence   **72 lose . . . complexion** grow so pale   **74 paper** i.e. white/easily read   **76 Out of appearance** away from sight/out of your faces

80   **KING HENRY V** The mercy that was quick in us but late,
      By your own counsel is suppressed and killed.
      You must not dare, for shame, to talk of mercy,
      For your own reasons turn into your bosoms,
      As dogs upon their masters, worrying you.—
85   See you, my princes, and my noble peers,
      These English monsters. My lord of Cambridge here,
      You know how apt our love was to accord
      To furnish him with all appertinents
      Belonging to his honour; and this man
90   Hath, for a few light crowns, lightly conspired
      And sworn unto the practices of France
      To kill us here in Hampton. To the which
      This knight, no less for bounty bound to us
      Than Cambridge is, hath likewise sworn.— But, O,
95   What shall I say to thee, Lord Scroop, thou cruel,
      Ingrateful, savage and inhuman creature?
      Thou that didst bear the key of all my counsels,
      That knew'st the very bottom of my soul,
      That almost mightst have coined me into gold,
100   Wouldst thou have practised on me for thy use?
      May it be possible that foreign hire
      Could out of thee extract one spark of evil
      That might annoy my finger? 'Tis so strange,
      That though the truth of it stands off as gross
105   As black and white, my eye will scarcely see it.
      Treason and murder, ever kept together,
      As two yoke-devils sworn to either's purpose,
      Working so grossly in a natural cause,
      That admiration did not whoop at them.
110   But thou gainst all proportion, didst bring in
      Wonder to wait on treason and on murder,
      And whatsoever cunning fiend it was
      That wrought upon thee so preposterously
      Hath got the voice in hell for excellence,
115   All other devils that suggest by treasons

---

80 quick alive/prompt   **83 reasons** i.e. the arguments you made about showing no mercy   **84 worrying** biting at   **87 accord** agree   **88 furnish** provide   **appertinents … honour** things appropriate for his dignified position   **90 light** of little value/immoral   **lightly** readily, easily   **91 practices** plots   **93 This knight** i.e. Grey   **bounty** (kingly) generosity   **97 counsels** secrets   **99 coined … gold** i.e. used me to make as much gold as you liked   **100 practised on** worked on, deceived   **use** profit   **103 annoy** harm   **104 off as gross** out as plainly   **107 yoke-devils** devils yoked together in evil   **108 grossly** blatantly **natural** i.e. natural to evil creatures   **109 whoop** exclaim   **110 proportion** natural order   **111 wait on** serve   **113 wrought** worked   **preposterously** unnaturally   **114 voice** vote   **115 suggest** tempt **treasons** suggesting treasonous acts

Do botch and bungle up damnation
With patches, colours and with forms being fetched
From glist'ring semblances of piety.
But he that tempered thee, bade thee stand up,
120   Gave thee no instance why thou shouldst do treason,
Unless to dub thee with the name of traitor.
If that same demon that hath gulled thee thus
Should with his lion gait walk the whole world,
He might return to vasty Tartar back,
125   And tell the legions 'I can never win
A soul so easy as that Englishman's.'
O, how hast thou with jealousy infected
The sweetness of affiance! Show men dutiful?
Why, so didst thou. Seem they grave and learnèd?
130   Why, so didst thou. Come they of noble family?
Why, so didst thou. Seem they religious?
Why, so didst thou. Or are they spare in diet,
Free from gross passion or of mirth or anger,
Constant in spirit, not swerving with the blood,
135   Garnished and decked in modest complement,
Not working with the eye without the ear,
And but in purgèd judgement trusting neither?
Such and so finely bolted didst thou seem:
And thus thy fall hath left a kind of blot,
140   To mark the full-fraught man and best indued
With some suspicion. I will weep for thee,
For this revolt of thine, methinks, is like
Another fall of man.— Their faults are open.   *To Exeter*
Arrest them to the answer of the law,
145   And God acquit them of their practices.
EXETER I arrest thee of high treason, by the name of
Richard Earl of Cambridge.— I arrest thee of high

116 **botch . . . up** clumsily patch   117 **patches** pieces of material/fools/rogues   **colours** outward appearances/excuses, pretexts/military flags denoting allegiance   **forms** outward behaviour
118 **glist'ring** shining, glittering   119 **tempered** shaped/made resolved (as a sword is hardened)   **stand up** make a stand, rebel   120 **instance** motive, evidence   121 **dub** invest, knight   122 **gulled** tricked
123 **lion gait** alludes to 1 Peter 5:8: 'Be sober, be vigilant; because your adversary the devil, as a roaring lion, walketh about, seeking whom he may devour'   124 **vasty Tartar** vast hell (Tartarus is hell in classical mythology)   125 **legions** multitudes of devils   126 **easy** easily   127 **jealousy** suspicion   128 **affiance** trust   **Show** appear   132 **spare** frugal, abstemious   133 **gross passion** powerful feeling, coarse emotion   134 **Constant in spirit** steadfast in disposition   **blood** passions   135 **complement** qualities, accomplishments/outward appearance   136 **working . . . ear** i.e. without observing and listening together
137 **purgèd** purified, refined   138 **bolted** sifted   140 **full-fraught** fully laden (with virtues)   **indued** endowed   143 **Another . . . man** i.e. the disobedience of the biblical Adam and Eve   **open** obvious/ revealed   144 **to . . . of** i.e. so that they will be answerable to the law   145 **practices** sinful plots, treacheries   146 **by . . . of** you who go by the name of

treason, by the name of Henry Lord Scroop of
Masham.— I arrest thee of high treason, by the name
150   of Thomas Grey, knight, of Northumberland.

SCROOP Our purposes God justly hath discovered,
        And I repent my fault more than my death,
        Which I beseech your highness to forgive,
        Although my body pay the price of it.

155 CAMBRIDGE For me, the gold of France did not seduce,
        Although I did admit it as a motive
        The sooner to effect what I intended.
        But God be thankèd for prevention,
        Which I in sufferance heartily will rejoice,
160   Beseeching God and you to pardon me.

GREY Never did faithful subject more rejoice
        At the discovery of most dangerous treason
        Than I do at this hour joy o'er myself,
        Prevented from a damnèd enterprise.
165   My fault, but not my body, pardon, sovereign.

KING HENRY V God quit you in his mercy! Hear your
            sentence:
        You have conspired against our royal person,
        Joined with an enemy proclaimed and from his
            coffers
        Received the golden earnest of our death,
170   Wherein you would have sold your king to slaughter,
        His princes and his peers to servitude,
        His subjects to oppression and contempt
        And his whole kingdom into desolation.
        Touching our person, seek we no revenge,
175   But we our kingdom's safety must so tender,
        Whose ruin you have sought, that to her laws
        We do deliver you. Get you therefore hence,
        Poor miserable wretches, to your death:
        The taste whereof, God of his mercy give
180   You patience to endure, and true repentance
        Of all your dear offences!— Bear them hence.—
                    Exeunt [Cambridge, Scroop and Grey, guarded]
        Now, lords, for France: the enterprise whereof

---

151 **discovered** revealed   157 **what I intended** Cambridge's main intention was to make Edmund
Mortimer king   159 **sufferance** patience/suffering   166 **quit** acquit, pardon   168 **enemy proclaimed** i.e.
France, an officially designated enemy of the state   169 **earnest** advance payment   173 **desolation** ruin,
destruction   174 **Touching our person** with regard to myself   175 **tender** hold dear, value   181 **dear**
dire/costly

Shall be to you, as us, like glorious.
We doubt not of a fair and lucky war,
185 Since God so graciously hath brought to light
This dangerous treason lurking in our way
To hinder our beginnings. We doubt not now
But every rub is smoothèd on our way.
Then forth, dear countrymen. Let us deliver
190 Our puissance into the hand of God,
Putting it straight in expedition.
Cheerly to sea, the signs of war advance:
No King of England, if not King of
            France.   *Flourish*   [*Exeunt*]

[Act 2 Scene 3]   *running scene 4*

Enter Pistol, Nym, Bardolph, Boy and Hostess [Quickly]

HOSTESS QUICKLY Prithee, honey-sweet husband, let me
      bring thee to Staines.
PISTOL No, for my manly heart doth yearn.
      Bardolph, be blithe: Nym, rouse thy vaunting veins:
5   Boy, bristle thy courage up, for Falstaff he is dead,
      And we must earn therefore.
BARDOLPH Would I were with him, wheresome'er he is,
      either in heaven or in hell.
HOSTESS QUICKLY Nay, sure, he's not in hell: he's in
10   Arthur's bosom, if ever man went to Arthur's bosom.
      A made a finer end and went away an it had been
      any christom child. A parted e'en just between
      twelve and one, e'en at the turning o'th'tide. For
      after I saw him fumble with the sheets and play with
15   flowers and smile upon his fingers' end, I knew there
      was but one way, for his nose was as sharp as a pen
      on a table of green fields. 'How now, Sir John?' quoth

183 **to . . . glorious** as glorious to you as to me   184 **fair** favoured/honourable/just   **lucky** successful,
fortunate   188 **rub** obstacle (bowling term)   190 **puissance** power   191 **straight in expedition** straight
away to speedy action   192 **Cheerly** heartily, cheerfully   **advance** move forward/raise banners
2.3 *Location: in London, but unspecified, probably a street*   2 **bring** accompany   **Staines** town
seventeen miles west of London, on the way to Southampton   3 **yearn** grieve   4 **blithe** merry
rouse . . . veins raise your lively spirits/drum up some courage   **vaunting** boasting   5 **bristle** arouse, cause
to stand on end   6 **earn** make money/grieve   10 **Arthur's bosom** malapropism for 'Abraham's bosom', i.e.
heaven   11 **A** he   **a finer end** as fine a death as there could be   **an** as if   12 **christom** innocent, newly
christened – literally, a child that died within a month of birth   13 **e'en** just   15 **flowers** used to keep the
sickroom sweet-smelling   **upon . . . end** at his own fingers   16 **pen** quill pen (i.e. white, cold and
pointed)   17 **table . . . fields** perhaps alluding to the fields on a green gaming (backgammon) table; also
biblical in tone ('he maketh me to lie down in green pastures', Psalm 23:2); many editors emend to 'and a
babbled/talked of green fields'

I. 'What, man? Be o'good cheer.' So a cried out, 'God,
God, God!' three or four times. Now I, to comfort him,
20   bid him a should not think of God; I hoped there was
no need to trouble himself with any such thoughts
yet. So a bade me lay more clothes on his feet. I put
my hand into the bed and felt them, and they were as
cold as any stone. Then I felt to his knees, and so up-
25   peered and upward, and all was as cold as any stone.

NYM They say he cried out of sack.

HOSTESS QUICKLY Ay, that a did.

BARDOLPH And of women.

HOSTESS QUICKLY Nay, that a did not.

30   **BOY** Yes, that a did, and said they were devils incarnate.

HOSTESS QUICKLY A could never abide carnation, 'twas
a colour he never liked.

BOY A said once the devil would have him about
women.

35   **HOSTESS QUICKLY** A did in some sort, indeed, handle
women, but then he was rheumatic, and talked of
the whore of Babylon.

BOY Do you not remember, a saw a flea stick upon
Bardolph's nose, and a said it was a black soul
40   burning in hell?

BARDOLPH Well, the fuel is gone that maintained that
fire: that's all the riches I got in his service.

NYM Shall we shog? The king will be gone from
Southampton.

45   **PISTOL** Come, let's away.— My love, give me thy lips.   *Kisses her*
Look to my chattels and my movables.
Let senses rule. The world is 'pitch and pay',
Trust none,
For oaths are straws, men's faiths are wafer-cakes,
50   And hold-fast is the only dog. My duck,
Therefore, *Caveto* be thy counsellor.

---

22 clothes bedclothes, blankets   **25 all . . . stone** plays on senses of 'penis' ('awl') and 'testicle'   **26 of** against   **sack** Spanish white wine   **30 incarnate** in human form   **31 carnation** shade of red   **33 about** concerning, because of   **35 handle** discuss/touch, feel   **36 rheumatic** feverish/malapropism for 'lunatic' (plays on 'Rome-atic', thus anticipating the **whore of Babylon**)   **37 whore of Babylon** a popular image for the Roman Catholic Church   **38 stick upon** cling to/pierce, bite   **40 burning** i.e. as Bardolph's nose is fiery red from drink   **41 the fuel** i.e. alcohol, supplied by Falstaff   **43 shog** be gone   **46 chattels . . . movables** movable possessions   **47 Let senses rule** i.e. be sensible, keep your wits about you   **world . . . pay'** i.e. in this world it's 'cash down, no credit' (proverbial)   **49 oaths** promises (to pay)   **straws** i.e. worthless   **wafer-cakes** thin, lightweight cakes   **50 hold-fast . . . dog** 'Brag is a good dog, but Holdfast is a better' (proverbial); a brag is a large nail, a **hold-fast** a clamp or bolt and a **dog** a vice or clamp   **51 Caveto** 'beware' (Latin)

Go, clear thy crystals. Yoke-fellows in arms,
Let us to France, like horse-leeches, my boys,
To suck, to suck, the very blood to suck!

55 BOY And that's but unwholesome food they say.
PISTOL Touch her soft mouth, and march.
BARDOLPH Farewell, hostess.   *Kisses her*
NYM I cannot kiss, that is the humour of it. But, adieu.
PISTOL Let housewifery appear. Keep close, I thee
        command.
60 HOSTESS QUICKLY Farewell. Adieu.   *Exeunt [separately]*

[Act 2 Scene 4]   *running scene 5*

*Flourish. Enter the French King, the Dauphin, the Dukes of
Berri and Brittany, [the Constable and others]*

FRENCH KING Thus comes the English with full power
        upon us,
And more than carefully it us concerns
To answer royally in our defences.
Therefore the Dukes of Berri and of Brittany,
5 Of Brabant and of Orléans, shall make forth,
And you, Prince Dauphin, with all swift dispatch
To line and new repair our towns of war
With men of courage and with means defendant,
For England his approaches makes as fierce
10 As waters to the sucking of a gulf.
It fits us then to be as provident
As fear may teach us, out of late examples
Left by the fatal and neglected English
Upon our fields.
15 DAUPHIN My most redoubted father,
It is most meet we arm us gainst the foe,
For peace itself should not so dull a kingdom,
Though war nor no known quarrel were in question,
But that defences, musters, preparations,
20 Should be maintained, assembled and collected,

52 **clear thy crystals** wipe your eyes **Yoke-fellows** comrades   53 **horse-leeches** large leeches
59 **housewifery** careful housekeeping   **close** indoors/reticent/chaste   2.4 *Location: the French royal
court, at Rouen, northern France   French King* i.e. Charles VI   *Constable* title of the commander-in-
chief of the French army   2 **more . . . defences** i.e. it is vitally important that we put up strong defences
6 **dispatch** haste   7 **line** reinforce   8 **defendant** defensive   9 **approaches** attacks   10 **gulf** whirlpool
11 **fits us** is appropriate   **provident** forward-thinking   12 **late examples** i.e. former French defeats, such
as Crécy (1346) and Poitiers (1356)   13 **neglected** underestimated by the French   15 **redoubted**
revered   16 **meet** right, fit   18 **Though** even if   19 **musters** lists or recruitment of soldiers

As were a war in expectation.
Therefore, I say 'tis meet we all go forth
To view the sick and feeble parts of France,
And let us do it with no show of fear —
25   No, with no more than if we heard that England
Were busied with a Whitsun morris-dance,
For, my good liege, she is so idly kinged,
Her sceptre so fantastically borne
By a vain, giddy, shallow, humorous youth,
30   That fear attends her not.
CONSTABLE O, peace, Prince Dauphin!
You are too much mistaken in this king.
Question your grace the late ambassadors,
With what great state he heard their embassy,
35   How well supplied with noble counsellors,
How modest in exception, and withal
How terrible in constant resolution,
And you shall find his vanities forespent
Were but the outside of the Roman Brutus,
40   Covering discretion with a coat of folly;
As gardeners do with ordure hide those roots
That shall first spring and be most delicate.
DAUPHIN Well, 'tis not so, my lord high constable.
· But though we think it so, it is no matter.
45   In cases of defence 'tis best to weigh
The enemy more mighty than he seems,
So the proportions of defence are filled,
Which of a weak and niggardly projection
Doth, like a miser, spoil his coat with scanting
50   A little cloth.
FRENCH KING Think we King Harry strong,
And, princes, look you strongly arm to meet him.
The kindred of him hath been fleshed upon us,
And he is bred out of that bloody strain

26 **Whitsun morris-dance** folk-dance, traditionally held at Whitsun (the seventh Sunday after Easter)
27 **idly** frivolously, uselessly   **kinged** ruled (by Henry)   28 **sceptre** staff carried as a symbol of sovereignty/
baton carried by the fool of a morris troupe, or possibly sceptre carried by the mock figure of a king that the
troupe used   **fantastically** fancifully, bizarrely   29 **humorous** capricious, whimsical   30 **attends**
accompanies, waits on   33 **late** recent   34 **state** dignity/ceremony/demeanour   36 **modest** moderate,
mild   **exception** i.e. taking exception, objecting   **withal** in addition   37 **terrible** frightening, inspiring
dread   38 **forespent** previous used up   39 **Roman . . . folly** Lucius Junius Brutus feigned stupidity to dupe
and expel Tarquinius Superbus, King of Rome   41 **ordure** manure   44 **though** even if   45 **weigh** judge,
estimate   47 **So . . . filled** so that the defences will be on an adequate scale   48 **of . . . projection** if planned
in too miserly a fashion   49 **scanting** witholding   51 **Think we** let us think   52 **look you** be prepared,
make sure you   53 **fleshed** hunting term referring to feeding hounds raw meat to excite them for the
chase   54 **bloody strain** bloodthirsty breed

55   That haunted us in our familiar paths.
        Witness our too much memorable shame
        When Crécy battle fatally was struck,
        And all our princes captived by the hand
        Of that black name, Edward, Black Prince of Wales,
60   Whiles that his mountain sire, on mountain
            standing,
        Up in the air, crowned with the golden sun,
        Saw his heroical seed, and smiled to see him
        Mangle the work of nature and deface
        The patterns that by God and by French fathers
65   Had twenty years been made. This is a stem
        Of that victorious stock, and let us fear
        The native mightiness and fate of him.

Enter a Messenger

MESSENGER Ambassadors from Harry King of England
        Do crave admittance to your majesty.
70   FRENCH KING We'll give them present audience. Go, and
            bring them.   [*Exeunt Messenger and others*]
        You see this chase is hotly followed, friends.
        DAUPHIN Turn head, and stop pursuit, for coward dogs
        Most spend their mouths when what they seem to
            threaten
        Runs far before them. Good my sovereign,
75   Take up the English short, and let them know
        Of what a monarchy you are the head.
        Self-love, my liege, is not so vile a sin
        As self-neglecting.

Enter Exeter [and others]

FRENCH KING From our brother of England?
80   EXETER From him, and thus he greets your majesty.
        He wills you, in the name of God Almighty,
        That you divest yourself and lay apart
        The borrowed glories that by gift of heaven,
        By law of nature and of nations, longs
85   To him and to his heirs, namely, the crown
        And all wide-stretchèd honours that pertain

---

55 haunted pursued **familiar** habitual/familial **57 struck** fought/stricken **60 mountain** i.e. ascendant/
immovable, sturdy; may also refer to Edward's birth in mountainous Wales **sire** father **62 seed**
offspring **63 Mangle** wound, hack at **64 patterns** exemplary models **65 This** i.e. Henry **67 native**
inborn **fate** destiny **70 present** immediate **71 chase . . . followed** hunt is urgently pursued **72 Turn**
head turn and face your pursuers (hunting term) **73 spend their mouths** bark, cry **75 Take . . . short**
take quick and decisive action towards the English **78 self-neglecting** a lack of self-respect **81 wills**
urges, demands **82 divest** undress **apart** aside **83 borrowed glories** i.e. the glories of kingship that are
not rightfully his **84 longs** appertains **86 wide-stretchèd** far-reaching

By custom and the ordinance of times
Unto the crown of France. That you may know
'Tis no sinister nor no awkward claim,
90 Picked from the worm-holes of long-vanished days,
Nor from the dust of old oblivion raked,
He sends you this most memorable line,   *Gives a paper*
In every branch truly demonstrative;
Willing you overlook this pedigree.
95 And when you find him evenly derived
From his most famed of famous ancestors,
Edward the Third, he bids you then resign
Your crown and kingdom, indirectly held
From him the native and true challenger.
100 FRENCH KING Or else what follows?
EXETER Bloody constraint. For if you hide the crown
Even in your hearts, there will he rake for it:
Therefore in fierce tempest is he coming,
In thunder and in earthquake, like a Jove,
105 That, if requiring fail, he will compel,
And bids you, in the bowels of the Lord,
Deliver up the crown, and to take mercy
On the poor souls for whom this hungry war
Opens his vasty jaws, and on your head
110 Turning the widows' tears, the orphans' cries
The dead men's blood, the pining maidens' groans,
For husbands, fathers and betrothèd lovers,
That shall be swallowed in this controversy.
This is his claim, his threatening and my message —
115 Unless the dauphin be in presence here,
To whom expressly I bring greeting too.
FRENCH KING For us, we will consider of this further:
Tomorrow shall you bear our full intent
Back to our brother of England.
120 DAUPHIN For the dauphin,
I stand here for him. What to him from England?
EXETER Scorn and defiance, slight regard, contempt,
And anything that may not misbecome
The mighty sender, doth he prize you at.

87 **ordinance of times** law established through long tradition   89 **sinister** irregular, unjust, deceitful
awkward oblique   90 **worm-holes** decay, incomplete remains   92 **line** family tree   95 **evenly derived**
directly descended   98 **indirectly** dishonestly, wrongfully   99 **native** natural/rightful by birth
101 **Bloody constraint** violent force, military compulsion   104 **Jove** ruler of the Roman gods, whose
weapon was a thunderbolt   105 **requiring** demanding   106 **bowels** inmost mercy   109 **on...Turning**
places responsibility with you for   122 **slight** disdainful   123 **misbecome** be unbecoming to   124 **prize**
you at consider you worth

125 Thus says my king: an if your father's highness
Do not, in grant of all demands at large,
Sweeten the bitter mock you sent his majesty,
He'll call you to so hot an answer of it,
That caves and womby vaultages of France
130 Shall chide your trespass and return your mock
In second accent of his ordinance.

DAUPHIN Say, if my father render fair return,
It is against my will, for I desire
Nothing but odds with England. To that end,
135 As matching to his youth and vanity,
I did present him with the Paris balls.

EXETER He'll make your Paris Louvre shake for it,
Were it the mistress-court of mighty Europe.
And be assured, you'll find a diff'rence,
140 As we his subjects have in wonder found,
Between the promise of his greener days
And these he masters now. Now he weighs time
Even to the utmost grain: that you shall read
In your own losses, if he stay in France.

145 FRENCH KING Tomorrow shall you know our mind at
full.   *Flourish*

EXETER Dispatch us with all speed, lest that our king
Come here himself to question our delay;
For he is footed in this land already.

FRENCH KING You shall be soon dispatched with fair
conditions:
150 A night is but small breath and little pause
To answer matters of this consequence.
                                        Flourish.   Exeunt

[Act 3]

Enter Chorus

CHORUS Thus with imagined wing our swift scene flies
In motion of no less celerity
Than that of thought. Suppose that you have seen

125 **an if** if   126 **at large** in full   129 **womby** womb-like, hollow   **vaultages** vaults, caverns
131 **second accent** echo   **ordinance** artillery (ordnance)/decree   132 **fair return** an agreeable reply
134 **odds** conflict   137 **Louvre** palace in Paris/puns on 'lover'   138 **mistress-court** principal court/
mistress, lover   141 **greener days** i.e. his wild youth   142 **masters** possesses/rules   **weighs ... grain** i.e.
makes careful use of his time   143 **read** see, learn   148 **footed** present, disembarked   150 **breath**
breathing space, break   3   1 **with imagined wing** i.e. the wings of imagination   2 **celerity** speed

The well-appointed king at Dover pier
5   Embark his royalty, and his brave fleet
With silken streamers, the young Phoebus fanning.
Play with your fancies, and in them behold
Upon the hempen tackle ship-boys climbing;
Hear the shrill whistle which doth order give
10   To sounds confused. Behold the threaden sails,
Borne with th'invisible and creeping wind,
Draw the huge bottoms through the furrowed sea,
Breasting the lofty surge. O, do but think
You stand upon the rivage and behold
15   A city on th'inconstant billows dancing;
For so appears this fleet majestical,
Holding due course to Harfleur. Follow, follow.
Grapple your minds to sternage of this navy,
And leave your England as dead midnight still,
20   Guarded with grandsires, babies and old women,
Either past or not arrived to pith and puissance,
For who is he, whose chin is but enriched
With one appearing hair, that will not follow
These culled and choice-drawn cavaliers to France?
25   Work, work your thoughts, and therein see a siege:
Behold the ordnance on their carriages,
With fatal mouths gaping on girded Harfleur.
Suppose th'ambassador from the French comes back,
Tells Harry that the king doth offer him
30   Katherine his daughter, and with her, to dowry,
Some petty and unprofitable dukedoms.
The offer likes not, and the nimble gunner
With linstock now the devilish cannon touches,

Alarum, and chambers go off

---

4 well-appointed well-equipped   **Dover** port on the south coast of England: Shakespeare seems to have forgotten that he had previously specified Southampton   **5 his royalty** his royal person, himself   **brave** bold/impressive, splendid   **6 streamers** banners, pennants   **the ... fanning** fanning the hot face of the sun (Phoebus, Roman god of the sun)   **7 Play with** indulge, exercise   **fancies** imaginations   **8 hempen tackle** rigging made from hemp   **9 whistle** i.e. that of the ship's chief officer   **order** command/harmony   **10 threaden** made of linen thread   **12 Draw** move, drag (perhaps with play on the sense of 'create, represent')   **bottoms** i.e. ships (literally hulls or keels)   **13 lofty surge** high, swelling waves   **14 rivage** shore   **15 inconstant billows** shifting waves   **17 Harfleur** French port at the mouth of the River Seine   **18 Grapple** fasten (nautical term; grappling hooks were used to attach one ship to another)   **sternage** the sterns of ships   **21 pith** strength   **22 whose ... hair** i.e. who has only just reached the early manhood (when stubble appears)   **24 culled** chosen   **choice-drawn** specially selected   **cavaliers** military gentlemen   **25 Work** be industrious/create, fashion   **26 ordnance** cannons   **carriages** wheeled frames that cannons are mounted on   **27 girded** besieged, surrounded   **28 Suppose** imagine   **32 likes not** displeases   **33 linstock** stick for holding the gunner's lighted match   ***Alarum*** a call to arms by trumpets or drums   ***chambers*** pieces of artillery, such as cannon

And down goes all before them. Still be kind,
35   And eke out our performance with your mind. *Exit*

Act 3 Scene 1

Enter the King, Exeter, Bedford and Gloucester. Alarum.
[Enter Soldiers with] scaling-ladders at Harfleur

KING HENRY V Once more unto the breach, dear friends,
    once more,
Or close the wall up with our English dead.
In peace there's nothing so becomes a man
As modest stillness and humility,
5   But when the blast of war blows in our ears,
Then imitate the action of the tiger:
Stiffen the sinews, conjure up the blood,
Disguise fair nature with hard-favoured rage,
Then lend the eye a terrible aspect:
10   Let it pry through the portage of the head
Like the brass cannon, let the brow o'erwhelm it
As fearfully as doth a gallèd rock
O'erhang and jutty his confounded base,
Swilled with the wild and wasteful ocean.
15   Now set the teeth and stretch the nostril wide,
Hold hard the breath and bend up every spirit
To his full height. On, on, you noblest English,
Whose blood is fet from fathers of war-proof,
Fathers that, like so many Alexanders,
20   Have in these parts from morn till even fought
And sheathed their swords for lack of argument.
Dishonour not your mothers: now attest
That those whom you called fathers did beget you.
Be copy now to men of grosser blood,
25   And teach them how to war. And you, good yeoman,

---

35 eke out supplement   **3.1** *Location: Harfleur, northern France*   **scaling-ladders** used by soldiers to climb defensive fortifications   **1 breach** gap in defensive fortifications   **7 the blood** i.e. heat, courage and ferocity   **8 hard-favoured** ugly   **9 lend** give   **terrible** terrifying   **aspect** appearance, gaze **10 portage** porthole   **11 o'erwhelm** overhang, project over   **12 fearfully** frighteningly   **gallèd** battered **13 jutty** jut out over   **confounded** ruined   **14 Swilled** washed   **wasteful** destructive   **15 set the teeth** i.e. bare/grit your teeth   **16 bend up** strain (from archery: to bring tension to the string of a bow) **18 fet** derived   **of war-proof** tested and proved in war   **19 Alexanders** i.e. Alexander the Great who lamented that he had no more worlds to conquer   **21 sheathed . . . argument** only stopped fighting because there was no opposition left   **22 Dishonour . . . mothers** i.e. by suggesting that they were unfaithful to your fathers   **23 beget** conceive   **24 copy** an example   **grosser** lesser, coarser   **25 yeoman** man of property who is not a gentleman

Whose limbs were made in England, show us here
The mettle of your pasture: let us swear
That you are worth your breeding, which I doubt
   not,
For there is none of you so mean and base,
30   That hath not noble lustre in your eyes.
I see you stand like greyhounds in the slips,
Straining upon the start. The game's afoot:
Follow your spirit, and upon this charge
Cry 'God for Harry, England, and Saint George!'
                            [Exeunt]
                Alarum, and chambers go off

[Act 3 Scene 2]

running scene 6 continues

Enter Nym, Bardolph, Pistol and Boy

BARDOLPH On, on, on, on, on! To the breach, to the
   breach!
NYM Pray thee, corporal, stay: the knocks are too hot,
   and for mine own part, I have not a case of lives. The
5   humour of it is too hot, that is the very plainsong
   of it.
PISTOL The plainsong is most just, for humours do
   abound.
   Knocks go and come, God's vassals drop and die,
     And sword and shield,   *Sings*
10   In bloody field,
     Doth win immortal fame.
BOY Would I were in an ale-house in London: I would
   give all my fame for a pot of ale and safety.
PISTOL And I:
15   If wishes would prevail with me,   *Sings*
      My purpose should not fail with me,
      But thither would I hie.
   BOY   As duly,   *Sings*
      But not as truly,
20   As bird doth sing on bough.

27 **mettle** quality   **your pasture** the land you were raised on i.e. your breeding   **29 so . . . base** of such low social status   **31 slips** leashes designed for quick release   **32 upon the start** in anticipation of release   **33 charge** order/report of the cannon   **34 Harry** i.e. Henry   **Saint George** patron saint of England   **3.2**   **3 knocks** hard blows   **4 case** box/set, pair (of pistols)   **5 plainsong** i.e. truth (literally, simple melody)   **7 humours** dampness, mist/emotions/bodily fluids, especially blood   **8 vassals** servants   **13 fame** reputation, honour   **15 prevail** succeed   **16 My . . . me** i.e. I would get what I want   **17 hie** hurry   **19 truly** honourably/in tune

Enter Fluellen

FLUELLEN Up to the breach, you dogs! Avaunt, you   *Drives them on*
cullions!

PISTOL Be merciful, great duke, to men of mould.
Abate thy rage, abate thy manly rage,
25   Abate thy rage, great duke!
Good bawcock, bate thy rage: use lenity, sweet
chuck!

NYM These be good humours! Your honour wins bad
humours.   *Exeunt [all but Boy]*

BOY As young as I am, I have observed these three
30   swashers. I am boy to them all three, but all they
three, though they would serve me, could not be
man to me; for indeed three such antics do not
amount to a man. For Bardolph, he is white-livered
and red-faced; by the means whereof a faces it out,
35   but fights not. For Pistol, he hath a killing tongue and
a quiet sword; by the means whereof a breaks words,
and keeps whole weapons. For Nym, he hath heard
that men of few words are the best men, and
therefore he scorns to say his prayers, lest a should be
40   thought a coward. But his few bad words are
matched with as few good deeds; for a never broke
any man's head but his own, and that was against a
post when he was drunk. They will steal anything,
and call it purchase. Bardolph stole a lute-case, bore
45   it twelve leagues, and sold it for three halfpence. Nym
and Bardolph are sworn brothers in filching, and in
Calais they stole a fire-shovel. I knew by that piece of
service the men would carry coals. They would have
me as familiar with men's pockets as their gloves or
50   their handkerchiefs, which makes much against my
manhood, if I should take from another's pocket to

Fluellen anglicized spelling of Llewellyn   21 **Avaunt** begone   22 **cullions** rascals/testicles   23 **duke** captain, leader   **mould** clay (perhaps with play on the sense of 'decay, rottenness')   26 **bawcock** fine fellow (from French *beau coq*)   **lenity** mildness   **chuck** chick   27 **Your . . . humours** perhaps 'you are making everyone unhappy, distempered'; many editors emend 'wins' to 'runs'   30 **swashers** swashbucklers, boasters   **boy** servant/youth   32 **man** man-servant/manly   **antics** buffoons   33 **white-livered** i.e. cowardly (the liver was thought to be the seat of the passions)   34 **a faces** he brazens, blusters   36 **breaks words** exchanges words/breaks promises/mangles vocabulary (puns on 'break swords', which Pistol fails to do)   37 **whole** i.e. unused   44 **purchase** plunder, booty   45 **twelve leagues** approximately thirty-six miles (a league was about three miles)   46 **sworn brothers** brothers-in-arms   **filching** stealing   47 **Calais** port on the northern coast of France, occupied by the English 1347–1558   **fire-shovel** shovel for placing coals on the fire   **piece of service** military exploit   48 **carry coals** show cowardice/submit to insults/do degrading work   49 **familiar . . . pockets** i.e. by picking them   51 **manhood** manliness

put into mine; for it is plain pocketing up of wrongs. I
must leave them, and seek some better service: their
villainy goes against my weak stomach, and
55   therefore I must cast it up.   *Exit*
Enter Gower [and Fluellen]

GOWER Captain Fluellen, you must come presently to
the mines; the Duke of Gloucester would speak with
you.

FLUELLEN To the mines? Tell you the duke, it is not so
60   good to come to the mines, for look you, the mines is
not according to the disciplines of the war: the
concavities of it is not sufficient, for look you,
th'athversary, you may discuss unto the duke, look
you, is digt himself, four yard under, the
65   countermines. By Cheshu, I think a will plow up
all, if there is not better directions.

GOWER The Duke of Gloucester, to whom the order of
the siege is given, is altogether directed by an
Irishman, a very valiant gentleman, i'faith.

70 **FLUELLEN** It is Captain MacMorris, is it not?
GOWER I think it be.

FLUELLEN By Cheshu, he is an ass, as in the world. I will
verify as much in his beard. He has no more
directions in the true disciplines of the wars, look
75   you, of the Roman disciplines, than is a puppy dog.
Enter MacMorris and Captain Jamy

GOWER Here a comes, and the Scots captain, Captain
Jamy, with him.

FLUELLEN Captain Jamy is a marvellous falorous
gentleman, that is certain, and of great expedition
80   and knowledge in th'aunchient wars, upon my
particular knowledge of his directions. By Cheshu,
he will maintain his argument as well as any military
man in the world, in the disciplines of the pristine
wars of the Romans.

---

52 pocketing . . . **wrongs** pocketing stolen goods/accepting insults   **54 goes** . . . **stomach** makes me sick/
goes against my valour   **55 cast it up** give it up/vomit it up   **56 presently** at once   **57 mines** tunnels dug
under besieged places and packed with explosives   **59 not** i.e. not constructed   **61 disciplines** proper
procedures   **62 concavities** hollowness, depth   **63 th'athversary** the adversary; Shakespeare attempts to
render his Welsh accent phonetically   **discuss** explain, declare   **64 is digt** has digged   **65 countermines**
passages dug by the besieged defenders as a means of trying to intercept enemies   **Chesu** Jesus (suggesting
Welsh pronunciation)   **plow up** blow up   **66 directions** instructions, plans   **67 order** control,
organization   **72 in** any in   **73 in his beard** i.e. to his face   **75 Roman disciplines** i.e. traditional military
tactics, not so heavily reliant on gunpowder   **78 falorous** i.e. valorous   **79 expedition** quickness of
argument; possibly an error for 'experience' and 'erudition'

85 **JAMY** I say gud day, Captain Fluellen.

FLUELLEN God-den to your worship, good Captain James.

GOWER How now, Captain MacMorris? Have you quit the mines? Have the pioneers given o'er?

MACMORRIS By Chrish, la, tish ill done: the work ish give
90 over, the trompet sound the retreat. By my hand, I swear, and my father's soul, the work ish ill done, it ish give over. I would have blowed up the town, so Chrish save me, la, in an hour. O, tish ill done, tish ill done. By my hand, tish ill done!

95 **FLUELLEN** Captain MacMorris, I beseech you now, will you voutsafe me, look you, a few disputations with you, as partly touching or concerning the disciplines of the war, the Roman wars, in the way of argument, look you, and friendly communication — partly to
100 satisfy my opinion, and partly for the satisfaction, look you, of my mind, as touching the direction of the military discipline, that is the point.

JAMY It sall be vary gud, gud feith, gud captains bath, and I sall quit you with gud leve, as I may pick
105 occasion; that sall I, marry.

MACMORRIS It is no time to discourse, so Chrish save me. The day is hot and the weather and the wars and the king and the dukes: it is no time to discourse. The town is beseeched, and the trumpet call us to the
110 breach, and we talk, and, be Chrish, do nothing. 'Tis shame for us all. So God sa' me, 'tis shame to stand still, it is shame, by my hand. And there is throats to be cut, and works to be done, and there ish nothing done, so Chrish sa' me, la!

115 **JAMY** By the mess, ere these eyes of mine take themselves to slomber, I'll de gud service, or I'll lig i'th'grund for it; ay, or go to death. And I'll pay't as valorously as I may, that sall I suerly do, that is the breff and the long. Marry, I wad full fain heard some
120 question 'tween you tway.

---

85 **gud** i.e. good; Jamy's Scottish accent is also rendered phonetically   86 **God-den** good day/evening
88 **pioneers** soldiers employed to dig trenches and tunnels   **given o'er** finished   89 **la** exclamation used as
a substitute for an oath   **tish** 'tis, i.e. it is (MacMorris' Irish pronunciation)   92 **give over** abandoned, given
up   96 **voutsafe** vouchsafe, i.e. permit   **disputations** conversations   103 **sall** shall   **feith** faith   **bath**
both   104 **quit** requite, answer   **gud leve** your good leave, i.e. permission   **pick occasion** find the
opportunity   105 **marry** by the Virgin Mary   109 **beseeched** besieged   110 **be** by   111 **sa'** save
115 **mess** mass (a common oath)   **ere** before   116 **lig** lie   118 **suerly** surely   119 **breff...long** i.e. the
long and the short of it   **breff** brief   **wad** would   **full fain** very gladly   **heard** have heard   120 **question**
discussion, debate   **tway** two (Scottish dialect)

FLUELLEN Captain MacMorris, I think, look you, under
   your correction, there is not many of your nation—
MACMORRIS Of my nation? What ish my nation? Ish a
   villain and a bastard and a knave and a rascal. What
125 ish my nation? Who talks of my nation?
FLUELLEN Look you, if you take the matter otherwise
   than is meant, Captain MacMorris, peradventure I
   shall think you do not use me with that affability as
   in discretion you ought to use me, look you, being as
130 good a man as yourself, both in the disciplines of war,
   and in the derivation of my birth, and in other
   particularities.
MACMORRIS I do not know you so good a man as myself.
   So Chrish save me, I will cut off your head.
135 GOWER Gentlemen both, you will mistake each other.
JAMY Ah, that's a foul fault.   *A parley*
GOWER The town sounds a parley.
FLUELLEN Captain MacMorris, when there is more better
   opportunity to be required, look you, I will be so bold
140 as to tell you I know the disciplines of war, and there
   is an end.   *Exeunt*

[Act 3 Scene 3]   *running scene 6 continues*

Enter the King and all his train before the gates

KING HENRY V How yet resolves the governor of the
      town?
   This is the latest parle we will admit:
   Therefore to our best mercy give yourselves,
   Or like to men proud of destruction
5 Defy us to our worst, for as I am a soldier,
   A name that in my thoughts becomes me best,
   If I begin the batt'ry once again,
   I will not leave the half-achieved Harfleur
   Till in her ashes she lie burièd.
10 The gates of mercy shall be all shut up,

121 **under your correction** i.e. with your permission   123 **Ish . . . rascal** either MacMorris declares that
anyone who criticizes the Irish is a villain etc.; or he anticipates the habitual terms of abuse levelled at the
Irish   127 **peradventure** perhaps   128 **use** treat   129 **discretion** good judgement   135 **will** are going
to/are determined to   *parley* trumpet call indicating a ceasefire whilst negotiation is to take place between
the opposing sides   139 **required** asked for, i.e. available   3.3   *Location: still outside Harfleur*   **gates**
town gates   1 **resolves** answers, determines   2 **latest** last   **parle** ceasefire and negotiation   **admit** allow,
grant   4 **destruction** their own ruin   6 **becomes** fits, suits   7 **batt'ry** bombardment   8 **half-achieved**
half-conquered

And the fleshed soldier, rough and hard of heart,
In liberty of bloody hand shall range
With conscience wide as hell, mowing like grass
Your fresh fair virgins and your flow'ring infants.
15 What is it then to me, if impious war,
Arrayed in flames like to the prince of fiends,
Do with his smirched complexion all fell feats
Enlinked to waste and desolation?
What is't to me, when you yourselves are cause,
20 If your pure maidens fall into the hand
Of hot and forcing violation?
What rein can hold licentious wickedness
When down the hill he holds his fierce career?
We may as bootless spend our vain command
25 Upon th'enragèd soldiers in their spoil
As send precepts to the leviathan
To come ashore. Therefore, you men of Harfleur,
Take pity of your town and of your people,
Whiles yet my soldiers are in my command,
30 Whiles yet the cool and temperate wind of grace
O'erblows the filthy and contagious clouds
Of heady murder, spoil and villainy.
If not, why, in a moment look to see
The blind and bloody soldier with foul hand
35 Defile the locks of your shrill-shrieking daughters,
Your fathers taken by the silver beards,
And their most reverend heads dashed to the walls,
Your naked infants spitted upon pikes,
Whiles the mad mothers with their howls confused
40 Do break the clouds, as did the wives of Jewry
At Herod's bloody-hunting slaughtermen.

---

11 fleshed used to war/eager for bloodshed   **12 liberty...range** shall be allowed total freedom to kill
14 flow'ring flourishing   **15 impious** sinful, wicked   **16 prince of fiends** i.e. the devil   **17 smirched**
discoloured, filthy   **fell** cruel, fierce   **18 Enlinked** joined, linked   **21 hot** lustful/eager/aggressive
violation violence/rape   **22 rein** puns on 'reign'   **hold** contain, restrain   **23 career** rapid gallop
24 bootless uselessly   **spend** waste   **vain** useless   **25 spoil** act of pillaging/booty   **26 precepts** legal
summons/moral instructions   **leviathan** biblical sea creature of enormous size   **28 of** on   **30 temperate**
moderate, restrained   **31 O'erblows** blows away   **contagious** noxious, infectious (clouds were thought to
harbour disease)   **32 heady** impulsive, violent   **spoil** pillaging   **33 look** expect   **35 locks** hair/guarded
chastity   **38 spitted** impaled   **pikes** weapons with long wooden handles and pointed metal heads
39 confused disordered/mingled together   **40 Jewry** Judaea (region in southern Palestine, now Israel)/the
Jewish people   **41 Herod's bloody-hunting slaughtermen** in an attempt to destroy the infant Jesus, King
Herod ordered the slaughter of all boys under the age of two in Bethlehem and surrounding areas (Matthew
2:16–18)

What say you? Will you yield, and this avoid?
Or, guilty in defence, be thus destroyed?
Enter Governor [above, on the walls]
GOVERNOR Our expectation hath this day an end.
45   The dauphin, whom of succours we entreated,
Returns us that his powers are yet not ready
To raise so great a siege: therefore, great king,
We yield our town and lives to thy soft mercy.
Enter our gates, dispose of us and ours,
50   For we no longer are defensible.
KING HENRY V Open your gates.— Come, uncle Exeter,
Go you and enter Harfleur; there remain,
And fortify it strongly gainst the French.
Use mercy to them all. For us, dear uncle,
55   The winter coming on and sickness growing
Upon our soldiers, we will retire to Calais.
Tonight in Harfleur will we be your guest;
Tomorrow for the march are we addressed.
        Flourish, and [the King and his train] enter the town

---

[Act 3 Scene 4]   *running scene 7*

Enter Katherine and [Alice,] an old gentlewoman

KATHERINE *Alice, tu as été en Angleterre, et tu bien parles le
        langage.*
ALICE *Un peu, madame.*
KATHERINE *Je te prie, m'enseignez: il faut que j'apprenne à*
5   *parler. Comment appelez-vous la main en anglais?*
ALICE *La main? Elle est appelée* de hand.
KATHERINE De hand. *Et les doigts?*
ALICE *Les doigts? Ma foi, j'oublie les doigts, mais je me
        souviendrai. Les doigts? Je pense qu'ils sont appelés* de
10   fingres. *Oui,* de fingres.

---

43 guilty in defence i.e. guilty of bringing about this slaughter through persisting in trying to defend the
town   **44 expectation** hopefulness   **45 succours** help/reinforcements   **46 Returns** replies to   **powers**
troops   **47 raise** put an end to   **48 soft** compassionate   **49 dispose** control, govern/make arrangements
for   **58 addressed** prepared, directed   **3.4**   *Location: not specified, but presumably the French royal
court, at Rouen, northern France*   **1** *Alice...langage* 'Alice, you have been in England, and you speak
the language well'   **3** *Un peu, madame* 'a little, my lady'   **4** *Je...anglais?* 'I pray you, teach me: I must
learn to speak [it]. What do you call the hand in English?'   **6** *La...*hand 'The hand? It is called "de hand"'
de mispronunciation of English 'the'   **7** De...*doigts?* ' "De hand". And the fingers?'   **8** *Les...*fingres
'The fingers? By my faith, I forget the fingers; but I will remember. The fingers? I think that they are called
"de fingres". Yes, "de fingres"'

KATHERINE *La main,* de hand, *les doigts,* de fingres. *Je pense que je suis le bon écolier. J'ai gagné deux mots d'anglais vitement. Comment appelez-vous les ongles?*

ALICE *Les ongles? Nous les appelons* de nails.

15 **KATHERINE** De nails. *Écoutez, dites-moi, si je parle bien:* de hand, de fingres, *et* de nails.

ALICE *C'est bien dit, madame. Il est fort bon anglais.*

KATHERINE *Dites-moi l'anglais pour le bras.*

ALICE De arm, *madame.*

20 **KATHERINE** *Et le coude?*

ALICE D'elbow.

KATHERINE D'elbow. *Je m'en fais la répétition de tous les mots que vous m'avez appris dès à présent.*

ALICE *Il est trop difficile, madame, comme je pense.*

25 **KATHERINE** *Excusez-moi, Alice, écoutez:* de hand, de fingres, de nails, de arma, de bilbow.

ALICE D'elbow, *madame.*

KATHERINE *O Seigneur Dieu, je m'en oublie!* D'elbow. *Comment appelez-vous le col?*

30 **ALICE** De neck, *madame.*

KATHERINE De nick. *Et le menton?*

ALICE De chin.

KATHERINE De sin. *Le col,* de nick, *le menton,* de sin.

ALICE *Oui. Sauf votre honneur, en vérité, vous prononcez les*
35 *mots aussi droit que les natifs d'Angleterre.*

KATHERINE *Je ne doute point d'apprendre, par la grâce de Dieu, et en peu de temps.*

ALICE *N'avez vous pas déjà oublié ce que je vous ai enseigné?*

KATHERINE *Non, je réciterai à vous promptement:* de hand,
40 de fingres, de mails—

ALICE De nails, *madame.*

---

11 *La . . . ongles?* 'The hand, "de hand"; the fingers, "de fingres". I think that I am a good pupil. I have learned two English words quickly. What do you call the nails?' **14** *Les . . .* **nails** 'The nails? We call them "de nails"' **15** *Écoutez . . . bien* 'Listen, tell me, if I speak well' **17** *C'est . . . anglais* 'That's well said, my lady. It is very good English' **18** *Dites-moi . . . bras* 'Tell me the English for the arm' **19** *De arm, madame* ' "De arm", my lady' **20** *Et le coude?* 'And the elbow?' **22** *Je . . . présent* 'I shall repeat all of the words that you have taught me so far' **24** *Il . . . pense* 'It is too difficult, my lady, I think' **25** *Excusez-moi, Alice, écoutez* 'Pardon me, Alice, listen' **26** **bilbow** type of sword/manacle for the ankles **28** *O . . . col?* 'O Lord God, I am forgetting! "D'elbow". What do you call the neck?' **31** **nick** puns on English slang sense of 'vagina' *Et le menton?* 'And the chin?' **33** **sin** given the slang sense of 'nick', 'sin' takes on a sense of 'sexual transgression' **34** *Oui . . . d'Angleterre* 'Yes. Saving your honour, in truth, you pronounce the words as correctly as the natives of England' **36** *Je . . . temps* 'I do not doubt that I shall learn [English], by the grace of God, and in a short space of time' **38** *N'avez . . . enseigné?* 'Have you not already forgotten what I have taught you?' **39** *Non . . . promptement* 'No, I will recite it to you promptly' **40** **mails** possible pun on 'males'

KATHERINE De nails, de arm, de ilbow.

ALICE *Sauf votre honneur,* d'elbow.

KATHERINE *Ainsi dis-je,* d'elbow, de nick, et de sin.

45   *Comment appelez-vous le pied et la robe?*

ALICE *Le* foot, *madame, et le* coun.

KATHERINE *Le* foot *et le* coun! *O Seigneur Dieu! Ce sont les mots de son mauvais, corruptible, gros, et impudique, et non pour les dames d'honneur d'user. Je ne voudrais*

50   *prononcer ces mots devant les seigneurs de France pour tout le monde. Foh! Le* foot *et le* coun! *Néanmoins, je réciterai une autre fois ma leçon ensemble:* de hand, de fingres, de nails, de arm, d'elbow, de nick, de sin, de foot, de coun.

55   **ALICE** *Excellent, madame!*

KATHERINE *C'est assez pour une fois. Allons-nous à dîner.*

Exeunt

[Act 3 Scene 5]   *running scene 7 continues*

Enter the King of France, the Dauphin, [the Duke of Brittany,] the Constable of France and others

FRENCH KING 'Tis certain he hath passed the River
        Somme.

CONSTABLE And if he be not fought withal, my lord,
        Let us not live in France, let us quit all
        And give our vineyards to a barbarous people.

5   **DAUPHIN** *O Dieu vivant!* Shall a few sprays of us,
        The emptying of our fathers' luxury,
        Our scions, put in wild and savage stock,
        Spirt up so suddenly into the clouds,
        And overlook their grafters?

---

43 *Sauf...*d'elbow 'Saving your honour, "d'elbow"' **44** *Ainsi...robe?* 'So I said, "d'elbow, de nick" and "de sin". What do you call the foot and the gown?' **46 foot** puns on French *foutre,* i.e. 'fuck' **coun** 'gown', puns on French *con,* i.e. 'cunt' **47 O...ensemble** 'O Lord God! These are words with a wicked sound, corrupting, coarse and lewd, and not for ladies of honour to use: I would not like to utter these words before the gentlemen of France for all the world. Fie! The "foot" and the "coun"! Nevertheless, I will recite my whole lesson once again' **55 Excellent, madame!** 'Excellent, my lady!' **56 C'est...dîner** 'That's enough for one time. Let us go to dinner.' **3.5 1 River Somme** just over halfway between Calais and Harfleur **2 withal** with **5 O Dieu vivant!** 'O living God!' (French) **sprays** offshoots/spurts of semen (refers to the fact that after the Norman Conquest of 1066, many English have some French heritage) **6 emptying** ejaculate **luxury** lust **7 scions** shoots used for grafting (when a shoot from one plant is fused to the stem of another) **stock** the plant which receives the graft (here, the English) **8 Spirt** sprout **9 overlook** rise above/look down on/ignore/bewitch **grafters** i.e. those who have done the grafting/the trees from which the grafted shoot was taken

10 **BRITTANY** Normans, but bastard Normans, Norman
                bastards!
        Mort de ma vie! If they march along
        Unfought withal, but I will sell my dukedom
        To buy a slobb'ry and a dirty farm
        In that nook-shotten isle of Albion.
15 **CONSTABLE** *Dieu de batailles*! Where have they this
                mettle?
        Is not their climate foggy, raw and dull,
        On whom, as in despite, the sun looks pale,
        Killing their fruit with frowns? Can sodden water,
        A drench for sur-reined jades, their barley broth,
20   Decoct their cold blood to such valiant heat?
        And shall our quick blood, spirited with wine,
        Seem frosty? O, for honour of our land,
        Let us not hang like roping icicles
        Upon our houses' thatch, whiles a more frosty people
25   Sweat drops of gallant youth in our rich fields!
        Poor we may call them in their native lords.
    DAUPHIN By faith and honour,
        Our madams mock at us, and plainly say
        Our mettle is bred out and they will give
30   Their bodies to the lust of English youth
        To new-store France with bastard warriors.
    BOURBON They bid us to the English dancing-schools,
        And teach lavoltas high and swift corantos,
        Saying our grace is only in our heels
35   And that we are most lofty runaways.
    FRENCH KING Where is Montjoy the herald? Speed him
                hence.
        Let him greet England with our sharp defiance.
        Up, princes, and with spirit of honour edged
        More sharper than your swords, hie to the field:
40   Charles Delabret, High Constable of France,
        You Dukes of Orléans, Bourbon, and of Berri,

---

10 **Normans** i.e. the English who have French ancestry   **bastard** illegitimate   11 *Mort . . . vie*! 'Death of
my life!'   13 **Slobb'ry** slimy, muddy   14 **nook-shotten** crookedly-shaped   **Albion** the island composed of
England, Scotland and Wales   15 *Dieu de batailles*! 'God of battles!'   **mettle** spirit, temperament,
courage   17 **despite** contempt, malice   **looks pale** i.e. barely shines   18 **sodden** boiled, stewed
19 **drench** drink/dose of medicine   **sur-reined** over-ridden   **jades** worn-out horses   **barley broth** strong
ale   20 **Decoct** heat up   23 **roping** hanging like ropes   26 **Poor . . . lords** i.e. whilst our fields are **rich** in
themselves, they may be called poor if they are owned by such spiritless masters as we are proving to be
28 **madams** ladies/wives   29 **bred out** weakened by generations of breeding   31 **new-store** freshly
populate   33 **lavoltas . . . corantos** dances which involve leaping, turning and running (implying
cowardice)   34 **our . . . heels** our only accomplishment is in dancing/running away   35 **lofty** high born/
proficient/high leaping   36 **herald** messenger   37 **England** the country/King Henry   39 **hie** hurry

Alençon, Brabant, Bar, and Burgundy;
Jaques Chatillion, Rambures, Vaudemont,
Beaumont, Grandpré, Roussi, and Fauconbridge,
45   Foix, Lestrale, Boucicault, and Charolais,
High dukes, great princes, barons, lords and knights,
For your great seats now quit you of great shames.
Bar Harry England, that sweeps through our land
With pennons painted in the blood of Harfleur.
50   Rush on his host, as doth the melted snow
Upon the valleys, whose low vassal seat
The Alps doth spit and void his rheum upon.
Go down upon him, you have power enough,
And in a captive chariot into Rouen
55   Bring him our prisoner.
CONSTABLE This becomes the great.
Sorry am I his numbers are so few,
His soldiers sick and famished in their march,
For I am sure, when he shall see our army,
60   He'll drop his heart into the sink of fear
And for achievement offer us his ransom.
FRENCH KING Therefore, lord constable, haste on
     Montjoy,
And let him say to England that we send
To know what willing ransom he will give.—
65   Prince Dauphin, you shall stay with us in Rouen.
DAUPHIN Not so, I do beseech your majesty.
FRENCH KING Be patient, for you shall remain with us.—
Now forth, lord constable and princes all,
And quickly bring us word of England's fall. *Exeunt*

[Act 3 Scene 6]   *running scene 8*

Enter Captains, English and Welsh: Gower and Fluellen

GOWER How now, Captain Fluellen? Come you from the
     bridge?
FLUELLEN I assure you, there is very excellent services
     committed at the bridge.

---

47 seats estates/ranks, status   **quit** absolve/avenge/rid   **48 Bar** obstruct   **49 pennons** banners,
streamers attached to lances   **50 host** army   **52 void** empty, cough-up, sneeze   **rheum** watery discharge,
mucus (here, melted snow)   **54 Rouen** town in northern France, capital of Normandy   **56 becomes the
great** befits kingly greatness   **60 heart** courage, spirit   **sink** cesspit   **61 for achievement** in exchange for
honour/as the only paltry thing to be achieved   **his ransom** amount that must be paid on his defeat
62 haste on dispatch with speed   **3.6** *Location: the English camp, northern France*   **2 bridge**
historically, this would have been over the River Ternoise, on the way to Calais   **3 services** military feats

5 **GOWER** Is the Duke of Exeter safe?

FLUELLEN The Duke of Exeter is as magnanimous as
  Agamemnon, and a man that I love and honour with
  my soul and my heart and my duty and my life and
  my living and my uttermost power. He is not — God
10 be praised and blessed! — any hurt in the world, but
  keeps the bridge most valiantly, with excellent
  discipline. There is an aunchient lieutenant there at
  the pridge, I think in my very conscience he is as
  valiant a man as Mark Antony, and he is a man of no
15 estimation in the world, but I did see him do as
  gallant service.

GOWER What do you call him?

FLUELLEN He is called Aunchient Pistol.

GOWER I know him not.

Enter Pistol

20 **FLUELLEN** Here is the man.

PISTOL Captain, I thee beseech to do me favours:
  The Duke of Exeter doth love thee well.

FLUELLEN Ay, I praise God, and I have merited some love
  at his hands.

25 **PISTOL** Bardolph, a soldier, firm and sound of heart,
  And of buxom valour, hath, by cruel fate,
  And giddy Fortune's furious fickle wheel,
  That goddess blind,
  That stands upon the rolling restless stone—

30 **FLUELLEN** By your patience, Aunchient Pistol. Fortune is
  painted blind, with a muffler afore her eyes, to signify
  to you that Fortune is blind; and she is painted also
  with a wheel, to signify to you, which is the moral of
  it, that she is turning and inconstant, and mutability,
35 and variation. And her foot, look you, is fixed upon a
  spherical stone, which rolls and rolls and rolls. In
  good truth, the poet makes a most excellent
  description of it. Fortune is an excellent moral.

---

6 magnanimous of great and generous spirit, nobly valiant   **7 Agamemnon** leader of the Greeks at the
siege of Troy   **13 pridge** bridge (Fluellen's Welsh accent renders 'b' as 'p')   **14 Mark Antony** famous
Roman general   **no estimation** reputation/social standing   **18 Aunchient** i.e. Ancient, an ensign or bearer
of military banners   **26 buxom** lively, vigorous/pliant   **27 giddy** fickle   **Fortune's . . . blind** Fortune was
traditionally depicted as a blind woman turning a wheel that raised humans up and cast them down
furious cruel/violently turning   **29 rolling restless stone** alternative image of Fortune, the possessor of a
rolling stone on which humans balanced precariously   **30 By your patience** i.e. forgive me for interrupting
31 muffler blindfold   **38 moral** symbolic figure, allegory

PISTOL Fortune is Bardolph's foe, and frowns on him,
40   For he hath stol'n a pax,
        And hangèd must a be — a damnèd death!
        Let gallows gape for dog, let man go free
        And let not hemp his wind-pipe suffocate.
        But Exeter hath given the doom of death
45   For pax of little price.
        Therefore, go speak — the duke will hear thy voice —
        And let not Bardolph's vital thread be cut
        With edge of penny cord and vile reproach.
        Speak, captain, for his life, and I will thee requite.
50 FLUELLEN Aunchient Pistol, I do partly understand your
        meaning.
    PISTOL Why then, rejoice therefore.
    FLUELLEN Certainly, aunchient, it is not a thing to
        rejoice at, for if, look you, he were my brother, I
55   would desire the duke to use his good pleasure and
        put him to execution; for discipline ought to be used.
    PISTOL Die and be damned! And *figo* for thy friendship!
    FLUELLEN It is well.
    PISTOL The fig of Spain!   *Exit*
60 FLUELLEN Very good.
    GOWER Why, this is an arrant counterfeit rascal. I
        remember him now: a bawd, a cutpurse.
    FLUELLEN I'll assure you, a uttered as prave words at the
        pridge as you shall see in a summer's day. But it is
65   very well. What he has spoke to me, that is well, I
        warrant you, when time is serve.
    GOWER Why, 'tis a gull, a fool, a rogue, that now and
        then goes to the wars to grace himself at his return
        into London under the form of a soldier; and such
70   fellows are perfect in the great commanders' names,
        and they will learn you by rote where services were
        done; at such and such a sconce, at such a breach, at
        such a convoy, who came off bravely, who was shot,

---

40 pax disc, usually of gold or silver, bearing an image of the crucifixion, kissed by those taking
Communion   **43 hemp** i.e. rope made of hemp   **44 doom** judgement   **47 vital thread** thread of life,
supposedly spun and cut by the three Fates   **48 penny cord** cheap rope   **reproach** blame, disgrace
49 requite repay (with a bribe)   **50 partly** i.e. because it is implied rather than stated/because Pistol's
speech is confusing   **54 if** even if   **57 *figo*** a fig (from old Spanish *figo* or Italian *fico*); exclamation of
contempt, often accompanied by an obscene gesture known as the **fig of Spain**, which consisted of thrusting
the thumb between the index and middle fingers or into the mouth   **61 arrant** downright   **counterfeit**
deceptive, feigning   **62 bawd** pimp   **cutpurse** pickpocket   **64 a summer's day** i.e. a long day
66 warrant assure   **time is serve** there is opportunity   **67 gull** fool, dupe/hoaxer   **70 perfect**
word-perfect   **71 learn you** teach/learn (**you** being emphatic)   **72 sconce** small fort   **73 convoy** armed
escort   **came off** acquitted himself

who disgraced, what terms the enemy stood on —
75   and this they con perfectly in the phrase of war,
which they trick up with new-tuned oaths. And
what a beard of the general's cut and a horrid suit of
the camp will do among foaming bottles and ale-
washed wits is wonderful to be thought on. But you
80   must learn to know such slanders of the age, or else
you may be marvellously mistook.

FLUELLEN I tell you what, Captain Gower, I do perceive
he is not the man that he would gladly make show to
the world he is: if I find a hole in his coat, I will tell
85   him my mind. Hark you, the king is coming and I   *Drum heard*
must speak with him from the pridge.

*Drum and colours. Enter the King and his poor Soldiers [and
Gloucester]*

God pless your majesty!

KING HENRY V How now, Fluellen? Cam'st thou from the
bridge?

90   **FLUELLEN** Ay, so please your majesty. The Duke of
Exeter has very gallantly maintained the pridge; the
French is gone off, look you, and there is gallant and
most prave passages. Marry, th'athversary was have
possession of the pridge, but he is enforced to retire,
95   and the Duke of Exeter is master of the pridge. I can
tell your majesty, the duke is a prave man.

KING HENRY V What men have you lost, Fluellen?

FLUELLEN The perdition of th'athversary hath been very
great, reasonable great. Marry, for my part, I think
100   the duke hath lost never a man, but one that is like to
be executed for robbing a church, one Bardolph, if
your majesty know the man: his face is all bubukles
and whelks and knobs and flames o' fire, and his lips
blows at his nose and it is like a coal of fire,
105   sometimes plue and sometimes red. But his nose is
executed and his fire's out.

---

74 **what . . . on** i.e. what conditions the enemy insisted on   75 **con** learn, memorize   **the . . . war** military
terminology   76 **trick up** adorn, dress up   **new-tuned** newly invented, fashionable   77 **general's cut**
same style as the general's   **horrid** fearful, intimidating   **suit** outfit, uniform/shout, battle cry
78 **ale-washed** drunken   80 **slanders . . . age** i.e. people who are a disgrace to current times   81 **mistook**
mistaken, mislead   84 **hole . . . coat** i.e. slip in the way he presents himself/chance to expose him   86 **from**
i.e. about   **colours** military banners or flags   **poor** shabby, tired, unwell   93 **passages** fights   **was have**
i.e. did have   94 **enforced** compelled   98 **perdition** loss/destruction   100 **never a man** no man
like likely   102 **bubukles** inflamed swellings   103 **whelks** pimples   **knobs** lumps, swellings   **flames o'**
fire i.e. red streaks or patches   104 **blows** i.e. like bellows on a fire

KING HENRY V We would have all such offenders so cut
off: and we give express charge, that in our marches
through the country, there be nothing compelled
110   from the villages, nothing taken but paid for, none of
the French upbraided or abused in disdainful
language; for when lenity and cruelty play for a
kingdom, the gentler gamester is the soonest winner.
Tucket. Enter Montjoy

MONTJOY You know me by my habit.

115   KING HENRY V Well then, I know thee: what shall I know
of thee?

MONTJOY My master's mind.

KING HENRY V Unfold it.

MONTJOY Thus says my king: 'Say thou to Harry of
120   England, though we seemed dead, we did but sleep.
Advantage is a better soldier than rashness. Tell him
we could have rebuked him at Harfleur, but that we
thought not good to bruise an injury till it were full
ripe. Now we speak upon our cue, and our voice is
125   imperial: England shall repent his folly, see his
weakness, and admire our sufferance. Bid him
therefore consider of his ransom, which must
proportion the losses we have borne, the subjects
we have lost, the disgrace we have digested; which in
130   weight to re-answer, his pettiness would bow under.
For our losses, his exchequer is too poor; for
th'effusion of our blood, the muster of his kingdom
too faint a number; and for our disgrace, his own
person, kneeling at our feet, but a weak and
135   worthless satisfaction. To this add defiance, and tell
him, for conclusion, he hath betrayed his followers,
whose condemnation is pronounced.' So far my king
and master; so much my office.

KING HENRY V What is thy name? I know thy quality.

140   MONTJOY Montjoy.

---

107 **cut off** killed   108 **charge** command   109 **compelled** forcibly taken   112 **lenity** gentleness,
mercifulness   113 **gamester** player/gambler   *Tucket* trumpet call   114 **habit** clothing (French herald's
uniform, which would bear his king's coat of arms)   116 **of** from   118 **Unfold** reveal, relate
121 **Advantage** superior position for a military attack/favourable circumstances/greater numbers
122 **rebuked** repressed, checked   123 **bruise an injury** squeeze a boil   124 **upon our cue** at the right
time for us   126 **sufferance** patience, endurance   128 **proportion** be proportionate to, compensate
for   129 **digested** endured   **in . . . re-answer** to pay back in full measure   130 **pettiness** weakness,
inadequacy   132 **muster** roll-call, number of soldiers (or total population)   137 **So far** i.e. this concludes
the message of   139 **quality** character/rank/occupation

KING HENRY V Thou dost thy office fairly. Turn thee
    back,
And tell thy king I do not seek him now,
But could be willing to march on to Calais
Without impeachment. For, to say the sooth,
145   Though 'tis no wisdom to confess so much
Unto an enemy of craft and vantage,
My people are with sickness much enfeebled,
My numbers lessened, and those few I have,
Almost no better than so many French;
150   Who when they were in health, I tell thee, herald,
I thought upon one pair of English legs
Did march three Frenchmen.— Yet, forgive me, God,
That I do brag thus. This your air of France
Hath blown that vice in me: I must repent.—
155   Go therefore, tell thy master here I am;
My ransom is this frail and worthless trunk;
My army but a weak and sickly guard:
Yet, God before, tell him we will come on,
Though France himself and such another neighbour
160   Stand in our way. There's for thy labour, Montjoy.   *Gives money*
Go bid thy master well advise himself.
If we may pass, we will. If we be hindered,
We shall your tawny ground with your red blood
Discolour. And so Montjoy, fare you well.
165   The sum of all our answer is but this:
We would not seek a battle, as we are,
Nor, as we are, we say we will not shun it.
So tell your master.
MONTJOY I shall deliver so. Thanks to your highness.
                                                  [Exit]
170   **GLOUCESTER** I hope they will not come upon us now.
KING HENRY V We are in God's hand, brother, not in
    theirs.
March to the bridge, it now draws toward night.
Beyond the river we'll encamp ourselves,
And on tomorrow, bid them march away.   *Exeunt*

---

144 impeachment hindrance   **sooth** truth   **146 craft and vantage** cunning and military advantage
156 trunk body   **158 God before** with God on our side   **163 tawny** yellowish-brown   **174 them** i.e. the
English soldiers

[Act 3 Scene 7]   *running scene 9*

Enter the Constable of France, the Lord Rambures, Orléans,
Dauphin with others

CONSTABLE Tut, I have the best armour of the world.
 Would it were day!

ORLÉANS You have an excellent armour, but let my
 horse have his due.

5 **CONSTABLE** It is the best horse of Europe.

ORLÉANS Will it never be morning?

DAUPHIN My lord of Orléans, and my lord high constable,
 you talk of horse and armour?

ORLÉANS You are as well provided of both as any prince
10   in the world.

DAUPHIN What a long night is this? I will not change my
 horse with any that treads but on four pasterns.
 Ch'ha! He bounds from the earth, as if his entrails
 were hairs: *le cheval volant*, the Pegasus, *chez les*
15   *narines de feu*! When I bestride him, I soar, I am a
 hawk: he trots the air, the earth sings when he
 touches it, the basest horn of his hoof is more musical
 than the pipe of Hermes.

ORLÉANS He's of the colour of the nutmeg.

20 **DAUPHIN** And of the heat of the ginger. It is a beast for
 Perseus: he is pure air and fire; and the dull elements
 of earth and water never appear in him, but only in
 patient stillness while his rider mounts him. He is
 indeed a horse, and all other jades you may call
25   beasts.

CONSTABLE Indeed, my lord, it is a most absolute and
 excellent horse.

DAUPHIN It is the prince of palfreys. His neigh is like the
 bidding of a monarch and his countenance enforces
30   homage.

ORLÉANS No more, cousin.

3.7 *Location: the French camp, near Agincourt*   **12 pasterns** i.e. hoofs (literally, part of the leg
between the fetlock and the hoof)   **13 Ch'ha!** exclamation of triumph and pride, or onomatopoeic sound of a
horse   **entrails were hairs** i.e. as if he weighed nothing   **entrails** intestines   **14 *le cheval volant*** 'the
flying horse'   **Pegasus** winged horse in classical mythology   ***chez . . . feu*** 'with fiery nostrils'   **17 basest
horn** lowest part (plays on the sense of 'musical instrument lowest in pitch')   **18 Hermes** in classical
mythology, Hermes played his **pipe** to charm the hundred-eyed giant Argus asleep   **21 Perseus** in classical
mythology, the hero who beheaded the gorgon Medusa; from her blood sprang the horse Pegasus   **24 jades**
worn-out horses   **26 absolute** perfect   **28 palfreys** horses for riding (particularly by women) as opposed to
war-horses; a word associated with romantic tales of wandering knights   **29 bidding** command
countenance appearance/bearing

DAUPHIN Nay, the man hath no wit that cannot, from
the rising of the lark to the lodging of the lamb, vary
deserved praise on my palfrey. It is a theme as fluent
35   as the sea: turn the sands into eloquent tongues and
my horse is argument for them all. 'Tis a subject for a
sovereign to reason on, and for a sovereign's
sovereign to ride on, and for the world, familiar to
us and unknown, to lay apart their particular
40   functions and wonder at him. I once writ a sonnet
in his praise and began thus: 'Wonder of nature'—

ORLÉANS I have heard a sonnet begin so to one's
mistress.

DAUPHIN Then did they imitate that which I composed to
45   my courser, for my horse is my mistress.

ORLÉANS Your mistress bears well.

DAUPHIN Me well, which is the prescript praise and
perfection of a good and particular mistress.

CONSTABLE Nay, for methought yesterday your mistress
50   shrewdly shook your back.

DAUPHIN So perhaps did yours.

CONSTABLE Mine was not bridled.

DAUPHIN O, then belike she was old and gentle, and you
rode like a kern of Ireland, your French hose off, and
55   in your straight strossers.

CONSTABLE You have good judgement in horsemanship.

DAUPHIN Be warned by me, then: they that ride so and
ride not warily, fall into foul bogs. I had rather have
my horse to my mistress.

60 CONSTABLE I had as lief have my mistress a jade.

DAUPHIN I tell thee, constable, my mistress wears his
own hair.

CONSTABLE I could make as true a boast as that, if I had
a sow to my mistress.

---

33 rising . . . lamb i.e. all day long   **lodging** going to bed, settling down   **vary** express a set **theme** in fresh
words (rhetorical term)   **35 the sands** i.e. infinite particles of sand   **39 lay . . . functions** set aside their
business or occupation   **45 courser** swift horse, charger   **46 bears** carries your weight in riding/during
sex   **47 Me** i.e. only me   **prescript** prescribed, appropriate   **48 particular** personal, private
50 shrewdly sharply, severely/shrewishly, bad-temperedly   **shook your back** jolted you/had sex with
you   **52 Mine . . . bridled** i.e. my mistress is a woman, not a horse   **53 belike** presumably   **54 rode** as a
horseman/sexually   **kern of Ireland** Irish foot-soldier/peasant   **hose** breeches   **55 straight strossers**
tight trousers (worn by the Irish)/bare skin   **56 horsemanship** perhaps with a pun on 'whores'   **58 foul
bogs** muddy mires/diseased vaginas/dirty anuses   **60 as lief** rather   **jade** worn-out horse/prostitute
(possibly picking up a pun in the dauphin's **horse** and rendering it 'whores')   **61 my . . . hair** implying that
the Constable's bewigged mistress does not, as she is bald from syphilis   **64 to** as

65 DAUPHIN '*Le chien est retourné à son propre vomissement, et
    la truie lavée au bourbier.*' Thou makest use of
    anything.

    CONSTABLE Yet do I not use my horse for my mistress, or
    any such proverb so little kin to the purpose.

70 RAMBURES My lord constable, the armour that I saw in
    your tent tonight, are those stars or suns upon it?

    CONSTABLE Stars, my lord.

    DAUPHIN Some of them will fall tomorrow, I hope.

    CONSTABLE And yet my sky shall not want.

75 DAUPHIN That may be, for you bear a many
    superfluously and 'twere more honour some were
    away.

    CONSTABLE Ev'n as your horse bears your praises, who
    would trot as well, were some of your brags
80 dismounted.

    DAUPHIN Would I were able to load him with his desert!
    Will it never be day? I will trot tomorrow a mile, and
    my way shall be paved with English faces.

    CONSTABLE I will not say so, for fear I should be faced
85 out of my way. But I would it were morning, for I
    would fain be about the ears of the English.

    RAMBURES Who will go to hazard with me for twenty
    prisoners?

    CONSTABLE You must first go yourself to hazard, ere you
90 have them.

    DAUPHIN 'Tis midnight, I'll go arm myself.   *Exit*

    ORLÉANS The dauphin longs for morning.

    RAMBURES He longs to eat the English.

    CONSTABLE I think he will eat all he kills.

95 ORLÉANS By the white hand of my lady, he's a gallant
    prince.

    CONSTABLE Swear by her foot, that she may tread out
    the oath.

    ORLÉANS He is simply the most active gentleman of
100 France.

    CONSTABLE Doing is activity, and he will still be doing.

---

65 'Le . . . bourbier' 'The dog is returned to his own vomit, and the washed sow to the mire' (proverbial)
68 use utilize/employ sexually   **69 kin . . . purpose** relevant   **73 fall** i.e. be knocked off   **74 want** lack
(stars)   **75 many** great many   **76 honour** honest/noble   **78 Ev'n** just   **81 desert** what he deserves
84 faced . . . way outfaced, shamed and driven away   **86 about the ears** i.e. beating the heads   **87 go to
hazard** place a bet   **89 hazard** risk, danger   **94 eat all he kills** implies that he won't kill anyone   **97 foot**
may play on the sense of 'vulva' or on French *foutre* ('fuck')   **tread out** trample on and erase, i.e. prove
wrong (with sexual connotations, to **tread** being also 'to have sex')   **99 active** energetic/sexually vigorous
101 Doing having sex   **still** constantly

ORLÉANS He never did harm, that I heard of.

CONSTABLE Nor will do none tomorrow: he will keep
that good name still.

105 ORLÉANS I know him to be valiant.

CONSTABLE I was told that by one that knows him better
than you.

ORLÉANS What's he?

CONSTABLE Marry, he told me so himself, and he said he
110 cared not who knew it.

ORLÉANS He needs not, it is no hidden virtue in him.

CONSTABLE By my faith, sir, but it is: never anybody saw
it but his lackey. 'Tis a hooded valour, and when it
appears, it will bate.

115 ORLÉANS Ill will never said well.

CONSTABLE I will cap that proverb with 'There is flattery
in friendship.'

ORLÉANS And I will take up that with 'Give the devil his
due.'

120 CONSTABLE Well placed: there stands your friend for the
devil. Have at the very eye of that proverb with 'A
pox of the devil.'

ORLÉANS You are the better at proverbs, by how much
'A fool's bolt is soon shot.'

125 CONSTABLE You have shot over.

ORLÉANS 'Tis not the first time you were overshot.

Enter a Messenger

MESSENGER My lord high constable, the English lie
within fifteen hundred paces of your tents.

CONSTABLE Who hath measured the ground?

130 MESSENGER The lord Grandpré.

CONSTABLE A valiant and most expert gentleman.
Would it were day! Alas, poor Harry of England: he
longs not for the dawning as we do.

ORLÉANS What a wretched and peevish fellow is this
135 king of England, to mope with his fat-brained
followers so far out of his knowledge!

---

102 did harm hurt, injured/upset anyone   **108 What's** who's   **109 he** i.e. the dauphin   **111 no hidden
virtue** i.e. it is obvious/it does not exist   **113 lackey** servant, who has presumably seen the dauphin's
supposed valour in the form of a beating   **hooded** concealed, masked (like a hunting falcon)   **114 bate**
flutter its wings/abate, diminish   **118 take up** counter   **121 Have . . . eye** I'll strike the very target/
tenderest part   **124 bolt** short blunt arrow suitable for use by a fool/penis   **soon shot** plays on the notion
of premature ejaculation   **125 shot over** overshot the target, i.e. your proverb does not fit the sequence
126 overshot outshot, beaten in archery   **134 peevish** foolish/headstrong   **135 mope** wander about
aimlessly   **fat-brained** thick-witted, stupid   **136 out . . . knowledge** i.e. out of known territory, familiar
affairs

CONSTABLE If the English had any apprehension, they
    would run away.
ORLÉANS That they lack, for if their heads had any
140   intellectual armour, they could never wear such
    heavy head-pieces.
RAMBURES That island of England breeds very valiant
    creatures; their mastiffs are of unmatchable courage.
ORLÉANS Foolish curs, that run winking into the mouth
145   of a Russian bear and have their heads crushed like
    rotten apples. You may as well say, that's a valiant
    flea that dare eat his breakfast on the lip of a lion.
CONSTABLE Just, just. And the men do sympathize with
    the mastiffs in robustious and rough coming on,
150   leaving their wits with their wives, and then give
    them great meals of beef and iron and steel; they will
    eat like wolves and fight like devils.
ORLÉANS Ay, but these English are shrewdly out of beef.
CONSTABLE Then shall we find tomorrow they have only
155   stomachs to eat and none to fight. Now is it time to
    arm. Come, shall we about it?
ORLÉANS It is now two o'clock, but let me see, by ten
    We shall have each a hundred Englishmen. *Exeunt*

[Act 4]

[Enter] Chorus

CHORUS Now entertain conjecture of a time
    When creeping murmur and the poring dark
    Fills the wide vessel of the universe.
    From camp to camp through the foul womb of night
5   The hum of either army stilly sounds,
    That the fixed sentinels almost receive
    The secret whispers of each other's watch.
    Fire answers fire, and through their paly flames
    Each battle sees the other's umbered face.
10   Steed threatens steed, in high and boastful neighs
    Piercing the night's dull ear, and from the tents,

---

137 **apprehension** understanding   141 **head-pieces** helmets   143 **mastiffs** strong and fierce breed of
dog   144 **run . . . bear** i.e. in bear-baiting with dogs   **winking** with eyes closed   147 **eat his breakfast** i.e.
suck blood from   149 **robustious** noisy, rough   **coming on** advancing   150 **give** if you give
153 **shrewdly** seriously, severely   155 **stomachs** appetite   4   1 **entertain conjecture of** i.e. imagine
conjecture supposition   2 **murmur** rumour   **poring** eye-straining (puns on 'pouring')   4 **foul** loathsome/
dark, dirty   5 **stilly** quietly   8 **paly** pale   9 **umbered** shadowed/orange-brown, as though stained with
umber (brown pigment made from earth)

The armourers, accomplishing the knights,
With busy hammers closing rivets up,
Give dreadful note of preparation.
15 The country cocks do crow, the clocks do toll,
And the third hour of drowsy morning name.
Proud of their numbers and secure in soul,
The confident and over-lusty French
Do the low-rated English play at dice;
20 And chide the cripple tardy-gaited night,
Who like a foul and ugly witch doth limp
So tediously away. The poor condemnèd English,
Like sacrifices, by their watchful fires
Sit patiently and inly ruminate
25 The morning's danger, and their gesture sad
Investing lank-lean cheeks and war-worn coats
Presented them unto the gazing moon
So many horrid ghosts. O, now, who will behold
The royal captain of this ruined band
30 Walking from watch to watch, from tent to tent,
Let him cry 'Praise and glory on his head!'
For forth he goes and visits all his host,
Bids them good morrow with a modest smile
And calls them brothers, friends and countrymen.
35 Upon his royal face there is no note
How dread an army hath enrounded him;
Nor doth he dedicate one jot of colour
Unto the weary and all-watchèd night,
But freshly looks and over-bears attaint
40 With cheerful semblance and sweet majesty,
That every wretch, pining and pale before,
Beholding him, plucks comfort from his looks.
A largess universal like the sun
His liberal eye doth give to every one,
45 Thawing cold fear, that mean and gentle all,
Behold, as may unworthiness define,

---

12 **accomplishing** equipping   13 **rivets** bolts for fastening armour   14 **note** sound/notice   17 **secure** overconfident   18 **over-lusty** overly lively and cheerful   19 **low-rated** little valued   **play** gamble for   20 **chide** scold   **tardy-gaited** slow-moving   22 **tediously** laboriously/painfully   24 **inly** inwardly   25 **gesture sad** serious/sorrowful bearing   26 **Investing** enveloping, clothing   **lank-lean** gaunt   28 **who** whoever   30 **watch** group of soldiers on guard   32 **host** army   35 **note** sign   36 **enrounded** surrounded   37 **dedicate** give up, sacrifice   38 **all-watchèd** i.e. spent entirely in watchfulness   39 **over-bears** overcomes   **attaint** sign of weariness (perhaps plays on the sense of 'false colour')   40 **semblance** appearance   41 **pining** wasting away   43 **largess** largesse (generosity, warmth)   44 **liberal** unrestrained, generous   45 **that . . . all** so that men of low and high ranks   46 **unworthiness** the Chorus refers to his own humble status or inadequate means of expression

A little touch of Harry in the night.
And so our scene must to the battle fly,
Where — O, for pity! — we shall much disgrace
50   With four or five most vile and ragged foils,
Right ill-disposed in brawl ridiculous,
The name of Agincourt. Yet sit and see,
Minding true things by what their mock'ries be.   *Exit*

[Act 4 Scene 1]   *running scene 10*

Enter the King, Bedford and Gloucester

KING HENRY V Gloucester, 'tis true that we are in great
         danger,
     The greater therefore should our courage be.—
     Good morrow, brother Bedford. God Almighty!
     There is some soul of goodness in things evil,
5   Would men observingly distil it out.
     For our bad neighbour makes us early stirrers,
     Which is both healthful and good husbandry.
     Besides, they are our outward consciences
     And preachers to us all, admonishing
10   That we should dress us fairly for our end.
     Thus may we gather honey from the weed,
     And make a moral of the devil himself.—
Enter Erpingham
     Good morrow, old Sir Thomas Erpingham:
     A good soft pillow for that good white head
15   Were better than a churlish turf of France.
ERPINGHAM Not so, my liege. This lodging likes me
         better,
     Since I may say 'Now lie I like a king.'
KING HENRY V 'Tis good for men to love their present
         pains
     Upon example, so the spirit is eased:
20   And when the mind is quickened, out of doubt,
     The organs, though defunct and dead before,

47 **touch** glimpse   50 **ragged** shabby   **foils** light, fencing swords   51 **ill-disposed** poorly handled
53 **Minding** calling to mind   **mock'ries** imitations   **4.1** *Location: the English camp, near Agincourt*
5 **Would men** if men would   **observingly** observantly   **distil** extract   6 **bad...stirrers** proverbial: 'he
that has an ill neighbour has oftentimes an ill morning' (the neighbours here being the French)
7 **husbandry** domestic management (here applies to life rather than a household)   10 **dress us** prepare
ourselves   11 **gather...weed** proverbial   12 **make...of** i.e. draw a moral from   15 **churlish** hard,
unyielding   16 **likes** pleases   19 **Upon example** by taking another's example   20 **quickened** revived

Break up their drowsy grave and newly move
With casted slough and fresh legerity.
Lend me thy cloak, Sir Thomas. Brothers both,
25 Commend me to the princes in our camp;
Do my good morrow to them, and anon
Desire them all to my pavilion.

GLOUCESTER We shall, my liege.

ERPINGHAM Shall I attend your grace?

30 **KING HENRY V** No, my good knight.
Go with my brothers to my lords of England:
I and my bosom must debate awhile   *Covers himself with*
And then I would no other company.   *Erpingham's cloak*

ERPINGHAM The Lord in heaven bless thee, noble Harry!
Exeunt [all but King Henry]

35 **KING HENRY V** God-a-mercy, old heart! Thou speak'st
cheerfully.

Enter Pistol

PISTOL *Che vous là?*

KING HENRY V A friend.

PISTOL Discuss unto me: art thou officer?
Or art thou base, common and popular?

40 **KING HENRY V** I am a gentleman of a company.

PISTOL Trail'st thou the puissant pike?

KING HENRY V Even so. What are you?

PISTOL As good a gentleman as the emperor.

KING HENRY V Then you are a better than the king.

45 **PISTOL** The king's a bawcock, and a heart of gold,
A lad of life, an imp of fame,
Of parents good, of fist most valiant.
I kiss his dirty shoe and from heartstring
I love the lovely bully. What is thy name?

50 **KING HENRY V** Harry le Roy.

PISTOL Le Roy? A Cornish name: art thou of Cornish
crew?

KING HENRY V No, I am a Welshman.

PISTOL Know'st thou Fluellen?

KING HENRY V Yes.

---

22 **Break up** break out of   23 **casted slough** cast off skin (like a snake's)   **legerity** lightness
25 **Commend me** convey my greetings   26 **anon** shortly   27 **pavilion** ceremonial tent   32 **bosom** i.e.
heart   36 ***Che vous là?*** Pistol's rendering of *Qui va la?*, French for 'Who goes there?'   38 **Discuss**
declare   39 **popular** of the common people   40 **gentleman … company** gentleman volunteer serving in
the ranks   41 **Trail'st … pike** i.e. are you in the infantry   42 **Even so** just so   45 **bawcock** fine
fellow   46 **imp** shoot, scion   49 **bully** fine fellow   50 **le Roy** the king (*roi* is French for 'king')   51 **crew**
group/military company

55 PISTOL Tell him I'll knock his leek about his pate
        Upon Saint Davy's day.
    KING HENRY V Do not you wear your dagger in your cap
        that day, lest he knock that about yours.
    PISTOL Art thou his friend?
60 KING HENRY V And his kinsman too.
    PISTOL The *figo* for thee, then!
    KING HENRY V I thank you. God be with you!
    PISTOL My name is Pistol called.
                        Exit. The King remains [and stands aside]
    KING HENRY V It sorts well with your fierceness.
    Enter Fluellen and Gower
65 GOWER Captain Fluellen!
    FLUELLEN So, in the name of Jesu Christ, speak fewer. It
        is the greatest admiration in the universal world,
        when the true and aunchient prerogatifes and laws
        of the wars is not kept: if you would take the pains
70   but to examine the wars of Pompey the Great, you
        shall find, I warrant you, that there is no tiddle taddle
        nor pibble babble in Pompey's camp. I warrant you,
        you shall find the ceremonies of the wars, and the
        cares of it, and the forms of it, and the sobriety of it,
75   and the modesty of it, to be otherwise.
    GOWER Why, the enemy is loud. You hear him all night.
    FLUELLEN If the enemy is an ass and a fool and a prating
        coxcomb, is it meet, think you, that we should also,
        look you, be an ass and a fool and a prating coxcomb,
80   in your own conscience, now?
    GOWER I will speak lower.
    FLUELLEN I pray you and beseech you that you will.
                        Exeunt [Gower and Fluellen]
    KING HENRY V Though it appear a little out of fashion,
        There is much care and valour in this Welshman.
    *Enter three soldiers: John Bates, Alexander Court and
    Michael Williams*
85 COURT Brother John Bates, is not that the morning
        which breaks yonder?

---

55 pate head   56 Saint Davy's day 1 March, when Welshmen wore leeks in their caps to commemorate
Saint David, the patron saint of Wales   64 sorts fits   66 fewer less/more quietly   67 admiration
wonder   68 prerogatifes i.e. prerogatives – principles, rights   70 Pompey the Great famous Roman
general   71 tiddle . . . babble tittle-tattle, babbling   73 ceremonies formalities   74 cares duties   forms
due procedures, codes of conduct   sobriety seriousness   75 modesty discipline   otherwise i.e. other
than as things are here   77 prating prattling   78 coxcomb fool   84 care responsibility

BATES I think it be. But we have no great cause to desire
the approach of day.

WILLIAMS We see yonder the beginning of the day, but I
90   think we shall never see the end of it.— Who goes
there?

KING HENRY V A friend.

WILLIAMS Under what captain serve you?

KING HENRY V Under Sir Thomas Erpingham.

95   **WILLIAMS** A good old commander and a most kind
gentleman. I pray you, what thinks he of our estate?

KING HENRY V Even as men wrecked upon a sand, that
look to be washed off the next tide.

BATES He hath not told his thought to the king?

100   **KING HENRY V** No, nor it is not meet he should. For,
though I speak it to you, I think the king is but a
man, as I am: the violet smells to him as it doth to
me: the element shows to him as it doth to me; all his
senses have but human conditions, his ceremonies

105   laid by, in his nakedness he appears but a man; and
though his affections are higher mounted than ours,
yet, when they stoop, they stoop with the like wing.
Therefore, when he sees reason of fears, as we do, his
fears, out of doubt, be of the same relish as ours are.

110   Yet, in reason, no man should possess him with any
appearance of fear, lest he, by showing it, should
dishearten his army.

BATES He may show what outward courage he will, but
I believe, as cold a night as 'tis, he could wish himself

115   in Thames up to the neck; and so I would he were,
and I by him, at all adventures, so we were quit here.

KING HENRY V By my troth, I will speak my conscience of
the king: I think he would not wish himself
anywhere but where he is.

120   **BATES** Then I would he were here alone; so should he be
sure to be ransomed, and a many poor men's lives
saved.

KING HENRY V I dare say you love him not so ill to wish
him here alone, howsoever you speak this to feel

---

96 estate situation, circumstances   **97 wrecked** shipwrecked   **sand** sandbank   **101 though . . . it** i.e.
though I myself say so (but should not)   **103 element** sky   **104 conditions** qualities, functions,
limitations   **ceremonies** kingly trappings   **105 laid by** put aside   **106 affections** emotions   **higher
mounted** more lofty and sophisticated   **107 stoop** swoop, descend (falconry term)   **like wing** i.e. in the
same way that ours do   **108 of** for   **109 relish** flavour   **110 possess him with** show him/induce in
him   **111 he** i.e. the king   **115 Thames** the River Thames, which runs through London   **116 at all
adventures** at all events, whatever the outcome   **quit** away from, finished   **124 feel** test

125   other men's minds. Methinks I could not die
          anywhere so contented as in the king's company;
          his cause being just and his quarrel honourable.
      WILLIAMS That's more than we know.
      BATES Ay, or more than we should seek after; for we
130   know enough, if we know we are the king's subjects.
          If his cause be wrong, our obedience to the king
          wipes the crime of it out of us.
      WILLIAMS But if the cause be not good, the king himself
          hath a heavy reckoning to make, when all those legs
135   and arms and heads, chopped off in a battle, shall join
          together at the latter day and cry all, 'We died at
          such a place' — some swearing, some crying for a
          surgeon, some upon their wives left poor behind
          them, some upon the debts they owe, some upon
140   their children rawly left. I am afeard there are few die
          well that die in a battle, for how can they charitably
          dispose of anything, when blood is their argument?
          Now, if these men do not die well, it will be a black
          matter for the king that led them to it — who to
145   disobey were against all proportion of subjection.
      KING HENRY V So, if a son that is by his father sent about
          merchandise do sinfully miscarry upon the sea, the
          imputation of his wickedness, by your rule, should be
          imposed upon his father that sent him. Or if a
150   servant, under his master's command transporting a
          sum of money, be assailed by robbers and die in
          many irreconciled iniquities, you may call the
          business of the master the author of the servant's
          damnation. But this is not so: the king is not bound
155   to answer the particular endings of his soldiers, the
          father of his son, nor the master of his servant; for
          they purpose not their death, when they purpose
          their services. Besides, there is no king, be his cause
          never so spotless, if it come to the arbitrement of

129 seek after try to find out   **134 reckoning** account of debts (both literal losses and spiritual debts)
135 join together remake whole bodies/unite in crying out   **136 latter day** Judgement Day   **138 upon** on
account of   **140 rawly** too young/unprovided for   **afeard** afraid   **141 charitably** i.e. with Christian
charity   **142 dispose of** make arrangements for/bestow (possessions in a will/souls to God)   **argument**
theme   **145 proportion** natural order   **subjection** the condition of being a subject   **147 merchandise**
trading, commerce   **sinfully miscarry** i.e. die in a state of sin   **148 imputation of** accusation of,
responsibility for   **152 irreconciled** unreconciled to God, unabsolved   **iniquities** wicked acts, sins
153 author person responsible for, creator of   **157 purpose** intend, plan   **159 arbitrement of swords**
arbitration, determining of the matter through war

160 swords, can try it out with all unspotted soldiers:
some peradventure have on them the guilt of
premeditated and contrived murder; some, of
beguiling virgins with the broken seals of perjury;
some, making the wars their bulwark, that have
165 before gored the gentle bosom of peace with pillage
and robbery. Now, if these men have defeated the law
and outrun native punishment, though they can
outstrip men, they have no wings to fly from God.
War is his beadle, war is his vengeance, so that here
170 men are punished for before-breach of the king's laws
in now the king's quarrel. Where they feared the
death, they have borne life away; and where they
would be safe, they perish. Then if they die
unprovided, no more is the king guilty of their
175 damnation than he was before guilty of those
impieties for the which they are now visited. Every
subject's duty is the king's, but every subject's soul is
his own. Therefore should every soldier in the wars
do as every sick man in his bed, wash every mote out
180 of his conscience, and dying so, death is to him
advantage; or not dying, the time was blessedly lost
wherein such preparation was gained. And in him
that escapes, it were not sin to think that, making
God so free an offer, he let him outlive that day to see
185 his greatness and to teach others how they should
prepare.

WILLIAMS 'Tis certain, every man that dies ill, the ill
upon his own head, the king is not to answer it.

BATES But I do not desire he should answer for me, and
190 yet I determine to fight lustily for him.

KING HENRY V I myself heard the king say he would not
be ransomed.

WILLIAMS Ay, he said so, to make us fight cheerfully. But
when our throats are cut, he may be ransomed, and
195 we ne'er the wiser.

---

160 **try it out** i.e. put his cause to the test   **unspotted** pure, sin-free   161 **peradventure** perhaps
163 **beguiling** deceiving   **perjury** oath-breaking   164 **bulwark** (military) fortification/safeguard,
means of escape (from punishment for crimes)   167 **native punishment** the punishment due to them at
home   169 **beadle** parish officer with the power to punish petty offenders   170 **before-breach** previous
breaking   171 **now...quarrel** the war that is now being fought on behalf of the king   172 **death** death
penalty   **borne life away** i.e. got away with their lives   174 **unprovided** unprepared   176 **visited**
punished   181 **blessedly** fortunately, in a holy manner   **lost** spent   183 **making...offer** in offering
himself to God   186 **prepare** i.e. for death   187 **ill** i.e. unprepared, in sin   188 **to answer it** responsible
for it   190 **lustily** heartily

KING HENRY V If I live to see it, I will never trust his word
after.

WILLIAMS You pay him then. That's a perilous shot out
of an elder-gun, that a poor and a private displeasure
200   can do against a monarch. You may as well go about
to turn the sun to ice with fanning in his face with a
peacock's feather. You'll never trust his word after!
Come, 'tis a foolish saying.

KING HENRY V Your reproof is something too round. I
205   should be angry with you, if the time were
convenient.

WILLIAMS Let it be a quarrel between us, if you live.

KING HENRY V I embrace it.

WILLIAMS How shall I know thee again?

210   **KING HENRY V** Give me any gage of thine, and I will wear
it in my bonnet: then, if ever thou darest
acknowledge it, I will make it my quarrel.

WILLIAMS Here's my glove. Give me another of thine.

KING HENRY V There.   *They exchange*
gloves

215   **WILLIAMS** This will I also wear in my cap. If ever thou
come to me and say, after tomorrow, 'This is my
glove', by this hand, I will take thee a box on the ear.

KING HENRY V If ever I live to see it, I will challenge it.

WILLIAMS Thou dar'st as well be hanged.

220   **KING HENRY V** Well, I will do it, though I take thee in the
king's company.

WILLIAMS Keep thy word. Fare thee well.

BATES Be friends, you English fools, be friends. We have
French quarrels enough, if you could tell how to
225   reckon.   *Exeunt Soldiers*

KING HENRY V Indeed, the French may lay twenty
French crowns to one, they will beat us; for they
bear them on their shoulders. But it is no English
treason to cut French crowns, and tomorrow the
230   king himself will be a clipper.

Upon the king! Let us our lives, our souls,

Our debts, our careful wives,

Our children and our sins lay on the king!

---

196 it i.e. that outcome   **198 pay** punish   **perilous** dangerous (said ironically)   **199 elder-gun** toy gun,
pellet gun (made from an elder stick)   **a . . . displeasure** the displeasure of a commoner   **200 go about**
try   **204 round** blunt, plain-spoken   **208 embrace** heartily accept   **210 gage** pledge (usually signifying a
commitment to duel; often a glove or gauntlet)   **211 bonnet** hat   **darest** dare to   **217 take** give
220 though even if   **take** find   **225 reckon** count   **227 crowns** coins/heads   **229 cut French crowns**
cut French heads off/shave silver or gold from French coins   **230 clipper** clipper of coins/barber
232 careful full of cares or grief   **233 lay on** burden/assault

We must bear all. O, hard condition,
235 Twin-born with greatness, subject to the breath
Of every fool, whose sense no more can feel
But his own wringing. What infinite heart's-ease
Must kings neglect, that private men enjoy?
And what have kings, that privates have not too,
240 Save ceremony, save general ceremony?
And what art thou, thou idle ceremony?
What kind of god art thou, that suffer'st more
Of mortal griefs than do thy worshippers?
What are thy rents? What are thy comings in?
245 O ceremony, show me but thy worth.
What? Is thy soul of adoration?
Art thou aught else but place, degree and form,
Creating awe and fear in other men?
Wherein thou art less happy being feared
250 Than they in fearing.
What drink'st thou oft, instead of homage sweet,
But poisoned flattery? O, be sick, great greatness,
And bid thy ceremony give thee cure!
Think'st thou the fiery fever will go out
255 With titles blown from adulation?
Will it give place to flexure and low bending?
Canst thou, when thou command'st the beggar's
    knee,
Command the health of it? No, thou proud dream,
That play'st so subtly with a king's repose.
260 I am a king that find thee, and I know
'Tis not the balm, the sceptre and the ball,
The sword, the mace, the crown imperial,
The intertissued robe of gold and pearl,
The farcèd title running 'fore the king,
265 The throne he sits on, nor the tide of pomp
That beats upon the high shore of this world.
No, not all these, thrice-gorgeous ceremony,

234 condition situation/social rank   **235 Twin-born** born at the same birth   **breath** i.e. opinion
237 wringing aches and pains   **heart's-ease** inner peace, contentment   **239 privates** men who do not
hold public office   **240 Save** except   **general** public   **241 idle** useless   **243 mortal** human
244 comings in income   **246 of adoration** made up of insubstantial admiration/of the things that provoke
admiration   **247 aught** anything   **place...form** i.e. social rank and eminence   **255 titles** puns on
'tittles', i.e. trifles   **blown** fanned, breathed (as if to cool fever)/corrupted, contaminated   **256 give place**
retreat, give way   **flexure** kneeling   **bending** bowing   **257 command'st...knee** claim it as your right
that the beggar kneels before you   **259 subtly** deceptively   **repose** rest   **260 find thee** find you out,
discover your true nature   **261 balm** consecrated oil (used at a coronation)   **ball** monarch's orb
262 mace official sceptre   **263 intertissued** interwoven   **264 farcèd** stuffed, pompous   **265 pomp**
ceremonious trappings, splendour

Not all these, laid in bed majestical,
Can sleep so soundly as the wretched slave,
270   Who with a body filled and vacant mind
Gets him to rest, crammed with distressful bread,
Never sees horrid night, the child of hell,
But like a lackey, from the rise to set,
Sweats in the eye of Phoebus and all night
275   Sleeps in Elysium: next day after dawn,
Doth rise and help Hyperion to his horse,
And follows so the ever-running year,
With profitable labour, to his grave.
And but for ceremony, such a wretch,
280   Winding up days with toil and nights with sleep,
Had the forehand and vantage of a king.
The slave, a member of the country's peace,
Enjoys it; but in gross brain little wots
What watch the king keeps to maintain the peace,
285   Whose hours the peasant best advantages.
Enter Erpingham
ERPINGHAM My lord, your nobles, jealous of your
        absence,
    Seek through your camp to find you.
KING HENRY V Good old knight,
    Collect them all together at my tent:
290   I'll be before thee.
ERPINGHAM I shall do't, my lord.   *Exit*
KING HENRY V O God of battles, steel my soldiers' hearts,
    Possess them not with fear. Take from them now
    The sense of reck'ning, ere th'opposèd numbers
295   Pluck their hearts from them. Not today, O lord,
    O, not today, think not upon the fault
    My father made in compassing the crown!
    I Richard's body have interrèd new,
    And on it have bestowed more contrite tears
300   Than from it issued forcèd drops of blood.

---

271 distressful earned by labour   **273 lackey** servant, specifically a footman who ran alongside his master's coach (here, Phoebus' chariot)   **the . . . set** sunrise to sunset   **274 in . . . Phoebus** under the sun (Phoebus, the Roman sun god)   **275 Elysium** i.e. perfect contentment (the heaven of classical mythology)   **276 Hyperion** in classical mythology, father of the sun; sometimes the sun itself   **278 profitable** useful, valuable (not 'remunerative')   **281 forehand . . . of** advantage over   **282 member** sharer in   **283 gross** dull   **wots** knows   **284 watch** sleeplessness/guard   **285 advantages** benefits from   **286 jealous of** anxious about   **294 sense of reck'ning** counting, calculation   **th'opposèd numbers** the numbers of enemy soldiers   **297 My . . . crown!** Henry's father, Henry IV, deposed **Richard** II, who was murdered whilst in captivity   **compassing** obtaining   **298 interrèd new** newly buried, with proper ceremony   **300 forcèd** violently shed

Five hundred poor I have in yearly pay,
Who twice a day their withered hands hold up
Toward heaven, to pardon blood, and I have built
Two chantries, where the sad and solemn priests
305   Sing still for Richard's soul. More will I do,
Though all that I can do is nothing worth,
Since that my penitence comes after all,
Imploring pardon.

Enter Gloucester

GLOUCESTER My liege.

310   **KING HENRY V** My brother Gloucester's voice?— Ay,
I know thy errand. I will go with thee.
The day, my friends, and all things stay for me.

Exeunt

[Act 4 Scene 2]   *running scene 11*

Enter the Dauphin, Orléans, Rambures and Beaumont

ORLÉANS The sun doth gild our armour. Up, my lords!
DAUPHIN *Monte à cheval!* My horse, varlet! *Laquais!* Ha!
ORLÉANS O brave spirit!
DAUPHIN *Via, les eaux et la terre.*
5   **ORLÉANS** *Rien puis? L'air et feu.*
DAUPHIN *Cieux*, cousin Orléans.

Enter Constable

Now, my lord constable?
CONSTABLE Hark, how our steeds for present service
neigh.
DAUPHIN Mount them, and make incision in their hides,
10   That their hot blood may spin in English eyes,
And dout them with superfluous courage. Ha!
RAMBURES What, will you have them weep our horses'
blood?
How shall we then behold their natural tears?

Enter Messenger

MESSENGER The English are embattled, you French
peers.

---

303 **blood** i.e. murder   304 **chantries** endowed chapels where **priests** sing masses for the founders or for
individuals specified by them (in this case, Richard)   **sad** serious, grave   305 **still** to this day/continually
312 **stay** wait   4.2   *Location: the French camp near Agincourt*   2 *Monte à cheval!* 'To horse!'   **varlet**
manservant/rascal   *Laquais!* 'Lackey!'   4 *Via...terre* 'Go through and over water and earth'
5 *Rien...feu* 'Nothing else? Air and fire'   6 *Cieux* 'the heavens'   8 **present service** immediate action
9 **make...hides** i.e. with spurs   10 **spin** spurt   11 **dout** extinguish, douse   **superfluous courage** an
excess of French courage (shown by the abundance of **blood**)   14 **embattled** arranged in battle formation
peers companions

15   CONSTABLE To horse, you gallant princes, straight to
              horse!
              Do but behold yond poor and starvèd band,
              And your fair show shall suck away their souls,
              Leaving them but the shales and husks of men.
              There is not work enough for all our hands,
20   Scarce blood enough in all their sickly veins
              To give each naked curtle-axe a stain,
              That our French gallants shall today draw out,
              And sheathe for lack of sport. Let us but blow on
                  them,
              The vapour of our valour will o'erturn them.
25   'Tis positive gainst all exceptions, lords,
              That our superfluous lackeys and our peasants,
              Who in unnecessary action swarm
              About our squares of battle, were enow
              To purge this field of such a hilding foe,
30   Though we upon this mountain's basis by
              Took stand for idle speculation:
              But that our honours must not. What's to say?
              A very little little let us do
              And all is done. Then let the trumpets sound
35   The tucket sonance and the note to mount,
              For our approach shall so much dare the field
              That England shall couch down in fear and yield.
          Enter Grandpré
          GRANDPRÉ Why do you stay so long, my lords of France?
              Yond island carrions, desperate of their bones,
40   Ill-favouredly become the morning field:
              Their ragged curtains poorly are let loose,
              And our air shakes them passing scornfully.
              Big Mars seems bankrupt in their beggared host
              And faintly through a rusty beaver peeps.
45   The horsemen sit like fixèd candlesticks,
              With torch-staves in their hand, and their poor jades

16 **yond . . . band** i.e. the English   17 **fair show** splendid appearance   18 **shales** shells   21 **curtle-axe**
cutlass, short sword   22 **gallants** fine, spirited young men   24 **o'erturn them** knock them over
25 **exceptions** objections   28 **squares of battle** square formations of soldiers   29 **hilding** worthless,
contemptible   30 **basis** base   **by** nearby   32 **honours** noble ranks/sense of honour   **What's** what's
left   35 **tucket sonance** trumpet sound   36 **dare** defy/daze, paralyse with fear   38 **stay** wait   39 **Yond**
yonder, those (over there)   **island** i.e. English   **carrions** carcasses   **desperate . . . bones** without hope of
saving their lives   40 **Ill-favouredly become** i.e. ill-befit, disgrace   41 **curtains** banners   42 **passing**
surpassingly, extremely   43 **Mars** Roman god of war   **beggared host** impoverished army   44 **beaver**
helmet's visor   45 **fixèd candlesticks** i.e. inanimate metal objects   46 **torch-staves** staffs for holding
torches

Lob down their heads, dropping the hides and hips,
The gum down-roping from their pale dead eyes
And in their pale dull mouths the gimmaled bit
50   Lies foul with chewed grass, still and motionless,
And their executors, the knavish crows,
Fly o'er them all, impatient for their hour.
Description cannot suit itself in words
To demonstrate the life of such a battle
55   In life so lifeless as it shows itself.
CONSTABLE They have said their prayers and they stay
    for death.
DAUPHIN Shall we go send them dinners and fresh suits
And give their fasting horses provender,
And after fight with them?
60   CONSTABLE I stay but for my guidon. To the field!
I will the banner from a trumpet take
And use it for my haste. Come, come, away!
The sun is high and we outwear the day.   *Exeunt*

[Act 4 Scene 3]

*Enter Gloucester, Bedford, Exeter, Erpingham with all his
host, Salisbury and Westmorland*

GLOUCESTER Where is the king?
BEDFORD The king himself is rode to view their battle.
WESTMORLAND Of fighting men they have full threescore
    thousand.
EXETER There's five to one. Besides, they all are fresh.
5   SALISBURY God's arm strike with us! 'Tis a fearful odds.
God buy' you, princes all; I'll to my charge.
If we no more meet till we meet in heaven,
Then joyfully, my noble Lord of Bedford,
My dear Lord Gloucester, and my good Lord Exeter,
10   And my kind kinsman, warriors all, adieu!
BEDFORD Farewell, good Salisbury, and good luck go
    with thee!

---

47 **Lob** hang heavily   48 **gum** rheum, gummy discharge   **down-roping** hanging in strings
49 **gimmaled** jointed   50 **foul** dirty, stained   51 **executors** those who dispose of what is left after
death   52 **hour** i.e. of death   53 **suit** clothe/befit   54 **demonstrate . . . battle** vividly depict such an
army   58 **fasting** starving   **provender** fodder   60 **guidon** pointed flag or pennant   63 **outwear** waste
4.3 *Location: the English camp, near Agincourt*   3 **threescore thousand** sixty thousand   6 **buy'** be
with   **charge** company   10 **kinsman** i.e. Westmorland, whose son was married to Salisbury's daughter

EXETER Farewell, kind lord. Fight valiantly today.
    And yet I do thee wrong to mind thee of it,
    For thou art framed of the firm truth of valour.
                        [Exit Salisbury]

15 BEDFORD He is as full of valour as of kindness,
    Princely in both.
Enter the King
WESTMORLAND O, that we now had here
    But one ten thousand of those men in England
    That do no work today!

20 KING HENRY V What's he that wishes so?
    My cousin Westmorland? No, my fair cousin,
    If we are marked to die, we are enough
    To do our country loss, and if to live,
    The fewer men, the greater share of honour.

25   God's will, I pray thee, wish not one man more.
    By Jove, I am not covetous for gold,
    Nor care I who doth feed upon my cost,
    It yearns me not if men my garments wear;
    Such outward things dwell not in my desires.

30   But if it be a sin to covet honour,
    I am the most offending soul alive.
    No, faith, my coz, wish not a man from England.
    God's peace, I would not lose so great an honour
    As one man more, methinks, would share from me

35   For the best hope I have. O, do not wish one more.
    Rather proclaim it, Westmorland, through my host,
    That he which hath no stomach to this fight,
    Let him depart, his passport shall be made
    And crowns for convoy put into his purse:

40   We would not die in that man's company
    That fears his fellowship to die with us.—
    This day is called the feast of Crispian: *To all*
    He that outlives this day, and comes safe home,
    Will stand a tiptoe when this day is named,

45   And rouse him at the name of Crispian.
    He that shall see this day, and live old age,
    Will yearly on the vigil feast his neighbours,

13 **mind** remind 14 **framed** composed **truth** principle 22 **we ... loss** there are enough of us for England to feel the loss 25 **wish** wish for 26 **Jove** supreme Roman god 27 **upon my cost** at my expense 28 **yearns** grieves 32 **coz** cousin 34 **share** take away as his share 36 **proclaim it** declare, announce 37 **stomach to** appetite/courage for 38 **passport** document of authorization (to pass through France and board a ship) 39 **convoy** i.e. his journey 41 **his fellowship** duty as a companion 42 **feast of Crispian** Saint Crispin's day, 25 October 44 **stand a tiptoe** i.e. feel uplifted, proud, eager 47 **vigil** evening before a feast day

And say, 'Tomorrow is Saint Crispian.'
Then will he strip his sleeve and show his scars,
50 And say, 'These wounds I had on Crispin's day.'
Old men forget; yet all shall be forgot,
But he'll remember with advantages
What feats he did that day. Then shall our names,
Familiar in his mouth as household words —
55 Harry the king, Bedford and Exeter,
Warwick and Talbot, Salisbury and Gloucester —
Be in their flowing cups freshly rememberèd.
This story shall the good man teach his son,
And Crispin Crispian shall ne'er go by,
60 From this day to the ending of the world,
But we in it shall be rememberèd;
We few, we happy few, we band of brothers.
For he today that sheds his blood with me
Shall be my brother, be he ne'er so vile,
65 This day shall gentle his condition.
And gentlemen in England now abed
Shall think themselves accursed they were not here,
And hold their manhoods cheap whiles any speaks
That fought with us upon Saint Crispin's day.
Enter Salisbury
70 **SALISBURY** My sovereign lord, bestow yourself with
    speed:
    The French are bravely in their battles set,
    And will with all expedience charge on us.
KING HENRY V All things are ready, if our minds be so.
WESTMORLAND Perish the man whose mind is backward
    now!
75 **KING HENRY V** Thou dost not wish more help from
    England, coz?
WESTMORLAND God's will, my liege, would you and I
    alone,
    Without more help, could fight this royal battle!
KING HENRY V Why, now thou hast unwished five
    thousand men,
    Which likes me better than to wish us one.—
80 You know your places. God be with you all!

51 **all** all else   52 **advantages** additions   57 **Be . . . rememberèd** i.e. a toast will be raised to them
59 **Crispin Crispian** Saint Crispin's day marks the martyring of two brothers, Crispin and Crispianus
62 **happy** fortunate   64 **vile** low-ranking   65 **gentle his condition** ennoble him   68 **manhoods**
manliness   **any** anyone   70 **bestow yourself** act, move   71 **bravely** showily, with great display
in . . . set in military formations   72 **expedience** speed   74 **backward** reluctant/not ready   79 **likes**
pleases

Tucket. Enter Montjoy

MONTJOY Once more I come to know of thee, King
        Harry,
    If for thy ransom thou wilt now compound,
    Before thy most assurèd overthrow,
    For certainly thou art so near the gulf,
85   Thou needs must be englutted. Besides, in mercy,
    The constable desires thee thou wilt mind
    Thy followers of repentance; that their souls
    May make a peaceful and a sweet retire
    From off these fields, where, wretches, their poor
        bodies
90   Must lie and fester.

KING HENRY V Who hath sent thee now?

MONTJOY The Constable of France.

KING HENRY V I pray thee bear my former answer back:
    Bid them achieve me and then sell my bones.
95   Good God, why should they mock poor fellows thus?
    The man that once did sell the lion's skin
    While the beast lived, was killed with hunting him.
    A many of our bodies shall no doubt
    Find native graves, upon the which, I trust,
100   Shall witness live in brass of this day's work.
    And those that leave their valiant bones in France,
    Dying like men, though buried in your dunghills,
    They shall be famed, for there the sun shall greet
        them,
    And draw their honours reeking up to heaven,
105   Leaving their earthly parts to choke your clime,
    The smell whereof shall breed a plague in France.
    Mark then abounding valour in our English,
    That being dead, like to the bullet's crazing,
    Break out into a second course of mischief,
110   Killing in relapse of mortality.
    Let me speak proudly: tell the constable
    We are but warriors for the working day.
    Our gayness and our gilt are all besmirched

82 **compound** agree terms   84 **gulf** whirlpool   85 **englutted** swallowed up   86 **mind** remind   88 **retire** retreat   94 **achieve** win, capture   96 **The . . . him** 'to sell the bear's (lion's) skin before the beast is caught' (proverbial) is foolish and dangerous   98 **many** great number   99 **native** English, i.e. they will survive the war   100 **in brass** inscribed on brass memorial plaques   104 **reeking** smelling (not necessarily unpleasantly)/blood-smeared   105 **clime** region/climate   107 **Mark** take notice of   108 **crazing** shattering (once lodged in the body); may also suggest 'grazing' – i.e. ricocheting   109 **mischief** damage, harm   110 **in . . . mortality** as their bodies decompose   112 **for the working day** i.e. dressed for work, not requiring finery   113 **gayness** showy appearance, brightness of colour   **besmirched** discoloured, stained

With rainy marching in the painful field.
115 There's not a piece of feather in our host —
Good argument, I hope, we will not fly —
And time hath worn us into slovenry.
But, by the mass, our hearts are in the trim,
And my poor soldiers tell me, yet ere night,
120 They'll be in fresher robes, or they will pluck
The gay new coats o'er the French soldiers' heads
And turn them out of service. If they do this —
As, if God please, they shall — my ransom then
Will soon be levied. Herald, save thou thy labour:
125 Come thou no more for ransom, gentle herald.
They shall have none, I swear, but these my joints,
Which if they have as I will leave 'em them,
Shall yield them little, tell the constable.
MONTJOY I shall, King Harry. And so fare thee well:
130 Thou never shalt hear herald any more.   *Exit*
KING HENRY V I fear thou wilt once more come again for
a ransom.

Enter York

YORK My lord, most humbly on my knee I beg   *Kneels*
The leading of the vanguard.
KING HENRY V Take it, brave York.— Now, soldiers,
march away.
135 And how thou pleasest, God, dispose the day! *Exeunt*

[Act 4 Scene 4]   *running scene 13*

Alarum. Excursions. Enter Pistol, French Soldier [and] Boy

PISTOL Yield, cur!
FRENCH SOLDIER *Je pense que vous êtes le gentilhomme de
bon qualité.*
PISTOL *Qualtitie calmie custure me?* Art thou a gentle-
5   man? What is thy name? Discuss.
FRENCH SOLDIER *O Seigneur Dieu!*

---

114 **painful field** arduous terrain   115 **feather** i.e. ornamental helmet feathers   116 **fly** flee
117 **slovenry** slovenliness, dirtiness   118 **in the trim** finely dressed/ready for action   120 **pluck ... service**
on dismissal from **service**, a servant would have his livery removed (additional play on sense of military
service)   124 **levied** raised   126 **joints** limbs   127 **as ... them** i.e. dead   135 **dispose** direct, govern
4.4   *Location: the battlefield at Agincourt   Excursions:* bouts of fighting across the stage
2 *Je ... qualité* 'I think that you are a gentleman of good quality'   4 *Qualtitie* uncomprehending repetition
of *qualité   calmie custure me* apparently a corruption of a fairly popular Irish refrain *cailin og a stor*
('maiden, my treasure'); Pistol seems to have picked up on the the 'qu/c' sound of the French   5 **Discuss**
declare   6 *O Seigneur Dieu!* 'O Lord God!'

PISTOL O, Signieur Dew should be a gentleman.
    Perpend my words, O Signieur Dew, and mark:
    O Signieur Dew, thou diest on point of fox,   *Draws his sword*
10   Except, O signieur, thou do give to me
    Egregious ransom.
FRENCH SOLDIER *O, prenez miséricorde! Ayez pitié de moi!*
PISTOL 'Moy' shall not serve. I will have forty moys,
    For I will fetch thy rim out at thy throat
15   In drops of crimson blood.
FRENCH SOLDIER *Est-il impossible d'échapper la force de ton*
    bras?
PISTOL Brass, cur?
    Thou damnèd and luxurious mountain goat,
20   Offer'st me brass?
FRENCH SOLDIER *O, pardonnez-moi!*
PISTOL Say'st thou me so? Is that a ton of moys?
    Come hither, boy. Ask me this slave in French
    What is his name.
25   BOY *Écoutez, comment êtes-vous appelé?*
FRENCH SOLDIER *Monsieur le Fer.*
BOY He says his name is Master Fer.
PISTOL Master Fer? I'll fer him, and firk him, and ferret
      him.
    Discuss the same in French unto him.
30   BOY I do not know the French for fer and ferret and firk.
PISTOL Bid him prepare, for I will cut his throat.
FRENCH SOLDIER *Que dit-il, monsieur?*
BOY *Il me commande à vous dire que vous faites vous prêt,*
    car ce soldat ici est disposé tout à cette heure de couper
35   *votre gorge.*
PISTOL *Owy, cuppele gorge, permafoy,*
    Peasant, unless thou give me crowns, brave crowns;
    Or mangled shalt thou be by this my sword.

---

8 Perpend consider   **mark** take note   **9 fox** type of sword   **10 Except** unless   **11 Egregious**
exceptionally large   **12 O … moi!** 'O, have mercy! Have pity on me!'   **13 Moy** mispronunciation of 'moi';
Pistol understands this to mean a type of coin, though it could also mean 'measurement of corn,
approximately a bushel'   **14 rim** stomach lining   **16 Est-il … bras?** 'Is it impossible to escape the strength
of your arm?'   **18 Brass** i.e. inferior metal; Pistol's misunderstanding of *bras*   **19 luxurious** lecherous
21 O pardonnez-moi! 'O spare me!'   **22 ton of moys** Pistol's interpretation of the French
25 Écoutez … appelé? 'Listen, what is your name?'   **26 le Fer** iron   **28 fer** a nonce usage of the word,
roughly intending 'beat'; possible play on 'fear', i.e. frighten   **firk** beat (puns on 'fuck')   **ferret** worry, tear at
(plays on sense of 'have sex with')   **32 Que … monsieur?** 'What did he say, sir?'   **33 Il … gorge** He
orders me to tell you that you are to make yourself ready, because this soldier here is disposed, at this very
hour, to cut your throat'   **36 Owy … permafoy** Pistol's mangled attempt to say *Oui, couper la gorge, par ma
foi*, i.e. 'yes, cut the throat, by my faith'   **37 brave** fine/worthy

FRENCH SOLDIER *O, je vous supplie, pour l'amour de Dieu,*
40   *me pardonner! Je suis gentilhomme de bonne maison.*
       Gardez ma vie, et je vous donnerai deux cents écus.

PISTOL What are his words?

BOY He prays you to save his life: he is a gentleman of a
      good house, and for his ransom he will give you two
45   hundred crowns.

PISTOL Tell him my fury shall abate, and I the crowns
       will take.

FRENCH SOLDIER *Petit monsieur, que dit-il?*

BOY *Encore qu'il est contre son jurement de pardonner aucun*
50   *prisonnier, néanmoins, pour les écus que vous l'avez*
       promis, il est content à vous donner la liberté, le
       franchisement.

FRENCH SOLDIER *Sur mes genoux je vous donne mille*   *Kneels*
       remerciements, et je m'estime heureux que j'ai tombé
55   *entre les mains d'un chevalier, je pense, le plus brave,*
       vaillant, et très distingué seigneur d'Angleterre.

PISTOL Expound unto me, boy.

BOY He gives you, upon his knees, a thousand thanks,
      and he esteems himself happy that he hath fallen into
60   the hands of one, as he thinks, the most brave,
      valorous, and thrice-worthy signieur of England.

PISTOL As I suck blood, I will some mercy show. Follow
       me!

BOY *Suivez-vous le grand capitaine!*   [*Exeunt Pistol and*
                                              French Soldier]
65   I did never know so full a voice issue from so empty a
      heart. But the saying is true, 'The empty vessel
      makes the greatest sound'. Bardolph and Nym had
      ten times more valour than this roaring devil i'th'old
      play, that everyone may pare his nails with a wooden
70   dagger, and they are both hanged, and so would this
      be, if he durst steal anything adventurously. I must
      stay with the lackeys, with the luggage of our camp.

---

39 O . . . écus 'O I beseech you, for the love of God, to spare me. I am a gentleman of a good house [i.e. family]. Save my life and I will give you two hundred crowns'   **48 Petit . . . dit-il?** 'Little sir, what does he say?'   **49 Encore . . . franchisement** 'Although it is contrary to his vow to spare any prisoner, nevertheless, for the crowns that you have promised him, he is content to give you liberty, freedom'   **53 Sur . . . d'Angleterre** the Boy's ensuing translation is accurate   **57 Expound** explain, translate   **61 thrice-worthy** most worthy   **62 suck blood** kill/am a leech   **64 Suivez-vous . . . capitaine!** 'Follow the great captain!'   **65 full** loud   **68 devil i'th'old play** i.e. one like the character of the devil in an old morality play   **69 pare** trim   **wooden dagger** the traditional prop of a morality-play devil   **70 this** this man, Pistol   **71 adventurously** in a manner involving genuine risk

The French might have a good prey of us, if he knew
of it, for there is none to guard it but boys.   *Exit*

[Act 4 Scene 5]   *running scene 13 continues*

Enter Constable, Orléans, Bourbon, Dauphin and Rambures

CONSTABLE *O diable!*
ORLÉANS *O Seigneur! Le jour est perdu, tout est perdu!*
DAUPHIN *Mort de ma vie!* All is confounded, all.
  Reproach and everlasting shame
5 Sits mocking in our plumes. *O méchante fortune!*
                                                                    A short alarum
  Do not run away.
CONSTABLE Why, all our ranks are broke.
DAUPHIN O, perdurable shame! Let's stab ourselves.
  Be these the wretches that we played at dice for?
10 **ORLÉANS** Is this the king we sent to for his ransom?
BOURBON Shame and eternal shame, nothing but
      shame!
  Let us die! In once more, back again.
  And he that will not follow Bourbon now,
  Let him go hence, and with his cap in hand,
15 Like a base pander, hold the chamber door
  Whilst by a base slave, no gentler than my dog,
  His fairest daughter is contaminated.
CONSTABLE Disorder that hath spoiled us, friend us now.
  Let us on heaps go offer up our lives.
20 **ORLÉANS** We are enough yet living in the field
  To smother up the English in our throngs,
  If any order might be thought upon.
BOURBON The devil take order now! I'll to the throng;
  Let life be short, else shame will be too long. *Exeunt*

---

73 prey plunder   **4.5   1 O diable!** 'O the devil!'   **2 O...perdu!** 'O Lord! The day is lost, all is lost!'
3 Mort...vie! 'Death of my life!'   **confounded** ruined   **5 in our plumes** i.e. over us (in their feathered
helmets)   **O méchante fortune!** 'O wicked fortune!'   **7 broke** broken, scattered   **8 perdurable**
everlasting   **12 In** i.e. into battle   **15 pander** go-between, pimp   **hold...door** guard the bedroom door
16 gentler nobler/kinder   **18 spoiled** ruined/plundered   **friend** befriend   **19 on** in   **22 upon** of

[Act 4 Scene 6]

Alarum. Enter the King and his train [Exeter and others,]
with prisoners

KING HENRY V Well have we done, thrice-valiant
    countrymen.
  But all's not done, yet keep the French the field.
EXETER The Duke of York commends him to your
    majesty.
KING HENRY V Lives he, good uncle? Thrice within this
    hour
5   I saw him down; thrice up again and fighting,
  From helmet to the spur all blood he was.
EXETER In which array, brave soldier, doth he lie,
  Larding the plain, and by his bloody side,
  Yoke-fellow to his honour-owing wounds,
10   The noble Earl of Suffolk also lies.
  Suffolk first died, and York, all haggled over,
  Comes to him, where in gore he lay insteeped,
  And takes him by the beard, kisses the gashes
  That bloodily did yawn upon his face,
15   And cries aloud, 'Tarry, my cousin Suffolk!
  My soul shall thine keep company to heaven.
  Tarry, sweet soul, for mine, then fly abreast,
  As in this glorious and well-foughten field
  We kept together in our chivalry.'
20   Upon these words I came and cheered him up.
  He smiled me in the face, raught me his hand
  And with a feeble grip says, 'Dear my lord,
  Commend my service to my sovereign.'
  So did he turn and over Suffolk's neck
25   He threw his wounded arm and kissed his lips,
  And so espoused to death, with blood he sealed
  A testament of noble-ending love.
  The pretty and sweet manner of it forced
  Those waters from me which I would have stopped,
30   But I had not so much of man in me,

4.6 *train* followers 2 **keep** remain (on) 8 **Larding** enriching 9 **honour-owing** i.e. honourable
11 **all haggled over** hacked all over 12 **insteeped** drenched 15 **Tarry** linger, wait 17 **abreast** side by
side 18 **well-foughten field** well-fought battle 19 **chivalry** knightly prowess/bravery in war
20 **cheered him up** spoke comfortingly to him 21 **raught** reached 23 **Commend** offer, remember
26 **espoused** married, united 27 **testament** will, bequest 29 **waters** i.e. tears

And all my mother came into mine eyes
And gave me up to tears.

KING HENRY V I blame you not,
For hearing this, I must perforce compound
35   With mixed-full eyes, or they will issue too. *Alarum*
But, hark, what new alarum is this same?
The French have reinforced their scattered men.
Then every soldier kill his prisoners.
Give the word through.   *Exeunt*

[Act 4 Scene 7]   *running scene 13 continues*

Enter Fluellen and Gower

FLUELLEN Kill the poys and the luggage! 'Tis expressly against the law of arms. 'Tis as arrant a piece of knavery, mark you now, as can be offer't, in your conscience, now, is it not?

5 **GOWER** 'Tis certain there's not a boy left alive, and the cowardly rascals that ran from the battle ha' done this slaughter. Besides, they have burned and carried away all that was in the king's tent, wherefore the king, most worthily, hath caused every soldier to cut
10   his prisoner's throat. O, 'tis a gallant king!

FLUELLEN Ay, he was porn at Monmouth, Captain Gower. What call you the town's name where Alexander the Pig was born?

GOWER Alexander the Great.

15 **FLUELLEN** Why, I pray you, is not 'pig' great? The pig, or the great, or the mighty, or the huge, or the magnanimous, are all one reckonings, save the phrase is a little variations.

GOWER I think Alexander the Great was born in
20   Macedon, his father was called Philip of Macedon, as I take it.

FLUELLEN I think it is in Macedon where Alexander is porn. I tell you, captain, if you look in the maps of the

---

31 my mother i.e. his tender, womanly side **34 perforce** necessarily **compound** come to terms (may play on the sense of 'mix') **35 mixed-full** unclear meaning, perhaps 'swimming confusedly with tears/fully mixed with tears' (some editors emend to 'mistful' or 'wilful') **issue** discharge (tears) **4.7** **1 poys** boys **luggage** perhaps 'those guarding the luggage' **3 offer't** attempted, dared **8 wherefore** because of which **9 worthily** deservedly, justly **11 Monmouth** town in south Wales, near the English border **13 Pig** i.e. Big (**Great**) **17 all one reckonings** all amount to the same thing **18 phrase ... variations** wording is slightly different **20 Macedon** Macedonia, a region in what is now northern Greece **21 take** understand

'orld, I warrant you sall find, in the comparisons
25   between Macedon and Monmouth, that the
situations, look you, is both alike. There is a river
in Macedon, and there is also moreover a river at
Monmouth: it is called Wye at Monmouth, but it is
out of my prains what is the name of the other river.
30   But 'tis all one, 'tis alike as my fingers is to my
fingers, and there is salmons in both. If you mark
Alexander's life well, Harry of Monmouth's life is
come after it indifferent well, for there is figures in all
things. Alexander, God knows, and you know, in his
35   rages and his furies and his wraths and his cholers
and his moods and his displeasures and his
indignations and also being a little intoxicates in
his prains, did, in his ales and his angers, look you,
kill his best friend, Cleitus.

40   **GOWER** Our king is not like him in that: he never killed
any of his friends.

    FLUELLEN It is not well done, mark you now, to take the
tales out of my mouth ere it is made and finished. I
speak but in the figures and comparisons of it: as
45   Alexander killed his friend Cleitus, being in his ales
and his cups, so also Harry Monmouth, being in his
right wits and his good judgements, turned away the
fat knight with the great belly-doublet. He was full of
jests and gipes and knaveries and mocks — I have
50   forgot his name.

    GOWER Sir John Falstaff.

    FLUELLEN That is he. I'll tell you there is good men porn
at Monmouth.

    GOWER Here comes his majesty.

    Alarum. Enter King Harry and Bourbon [and others] with
    prisoners. Flourish

55   **KING HENRY V** I was not angry since I came to France
    Until this instant. Take a trumpet, herald,
    Ride thou unto the horsemen on yond hill:
    If they will fight with us, bid them come down,

---

24 **'orld** world   26 **situations** geographical layout   28 **Wye** the River Wye, on the Welsh-English border   31 **both** i.e. both rivers   32 **is . . . it** follows, resembles   33 **figures** comparisons, parallels 35 **cholers** fits of anger (governed by choler, one of the four bodily humours controlling mood) 37 **intoxicates** intoxicated, drunk   38 **in his ales** i.e. whilst drunk   39 **Cleitus** friend and general to Alexander the Great (killed in a drunken argument by Alexander)   46 **his cups** i.e. drunk   48 **belly-doublet** close-fitting jacket with the lower part padded (in Falstaff's case, with his fat)   49 **gipes** jibes   **knaveries** roguish tricks   **mocks** jeers, acts of mockery   56 **this instant** i.e. at the death of the boys   **trumpet** trumpeter

Or void the field: they do offend our sight.
₆₀ If they'll do neither, we will come to them
And make them skirr away, as swift as stones
Enforcèd from the old Assyrian slings.
Besides, we'll cut the throats of those we have,
And not a man of them that we shall take
₆₅ Shall taste our mercy. Go and tell them so.
Enter Montjoy
EXETER Here comes the herald of the French, my liege.
GLOUCESTER His eyes are humbler than they used to be.
KING HENRY V How now? What means this, herald?
      Know'st thou not
That I have fined these bones of mine for ransom?
₇₀ Com'st thou again for ransom?
MONTJOY No, great king:
I come to thee for charitable licence,
That we may wander o'er this bloody field
To book our dead and then to bury them,
₇₅ To sort our nobles from our common men.
For many of our princes — woe the while! —
Lie drowned and soaked in mercenary blood,
So do our vulgar drench their peasant limbs
In blood of princes, and our wounded steeds
₈₀ Fret fetlock-deep in gore and with wild rage
Yerk out their armèd heels at their dead masters,
Killing them twice. O, give us leave, great king,
To view the field in safety and dispose
Of their dead bodies!
₈₅ **KING HENRY V** I tell thee truly, herald,
I know not if the day be ours or no,
For yet a many of your horsemen peer
And gallop o'er the field.
MONTJOY The day is yours.
₉₀ **KING HENRY V** Praised be God, and not our strength, for
      it!—
What is this castle called that stands hard by?
MONTJOY They call it Agincourt.

---

61 skirr scurry, flee **62 Enforcèd** forcibly flung **63 Besides** in addition **those** i.e. those French prisoners **64 take** capture **69 fined** undertaken to pay **bones** i.e. and nothing more **72 licence** permission **74 book** record **77 mercenary** belonging to paid soldiers **78 vulgar** common people **80 Fret** struggle, chafe **fetlock-deep** up to the fetlock (back of a horse's leg, above the hoof) **81 Yerk** lash, jerk **armèd heels** iron-shod hooves **86 day** i.e. victory **87 peer** appear/look carefully **91 hard** close

KING HENRY V Then call we this the field of Agincourt,
Fought on the day of Crispin Crispianus.

95 **FLUELLEN** Your grandfather of famous memory, an't
please your majesty, and your great-uncle Edward
the Plack Prince of Wales, as I have read in the
chronicles, fought a most prave pattle here in France.

KING HENRY V They did, Fluellen.

100 **FLUELLEN** Your majesty says very true: if your majesties
is remembered of it, the Welshmen did good service
in a garden where leeks did grow, wearing leeks in
their Monmouth caps, which, your majesty know, to
this hour is an honourable badge of the service, and I

105 do believe your majesty takes no scorn to wear the
leek upon Saint Tavy's day.

KING HENRY V I wear it for a memorable honour,
For I am Welsh, you know, good countryman.

FLUELLEN All the water in Wye cannot wash your

110 majesty's Welsh plood out of your pody, I can tell you
that. God pless it and preserve it, as long as it pleases
his grace, and his majesty too!

KING HENRY V Thanks, good my countryman.

FLUELLEN By Jeshu, I am your majesty's countryman, I

115 care not who know it. I will confess it to all the 'orld.
I need not to be ashamed of your majesty, praised be
God, so long as your majesty is an honest man.

KING HENRY V God keep me so!

Enter Williams

Our heralds go with him.
Bring me just notice of the numbers dead

120 On both our parts.— [*Exeunt Heralds with Montjoy*]
Call yonder fellow hither.   *Points to Williams*

EXETER Soldier, you must come to the king.

KING HENRY V Soldier, why wear'st thou that glove in
thy cap?

WILLIAMS An't please your majesty, 'tis the gage of one

125 that I should fight withal, if he be alive.

KING HENRY V An Englishman?

WILLIAMS An't please your majesty, a rascal that
swaggered with me last night, who, if alive and

---

95 grandfather . . . memory i.e. Edward III   **an't** if it   **98 chronicles** historical accounts
103 Monmouth caps round brimless caps with tapering crowns, originally made in Monmouth
104 badge emblem, insignia   **106 Tavy's** i.e. David's   **107 memorable honour** honour well worth
commemorating   **112 his grace** i.e. the king (or possibly 'God's grace')   **124 gage** pledge
128 swaggered quarrelled, blustered

ever dare to challenge this glove, I have sworn to
130   take him a box o'th'ear, or if I can see my glove in his
cap, which he swore as he was a soldier he would
wear if alive, I will strike it out soundly.

KING HENRY V What think you, Captain Fluellen? Is it fit
this soldier keep his oath?

135   **FLUELLEN** He is a craven and a villain else, an't please
your majesty, in my conscience.

KING HENRY V It may be his enemy is a gentleman of
great sort, quite from the answer of his degree.

FLUELLEN Though he be as good a gentleman as the
140   devil is, as Lucifer and Beelzebub himself, it is
necessary, look your grace, that he keep his vow
and his oath: if he be perjured, see you now, his
reputation is as arrant a villain and a jack-sauce as
ever his black shoe trod upon God's ground and his
145   earth, in my conscience, la!

KING HENRY V Then keep thy vow, sirrah, when thou
meet'st the fellow.

WILLIAMS So I will, my liege, as I live.

KING HENRY V Who servest thou under?

150   **WILLIAMS** Under Captain Gower, my liege.

FLUELLEN Gower is a good captain, and is good
knowledge and literatured in the wars.

KING HENRY V Call him hither to me, soldier.

WILLIAMS I will, my liege.   *Exit*

155   **KING HENRY V** Here, Fluellen, wear thou this favour for   *Gives him*
me and stick it in thy cap. When Alençon and myself   *Williams' glove*
were down together, I plucked this glove from his
helm: if any man challenge this, he is a friend to
Alençon and an enemy to our person; if thou
160   encounter any such, apprehend him, an thou dost
me love.

FLUELLEN Your grace does me as great honours as can
be desired in the hearts of his subjects. I would fain
see the man that has but two legs that shall find
165   himself aggriefed at this glove; that is all. But I would

---

129 **challenge** claim   133 **fit** appropriate   135 **craven** coward   **else** otherwise   138 **sort** rank
quite . . . degree of too high a rank to have to answer Williams' challenge   140 **Lucifer and Beelzebub**
the devil   143 **jack-sauce** saucy, impudent fellow   144 **black** dirty/wicked, damned   146 **sirrah** sir (used
to an inferior)   151 **is** has   152 **literatured** is well-read   155 **favour** token worn as mark of favour
156 **Alençon** a French duke   157 **down** i.e. on the ground   158 **helm** helmet   160 **apprehend**
arrest   161 **love** an act of love and loyalty   163 **fain** eagerly   164 **that . . . legs** i.e. whoever he might be

fain see it once, an please God of his grace that I
might see.

KING HENRY V Know'st thou Gower?

FLUELLEN He is my dear friend, an please you.

170 **KING HENRY V** Pray thee go seek him, and bring him to
my tent.

FLUELLEN I will fetch him. *Exit*

KING HENRY V My lord of Warwick, and my brother
Gloucester,

Follow Fluellen closely at the heels.

175 The glove which I have given him for a favour
May haply purchase him a box o'th'ear.
It is the soldier's, I by bargain should
Wear it myself. Follow, good cousin Warwick:
If that the soldier strike him, as I judge

180 By his blunt bearing he will keep his word,
Some sudden mischief may arise of it,
For I do know Fluellen valiant
And, touched with choler, hot as gunpowder,
And quickly will return an injury.

185 Follow and see there be no harm between them.
Go you with me, uncle of Exeter. *Exeunt*

[Act 4 Scene 8]   *running scene 13 continues*

Enter Gower and Williams

WILLIAMS I warrant it is to knight you, captain.

Enter Fluellen

FLUELLEN God's will and his pleasure, captain, I beseech
you now, come apace to the king: there is more good
toward you peradventure, than is in your knowledge

5 to dream of.

WILLIAMS Sir, know you this glove?

FLUELLEN Know the glove? I know the glove is a glove.

WILLIAMS I know this, and thus I challenge it. *Strikes him*

FLUELLEN 'Sblood, an arrant traitor as any's in the

10 universal world, or in France, or in England!

GOWER How now, sir? You villain!   *To Williams*

WILLIAMS Do you think I'll be forsworn?

166 it him   **176 haply** perhaps   **180 blunt** forthright   **181 mischief** harm   **183 touched** affected/lit,
fired (like **gunpowder**)   **choler** anger   **4.8   3 apace** quickly   **4 peradventure** perhaps   **6 know you** do
you recognize   **9 'Sblood** God's blood   **12 be forsworn** break my word

FLUELLEN Stand away, Captain Gower. I will give treason his payment into ploughs, I warrant you.

15 **WILLIAMS** I am no traitor.

FLUELLEN That's a lie in thy throat. I charge you in his majesty's name, apprehend him. He's a friend of the Duke Alençon's.

Enter Warwick and Gloucester

WARWICK How now, how now? What's the matter?

20 **FLUELLEN** My lord of Warwick, here is — praised be God for it! — a most contagious treason come to light, look you, as you shall desire in a summer's day. Here is his majesty.

Enter King and Exeter

KING HENRY V How now? What's the matter?

25 **FLUELLEN** My liege, here is a villain and a traitor, that, look your grace, has struck the glove which your majesty is take out of the helmet of Alençon.

WILLIAMS My liege, this was my glove, here is the fellow of it. And he that I gave it to in change promised to *Shows other* wear it in his cap. I promised to strike him, if he did. I *glove*

30 met this man with my glove in his cap, and I have been as good as my word.

FLUELLEN Your majesty hear now, saving your majesty's manhood, what an arrant, rascally, beggarly, lousy

35 knave it is. I hope your majesty is pear me testimony and witness, and will avouchment, that this is the glove of Alençon that your majesty is give me, in your conscience, now.

KING HENRY V Give me thy glove, soldier. Look, here is *Shows his glove* the fellow of it.

40 'Twas I, indeed, thou promisèd'st to strike,
And thou hast given me most bitter terms.

FLUELLEN An please your majesty, let his neck answer for it, if there is any martial law in the world.

KING HENRY V How canst thou make me satisfaction?

45 **WILLIAMS** All offences, my lord, come from the heart. Never came any from mine that might offend your majesty.

KING HENRY V It was ourself thou didst abuse.

WILLIAMS Your majesty came not like yourself: you

50 appeared to me but as a common man; witness the

---

13 away aside   **14 into ploughs** in blows (perhaps 'in two blows')   **16 lie . . . throat** deliberate lie
22 summer's day i.e. long day   **27 is take out** took out   **35 is pear** will bear   **36 avouchment** avouch,
affirm   **37 is give** gave   **41 terms** language, words   **44 satisfaction** amends   **48 abuse** insult

night, your garments, your lowliness. And what your
highness suffered under that shape, I beseech you
take it for your own fault and not mine, for had you
been as I took you for, I made no offence: therefore, I
55   beseech your highness, pardon me.
KING HENRY V Here, uncle Exeter, fill this glove with
    crowns,
    And give it to this fellow.— Keep it, fellow,
    And wear it for an honour in thy cap
    Till I do challenge it.— Give him the crowns.—   *Exeter gives*
60   And captain, you must needs be friends with him.   *Williams money*
FLUELLEN By this day and this light, the fellow has
    mettle enough in his belly.— Hold, there is twelve-   *Offers Williams*
    pence for you, and I pray you to serve God, and   *money*
    keep you out of prawls and prabbles and quarrels and
65   dissensions and, I warrant you, it is the better for
    you.
WILLIAMS I will none of your money.
FLUELLEN It is with a good will. I can tell you, it will
    serve you to mend your shoes. Come, wherefore
70   should you be so pashful? Your shoes is not so good.
    'Tis a good silling, I warrant you, or I will change it.
Enter Herald
KING HENRY V Now, herald, are the dead numbered?
HERALD Here is the number of the slaughtered French.   *Gives a paper*
KING HENRY V What prisoners of good sort are taken,
    uncle?
75   EXETER 'Charles Duke of Orléans, nephew to the king,   *Reads*
    John Duke of Bourbon, and Lord Bouciqualt.
    Of other lords and barons, knights and squires,
    Full fifteen hundred, besides common men.'
KING HENRY V This note doth tell me of ten thousand
    French
80   That in the field lie slain: of princes, in this number,
    And nobles bearing banners, there lie dead
    One hundred twenty six: added to these,
    Of knights, esquires, and gallant gentlemen,
    Eight thousand and four hundred, of the which,
85   Five hundred were but yesterday dubbed knights.
    So that in these ten thousand they have lost,
    There are but sixteen hundred mercenaries:

---

51 **lowliness** apparent low rank   **62 mettle** spirit, courage   **64 prawls and prabbles** brawls and brabbles
(i.e. petty quarrels)   **65 dissensions** quarrels, disputes   **67 will** want   **71 good** genuine, not counterfeit
74 good sort high rank

The rest are princes, barons, lords, knights, squires,
And gentlemen of blood and quality.
90 The names of those their nobles that lie dead:
Charles Delabreth, High Constable of France,
Jaques of Chatillion, Admiral of France,
The master of the cross-bows, Lord Rambures,
Great Master of France, the brave Sir Guichard
    Dolphin,
95 John Duke of Alençon, Anthony Duke of Brabant,
The brother to the Duke of Burgundy,
And Edward Duke of Bar. Of lusty earls,
Grandpré and Roussi, Fauconbridge and Foix,
Beaumont and Marle, Vaudemont and Lestrale.
100 Here was a royal fellowship of death.—
Where is the number of our English dead?—   *Herald gives him*
                                                   another paper
                                                   Reads
'Edward the Duke of York, the Earl of Suffolk,
Sir Richard Ketly, Davy Gam, Esquire';
None else of name, and of all other men
105 But five-and-twenty. O God, thy arm was here.
And not to us, but to thy arm alone,
Ascribe we all! When, without stratagem,
But in plain shock and even play of battle,
Was ever known so great and little loss
110 On one part and on th'other? Take it, God,
For it is none but thine.
EXETER 'Tis wonderful.
KING HENRY V Come, go we in procession to the village.
And be it death proclaimèd through our host
115 To boast of this or take that praise from God
Which is his only.
FLUELLEN Is it not lawful, an please your majesty, to tell
how many is killed?
KING HENRY V Yes, captain, but with this
    acknowledgement:
120 That God fought for us.
FLUELLEN Yes, my conscience, he did us great good.
KING HENRY V Do we all holy rites.
Let there be sung *Non nobis* and *Te Deum*,

---

89 blood nobility   **92 Admiral** commander-in-chief of the navy   **94 Great Master** chief official of the royal
household   **97 lusty** strong, vigorous   **104 name** note, rank   **105 arm** i.e. might, power   **107 stratagem**
tricks designed to outwit the enemy   **108 plain shock** direct clash of forces   **even play** straightforward
contest   **112 wonderful** to be marvelled at, extraordinary   **123** *Non nobis* opening words of Psalm
115 ('Give praise not unto us, O God')   *Te Deum* thanksgiving hymn 'Te Deum laudamus' ('We praise
thee O God')

The dead with charity enclosed in clay,
125 And then to Calais, and to England then,
Where ne'er from France arrived more happy men.

Exeunt

Act 5

Enter Chorus

CHORUS Vouchsafe to those that have not read the
story,
That I may prompt them: and of such as have,
I humbly pray them to admit th'excuse
Of time, of numbers and due course of things,
5 Which cannot in their huge and proper life
Be here presented. Now we bear the king
Toward Calais: grant him there; there seen,
Heave him away upon your wingèd thoughts
Athwart the sea. Behold, the English beach
10 Pales in the flood with men, wives and boys,
Whose shouts and claps out-voice the deep-mouthed
sea,
Which like a mighty whiffler 'fore the king
Seems to prepare his way. So let him land,
And solemnly see him set on to London.
15 So swift a pace hath thought that even now
You may imagine him upon Blackheath,
Where that his lords desire him to have borne
His bruisèd helmet and his bended sword
Before him through the city. He forbids it,
20 Being free from vainness and self-glorious pride;
Giving full trophy, signal and ostent
Quite from himself to God. But now behold,
In the quick forge and working-house of thought,
How London doth pour out her citizens.
25 The mayor and all his brethren in best sort,

---

124 **with ... clay** i.e. given a Christian burial **5 1 Vouchsafe** grant **2 prompt them** i.e. remind them
what comes next **4 time** the (five-year) time lapse between the last scene and the next/the limited time in
which to perform a play **numbers** limited number of actors and the multitude they are called on to
represent **due ... things** the nature of historical events **5 huge ... life** i.e. true enormous scale **7 grant**
acknowledge, allow imaginatively **9 Athwart** across **10 Pales** fences **flood** sea **11 claps** applause
deep-mouthed loud, deep-voiced **12 whiffler** attendant who clears the way at a procession
14 solemnly ceremoniously **16 Blackheath** a large common, just south of London **17 Where that**
where **18 bruisèd** dented **bended** bent **20 vainness** personal vanity, pride **21 trophy** token of
victory **signal** symbol, sign **ostent** display **23 working-house** workshop **25 brethren** fellow
councillors **best sort** i.e. civic robes

Like to the senators of th'antique Rome,
With the plebeians swarming at their heels,
Go forth and fetch their conqu'ring Caesar in:
As by a lower but by loving likelihood,
30   Were now the general of our gracious empress,
As in good time he may, from Ireland coming,
Bringing rebellion broachèd on his sword,
How many would the peaceful city quit,
To welcome him? Much more, and much more
        cause,
35   Did they this Harry. Now in London place him,
As yet the lamentation of the French
Invites the King of England's stay at home:
The emperor's coming in behalf of France,
To order peace between them. And omit
40   All the occurrences, whatever chanced,
Till Harry's back return again to France:
There must we bring him; and myself have played
The interim, by rememb'ring you 'tis past.
Then brook abridgment, and your eyes advance,
45   After your thoughts, straight back again to France.

Exit

[Act 5 Scene 1]   *running scene 14*

Enter Fluellen and Gower

GOWER Nay, that's right. But why wear you your leek
    today? Saint Davy's day is past.
FLUELLEN There is occasions and causes why and
    wherefore in all things. I will tell you, asse my
5   friend, Captain Gower: the rascally, scald, beggarly,
    lousy, pragging knave, Pistol, which you and yourself
    and all the world know to be no petter than a fellow,
    look you now, of no merits, he is come to me and
    prings me pread and salt yesterday, look you, and bid

26 **th'antique** ancient   29 **lower . . . likelihood** i.e. less glorious, but as loving, similar circumstance
30 **general . . . empress** apparently a reference to the Earl of Essex, for much of 1599 the commander of
English troops in **Ireland** on behalf of Elizabeth I   32 **broachèd** pierced, speared   34 **Much** many   **and**
and with   36 **lamentation** mourning, grievances   37 **Invites** requires   38 **emperor's coming** the Holy
Roman Emperor Sigismund came to England in 1416   39 **them** editors have conjectured that there may be
a line or so missing at this point in the text   **omit** let us pass over, ignore   42 **played The interim**
performed, represented the intervening period   44 **brook** tolerate   **5.1** *Location: the English camp,*
France   4 **wherefore** how, why   **asse** as (plays on 'ass/arse')   5 **scald** vile/scabby

10 me eat my leek. It was in a place where I could not
breed no contention with him, but I will be so bold as
to wear it in my cap till I see him once again, and
then I will tell him a little piece of my desires.

Enter Pistol

GOWER Why, here he comes, swelling like a turkey-cock.

15 FLUELLEN 'Tis no matter for his swellings nor his turkey-
cocks.— God pless you, aunchient Pistol. You scurvy,
lousy knave, God pless you!

PISTOL Ha, art thou bedlam? Dost thou thirst, base
Trojan,
To have me fold up Parcas fatal web?

20 Hence, I am qualmish at the smell of leek.

FLUELLEN I peseech you heartily, scurvy, lousy knave, at
my desires, and my requests, and my petitions, to eat,
look you, this leek; because, look you, you do not love
it, nor your affections and your appetites and your

25 disgestions doo's not agree with it, I would desire you
to eat it.

PISTOL Not for Cadwallader and all his goats.

FLUELLEN There is one goat for you.   *Strikes him*
Will you be so good, scald knave, as eat it?

30 PISTOL Base Trojan, thou shalt die.

FLUELLEN You say very true, scald knave, when God's
will is: I will desire you to live in the meantime, and
eat your victuals. Come, there is sauce for it. You   *Strikes him*
called me yesterday 'mountain squire', but I will

35 make you today a squire of low degree. I pray you fall
to: if you can mock a leek, you can eat a leek.

GOWER Enough, captain, you have astonished him.

FLUELLEN I say, I will make him eat some part of my
leek, or I will peat his pate four days.— Bite, I pray

40 you, it is good for your green wound and your ploody
coxcomb.

PISTOL Must I bite?

---

11 breed no contention start any argument   **14 swelling . . . turkey-cock** i.e. puffed up with self-
importance (in Fluellen's response **swellings** and **cock** have potentially phallic resonances)   **16 scurvy**
contemptible, worthless   **18 bedlam** mad   **thirst** i.e. long   **base Trojan** knave   **19 fold . . . web** i.e. end
your life (in classical mythology, the Parcae are the three Fates, who spin, reel out and cut the thread of each
human life)   **20 qualmish** made sick   **25 disgestions** digestions, perhaps implying 'hard-earned', 'difficult
to digest'   **27 Cadwallader** seventh-century Welsh warrior king   **goats** traditionally associated with
Wales   **28 goat** possible pun on 'goad' (i.e. rod for driving cattle/powerful incitement)   **29 scald** scabby
31 God's will is God decides   **33 victuals** food   **sauce** flavouring/a rebuke   **35 fall to** begin eating
37 astonished stunned   **40 green** fresh/festering, infected   **ploody coxcomb** bloody head

FLUELLEN Yes, certainly, and out of doubt and out of
question too, and ambiguities.

45 **PISTOL** By this leek, I will most horribly revenge. I eat   *Eats*
and eat, I swear—

FLUELLEN Eat, I pray you. Will you have some more   *Fluellen*
sauce to your leek? There is not enough leek to swear *threatens him or*
by.   *strikes him*

50 **PISTOL** Quiet thy cudgel, thou dost see I eat.   *Eats*

FLUELLEN Much good do you, scald knave, heartily. Nay,
pray you throw none away, the skin is good for your
broken coxcomb. When you take occasions to see
leeks hereafter, I pray you mock at 'em, that is all.

55 **PISTOL** Good.

FLUELLEN Ay, leeks is good. Hold you, there is a groat to   *Offers a coin*
heal your pate.

PISTOL Me a groat?

FLUELLEN Yes, verily and in truth, you shall take it, or I
60 have another leek in my pocket, which you shall eat.

PISTOL I take thy groat in earnest of revenge.

FLUELLEN If I owe you anything, I will pay you in
cudgels. You shall be a woodmonger, and buy
nothing of me but cudgels. God buy you, and keep
65 you, and heal your pate.   *Exit*

PISTOL All hell shall stir for this.

GOWER Go, go, you are a counterfeit cowardly knave.
Will you mock at an ancient tradition, begun upon
an honourable respect, and worn as a memorable
70 trophy of predeceased valour and dare not avouch in
your deeds any of your words? I have seen you
gleeking and galling at this gentleman twice or
thrice. You thought because he could not speak
English in the native garb, he could not therefore
75 handle an English cudgel: you find it otherwise, and
henceforth let a Welsh correction teach you a good
English condition. Fare ye well.   *Exit*

PISTOL Doth Fortune play the hussy with me now?
News have I, that my Doll is dead i'th'spital
80 Of a malady of France,

---

45 revenge have my revenge   **53 take occasions** should happen, have the opportunity   **55 Good** very well   **56 groat** small coin worth four old pence   **61 in earnest of** as a down-payment for   **62 pay** punish   **63 cudgels** beatings   **woodmonger** one who deals in wood   **64 buy** be with   **67 counterfeit** deceitful   **70 predeceased** former, past   **72 gleeking** taunting, insulting   **galling** harassing, scoffing   **74 garb** fashion   **77 condition** disposition   **79 Doll** some editors emend to 'Nell', assuming that Pistol refers to his wife Nell Quickly   **i'th'spital** in the hospital   **80 malady of France** syphilis, the 'French disease'

And there my rendezvous is quite cut off.
Old I do wax, and from my weary limbs
Honour is cudgelled. Well, bawd I'll turn,
And something lean to cutpurse of quick hand.
85 To England will I steal, and there I'll steal,
And patches will I get unto these cudgelled scars,
And swear I got them in the Gallia wars.   *Exit*

Act 5 [Scene 2]   *running scene 15*

Enter, at one door King Henry, Exeter, Bedford, Warwick,
[Gloucester, Clarence, Westmorland] and other Lords: at
another, Queen Isabel, the [French] King, the Duke of
Burgundy and other French [including Katherine and Alice]

KING HENRY V Peace to this meeting, wherefore we are
        met.
Unto our brother France, and to our sister,
Health and fair time of day, joy and good wishes
To our most fair and princely cousin Katherine,
5 And, as a branch and member of this royalty,
By whom this great assembly is contrived,
We do salute you, Duke of Burgundy,
And princes French and peers, health to you all!
FRENCH KING Right joyous are we to behold your face,
10 Most worthy brother England, fairly met.
So are you, princes English, every one.
QUEEN ISABEL So happy be the issue, brother England,
Of this good day and of this gracious meeting,
As we are now glad to behold your eyes —
15 Your eyes, which hitherto have borne in them
Against the French, that met them in their bent,
The fatal balls of murdering basilisks.
The venom of such looks, we fairly hope,
Have lost their quality, and that this day
20 Shall change all griefs and quarrels into love.
KING HENRY V To cry amen to that, thus we appear.

---

81 rendezvous refuge, haven, perhaps with play on 'sexual encounter' **82 wax** grow **83 bawd** pimp
84 something...hand am somewhat inclined to become a deft pickpocket **85 steal** steal away (plays on
the sense of 'rob') **86 patches** bandages (also with suggestion of patches to conceal syphilitic scars)
87 Gallia i.e. French **5.2** *Location: the royal court, France* **1 wherefore** for which **2 brother** fellow
monarch **sister** i.e. Queen Isabel, wife of the French king **3 fair...day** i.e. good day **4 princely**
royal **5 royalty** collection of royal persons **12 issue** outcome **13 gracious** happy/prosperous **16 bent**
line of sight/direction of fire **17 balls** eyeballs/cannonballs **basilisks** large cannon/mythical reptiles
whose gaze could kill **19 quality** i.e. deadly nature

QUEEN ISABEL You English princes all, I do salute you.
BURGUNDY My duty to you both, on equal love,
    Great Kings of France and England! That I have
      laboured,
25   With all my wits, my pains and strong endeavours,
    To bring your most imperial majesties
    Unto this bar and royal interview,
    Your mightiness on both parts best can witness.
    Since then my office hath so far prevailed
30   That, face to face and royal eye to eye,
    You have congreeted, let it not disgrace me,
    If I demand, before this royal view,
    What rub or what impediment there is,
    Why that the naked, poor and mangled Peace,
35   Dear nurse of arts, plenties and joyful births,
    Should not in this best garden of the world,
    Our fertile France, put up her lovely visage?
    Alas, she hath from France too long been chased,
    And all her husbandry doth lie on heaps,
40   Corrupting in it own fertility.
    Her vine, the merry cheerer of the heart,
    Unprunèd dies: her hedges even-pleached,
    Like prisoners wildly overgrown with hair,
    Put forth disordered twigs: her fallow leas
45   The darnel, hemlock and rank fumitory
    Doth root upon, while that the coulter rusts
    That should deracinate such savagery.
    The even mead, that erst brought sweetly forth
    The freckled cowslip, burnet and green clover,
50   Wanting the scythe, withal uncorrected, rank,
    Conceives by idleness and nothing teems
    But hateful docks, rough thistles, kecksies, burs,
    Losing both beauty and utility;
    And all our vineyards, fallows, meads and hedges,
55   Defective in their natures, grow to wildness.

---

23 on based on   **25 pains** efforts   **27 bar** court, tribunal **interview** meeting   **30 That** in the sense that   **31 congreeted** greeted each other   **32 before**...**view** in such royal company   **33 rub** obstacle (bowling term)   **35 nurse** nourisher **arts** learning, scholarship   **37 put up** raise **visage** face   **39 husbandry** agricultural cultivation and produce **on heaps** in a mess   **40 Corrupting**...**fertility** rotting for being overripe/ruining itself by being overgrown **it its**   **42 even-pleached** regularly interwoven   **44 fallow leas** unploughed arable fields   **45 darnel**...**fumitory** weeds **rank** overabundant   **46 root upon** take root, grow **coulter** blade on a plough   **47 deracinate** uproot **savagery** wild plants   **48 even mead** level meadow **erst** formerly   **49 freckled**...**clover** i.e. all useful plants or herbs   **50 Wanting** lacking **withal uncorrected** unchecked by it   **51 Conceives** germinates, breeds **teems** is fertile, flourishes   **52 docks**...**burs** all types of weed **kecksies** dry hollow stems   **54 fallows** arable lands   **55 natures** proper functions

Even so our houses and ourselves and children
Have lost, or do not learn for want of time,
The sciences that should become our country,
But grow like savages — as soldiers will
60   That nothing do but meditate on blood —
To swearing and stern looks, diffused attire
And everything that seems unnatural.
Which to reduce into our former favour
You are assembled, and my speech entreats
65   That I may know the let, why gentle Peace
Should not expel these inconveniences
And bless us with her former qualities.

KING HENRY V If, Duke of Burgundy, you would the
      peace,
Whose want gives growth to th'imperfections
70   Which you have cited, you must buy that peace
With full accord to all our just demands,
Whose tenors and particular effects
You have enscheduled briefly in your hands.

BURGUNDY The king hath heard them, to the which as
      yet
75   There is no answer made.

KING HENRY V Well then, the peace,
Which you before so urged, lies in his answer.

FRENCH KING I have but with a cursitory eye
O'erglanced the articles. Pleaseth your grace
80   To appoint some of your council presently
To sit with us once more, with better heed
To re-survey them, we will suddenly
Pass our accept and peremptory answer.

KING HENRY V Brother, we shall.— Go, uncle Exeter,
85   And brother Clarence, and you, brother Gloucester,
Warwick and Huntingdon, go with the king,
And take with you free power to ratify,
Augment, or alter, as your wisdoms best
Shall see advantageable for our dignity,
90   Anything in or out of our demands,

---

58 sciences knowledge, skills   **61 diffused** disordered   **63 reduce** restore   **favour** appearance/approval,
good grace   **65 let** hindrance   **68 would** desire   **69 want** lack   **71 accord** agreement   **just** exact/
legitimate   **72 tenors** substances, contents   **effects** purposes/drifts   **73 enscheduled** listed, written
down   **78 cursitory eye** cursory glance   **79 O'erglanced** looked over   **Pleaseth** if it please   **81 better
heed** greater care, attention   **82 suddenly** in a short time   **83 Pass** pronounce   **accept** acceptable (to
us), agreed   **peremptory** final, resolved   **87 ratify** confirm

And we'll consign thereto.— Will you, fair sister,   *To Queen Isabel*
Go with the princes, or stay here with us?
QUEEN ISABEL Our gracious brother, I will go with them:
Haply a woman's voice may do some good,
95   When articles too nicely urged be stood on.
KING HENRY V Yet leave our cousin Katherine here with
us.
She is our capital demand comprised
Within the fore-rank of our articles.
QUEEN ISABEL She hath good leave.   *Exeunt all. Henry,*
Katherine [and Alice] remain
100 **KING HENRY V** Fair Katherine, and most fair,
Will you vouchsafe to teach a soldier terms
Such as will enter at a lady's ear
And plead his love-suit to her gentle heart?
KATHERINE Your majesty shall mock at me: I cannot
105 speak your England.
KING HENRY V O fair Katherine, if you will love me
soundly with your French heart, I will be glad to hear
you confess it brokenly with your English tongue. Do
you like me, Kate?
110 **KATHERINE** *Pardonnez-moi*, I cannot tell vat is 'like me'.
KING HENRY V An angel is like you, Kate, and you are
like an angel.
KATHERINE *Que dit-il? Que je suis semblable à les anges?*   *To Alice*
ALICE *Oui, vraiment, sauf votre grâce, ainsi dit-il.*
115 **KING HENRY V** I said so, dear Katherine, and I must not
blush to affirm it.
KATHERINE *O bon Dieu! Les langues des hommes sont*
pleines de tromperies.
KING HENRY V What says she, fair one? That the tongues   *To Alice*
120 of men are full of deceits?
ALICE *Oui*, dat de tongues of de mans is be full of deceits:
dat is de princess.
KING HENRY V The princess is the better Englishwoman.
I'faith, Kate, my wooing is fit for thy understanding. I
125 am glad thou canst speak no better English, for, if

91 **consign** subscribe, agree 94 **Haply** perhaps 95 **nicely** strictly, fastidiously **stood on** insisted
97 **capital** principal **comprised** included 98 **fore-rank** front row **articles** conditions 101 **terms**
words, expressions (plays on the sense of 'conditions of a truce') 103 **love-suit** courtship
110 *Pardonnez-moi* 'excuse me' 113 *Que . . . anges?* 'What does he say? That I resemble angels?'
114 *Oui . . . dit-il* 'Yes, truly, saving your grace, he says so' 117 *O . . . tromperies* 'O good God! The tongues
of men are full of deceits' 122 **is de princess** i.e. is what the princess said 123 **the better**
Englishwoman i.e. like an Englishwoman for mistrusting his flattery 124 **fit** appropriate, suitable

thou couldst, thou wouldst find me such a plain king
that thou wouldst think I had sold my farm to buy
my crown. I know no ways to mince it in love, but
directly to say 'I love you.' Then if you urge me
130 further than to say, 'Do you in faith?', I wear out my
suit. Give me your answer, i'faith, do, and so clap
hands and a bargain. How say you, lady?

KATHERINE *Sauf votre honneur*, me understand vell.

KING HENRY V Marry, if you would put me to verses or to
135 dance for your sake, Kate, why you undid me, for the
one I have neither words nor measure; and for the
other, I have no strength in measure, yet a
reasonable measure in strength. If I could win a
lady at leap-frog, or by vaulting into my saddle with
140 my armour on my back, under the correction of
bragging be it spoken, I should quickly leap into a
wife. Or if I might buffet for my love, or bound my
horse for her favours, I could lay on like a butcher
and sit like a jackanapes, never off. But, before God,
145 Kate, I cannot look greenly nor gasp out my
eloquence, nor I have no cunning in protestation;
only downright oaths, which I never use till urged,
nor never break for urging. If thou canst love a fellow
of this temper, Kate, whose face is not worth
150 sunburning, that never looks in his glass for love of
anything he sees there, let thine eye be thy cook. I
speak to thee plain soldier: if thou canst love me for
this, take me: if not, to say to thee that I shall die, is
true; but for thy love, by the lord, no. Yet I love thee
155 too. And while thou liv'st, dear Kate, take a fellow of
plain and uncoined constancy, for he perforce must
do thee right, because he hath not the gift to woo in

---

126 plain plain-spoken/simple   **128 mince** speak in a delicate or pretentious way/behave affectedly
131 suit courtship (perhaps with suggestion of worn-out clothing)   **clap** . . . **bargain** shake hands on a
deal   **133** *Sauf votre honneur* 'saving your honour'   **134 put** . . . **verses** have me write love poetry
135 undid would ruin   **136 measure** poetic metre   **137 strength in measure** i.e. ability in dancing
measure slow, stately dance   **138 measure in strength** amount of physical strength
140 under . . . **spoken** at the risk of punishment for boasting, let it be said   **141 leap into** gain/have sex
with   **142 buffet** box   **bound** make jump   **143 lay on** strike vigorously/lie upon during sex   **144 sit** on
his horse/on his wife   **jackanapes** monkey (or someone acting like one)   **off** falling off   **145 look greenly**
i.e. as an inexperienced young lover does   **146 cunning in protestation** skill in declarations (of
love)   **147 downright** plain   **urged** provoked   **148 urging** being persuaded by others   **149 temper**
temperament, disposition   **not worth sunburning** i.e. so ugly that the sun could not make it worse
(Elizabethans considered fair skin a particular mark of beauty)   **150 glass** mirror   **151 be thy cook** i.e.
dress the dish (his face) to make it appetizing   **156 uncoined** genuine, freshly minted and uncirculated
(amongst women)

other places. For these fellows of infinite tongue, that
can rhyme themselves into ladies' favours, they do
160   always reason themselves out again. What! A
speaker is but a prater, a rhyme is but a ballad. A
good leg will fall, a straight back will stoop, a black
beard will turn white, a curled pate will grow bald, a
fair face will wither, a full eye will wax hollow: but a
165   good heart, Kate, is the sun and the moon — or
rather the sun and not the moon, for it shines bright
and never changes, but keeps his course truly. If thou
would have such a one, take me: and take me, take a
soldier: take a soldier, take a king. And what say'st
170   thou then to my love? Speak, my fair, and fairly, I
pray thee.

KATHERINE Is it possible dat I should love de enemy of
France?

KING HENRY V No, it is not possible you should love the
175   enemy of France, Kate; but in loving me, you should
love the friend of France, for I love France so well
that I will not part with a village of it; I will have it all
mine: and, Kate, when France is mine and I am
yours, then yours is France and you are mine.

180 **KATHERINE** I cannot tell vat is dat.

KING HENRY V No, Kate? I will tell thee in French, which
I am sure will hang upon my tongue like a new-
married wife about her husband's neck, hardly to be
shook off. *Je quand sur le possession de France, et quand*
185   *vous avez le possession de moi* — let me see, what then?
Saint Denis be my speed! — *donc vôtre est France et
vous êtes mienne.* It is as easy for me, Kate, to conquer
the kingdom as to speak so much more French. I
shall never move thee in French, unless it be to laugh
190   at me.

KATHERINE *Sauf votre honneur, le français que vous parlez,
il est meilleur que l'anglais lequel je parle.*

KING HENRY V No, faith, is't not, Kate. But thy speaking
of my tongue, and I thine, most truly-falsely, must

---

158 infinite tongue clever, unlimited speech   **159 favours** sexual benevolence   **160 What!** exclamation of
scorn   **161 prater** chatterbox   **ballad** popular, common form of poetry   **162 fall** waste away   **164 full**
perfect, lustrous   **wax hollow** sunken/insincere   **170 fairly** favourably   **176 friend** also has sense of
'lover'   **184 *Je...moi*** 'I, when I have possession of France, and when you have the possession of me'
(imperfect but generally comprehensible French)   **186 Saint...speed!** Saint Denis help me!   **Saint Denis**
patron saint of France   ***donc...mienne*** 'therefore yours is France and you are mine'   **189 move** i.e. stir
emotion in   **191 *Sauf...parle*** 'Saving your honour, the French that you speak, it is better than the English
that I speak'   **194 truly-falsely** sincerely and inaccurately

195   needs be granted to be much at one. But, Kate, dost
      thou understand thus much English, canst thou love
      me?

KATHERINE I cannot tell.

KING HENRY V Can any of your neighbours tell, Kate? I'll
200   ask them. Come, I know thou lovest me. And at
      night, when you come into your closet, you'll
      question this gentlewoman about me; and I know,
      Kate, you will to her dispraise those parts in me that
      you love with your heart, but, good Kate, mock me
205   mercifully, the rather, gentle princess, because I love
      thee cruelly. If ever thou beest mine, Kate, as I have a
      saving faith within me tells me thou shalt, I get thee
      with scambling, and thou must therefore needs prove
      a good soldier-breeder. Shall not thou and I, between
210   Saint Denis and Saint George, compound a boy, half
      French, half English, that shall go to Constantinople
      and take the Turk by the beard? Shall we not? What
      say'st thou, my fair flower-de-luce?

KATHERINE I do not know dat.

215   **KING HENRY V** No, 'tis hereafter to know, but now to
      promise: do but now promise, Kate, you will
      endeavour for your French part of such a boy; and
      for my English moiety take the word of a king and a
      bachelor. How answer you, *la plus belle Katherine du*
220   *monde, mon très chère et devin déesse?*

KATHERINE Your majestee 'ave *fausse* French enough to
      deceive de most sage *demoiselle* dat is *en France*.

KING HENRY V Now, fie upon my false French! By mine
      honour, in true English, I love thee, Kate: by which
225   honour I dare not swear thou lovest me, yet my
      blood begins to flatter me that thou dost,
      notwithstanding the poor and untempering effect of
      my visage. Now, beshrew my father's ambition! He
      was thinking of civil wars when he got me: therefore

195 **at one** the same   **199 neighbours** close acquaintances   **201 closet** private room   **203 dispraise**
belittle   **206 cruelly** extremely   **beest** be   **207 saving faith** faith deep enough for salvation
208 scambling struggling, scuffling   **210 compound** compose, create   **212 take…beard** humiliate,
drive the Turks out   **213 flower-de-luce** fleur-de-lis (lily), emblem on the French coat of arms
215 hereafter in time to come   **know** plays on sense of 'have sex'   **217 part** behalf (plays on sense of
'genitals')   **218 moiety** half, portion   **219 *la*…*déesse*** 'the most fair Katherine of the world, my most dear
and divine goddess'   **221 'ave** have, i.e. has   ***fausse*** 'false' – i.e. 'incorrect/insincere'   **222 sage** prudent,
wise   ***demoiselle*** 'young lady'   **226 blood** passion/sexual desire   **227 notwithstanding** in spite of
untempering unsoftening, unsettling   **228 beshrew** curse   **229 civil wars** i.e. Richard II's deposition
got conceived

230   was I created with a stubborn outside, with an aspect
       of iron, that when I come to woo ladies, I fright them.
       But, in faith, Kate, the elder I wax, the better I shall
       appear. My comfort is that old age, that ill layer-up of
       beauty, can do no more spoil upon my face. Thou
235   hast me, if thou hast me, at the worst; and thou shalt
       wear me, if thou wear me, better and better. And
       therefore tell me, most fair Katherine, will you have
       me? Put off your maiden blushes, avouch the
       thoughts of your heart with the looks of an
240   empress, take me by the hand, and say, 'Harry of
       England I am thine.' Which word thou shalt no
       sooner bless mine ear withal, but I will tell thee
       aloud, 'England is thine, Ireland is thine, France is
       thine, and Henry Plantagenet is thine'; who though I
245   speak it before his face, if he be not fellow with the
       best king, thou shalt find the best king of good
       fellows. Come, your answer in broken music; for thy
       voice is music and thy English broken: therefore,
       queen of all, Katherine, break thy mind to me in
250   broken English; wilt thou have me?

       KATHERINE Dat is as it sall please *de roi mon père.*

       KING HENRY V Nay, it will please him well, Kate; it shall
       please him, Kate.

       KATHERINE Den it sall also content me.

255   KING HENRY V Upon that I kiss your hand, and I call you   *Tries to kiss*
       my queen.   *her hand*

       KATHERINE *Laissez, mon seigneur, laissez, laissez: ma foi, je*
       ne veux point que vous abaissiez votre grandeur en
       baisant la main d'une, de votre seigneurie, indigne
260   *serviteur. Excusez-moi, je vous supplie, mon très-*
       puissant seigneur.

       KING HENRY V Then I will kiss your lips, Kate.

       KATHERINE *Les dames et demoiselles pour être baisées devant*
       leur noces, il n'est pas la coutume de France.

265   KING HENRY V Madam my interpreter, what says she?

       ALICE Dat it is not be de fashion *pour les* ladies of France
       — I cannot tell vat is *baiser* en Anglish.

---

230 **aspect** facial appearance   233 **ill layer-up** poor preserver/wrinkler   234 **spoil** damage   236 **wear**
use, possess (plays on sense of 'exhaust sexually')   244 **Plantagenet** name of the dynasty to which Henry V
belonged   245 **fellow with** equal to   249 **break** open, broach   251 *de . . . pere* 'the king my father'
257 *Laissez . . . seigneur* 'Desist, my lord, desist, desist: my faith, I do not at all wish you to abase your
greatness in kissing the hand of one [who is] your lordship's unworthy servant. Excuse me, I beg of you, my
most mighty lord'   263 *Les . . . France* 'In France it is not the custom for ladies and young ladies to be
kissed before their marriages'

KING HENRY V To kiss.

ALICE Your majesty *entendre* bettre *que moi.*

270 **KING HENRY V** It is not a fashion for the maids in France
to kiss before they are married, would she say?

ALICE *Oui, vraiment.*

KING HENRY V O, Kate, nice customs curtsy to great
kings. Dear Kate, you and I cannot be confined
275 within the weak list of a country's fashion: we are the
makers of manners, Kate; and the liberty that follows
our places stops the mouth of all find-faults, as I will
do yours, for upholding the nice fashion of your
country in denying me a kiss: therefore, patiently and
280 yielding. You have witchcraft in your lips, Kate: there   *Kisses her*
is more eloquence in a sugar touch of them than in
the tongues of the French council; and they should
sooner persuade Harry of England than a general
petition of monarchs. Here comes your father.

*Enter the French power [King, Queen, Burgundy] and the
English Lords*

285 **BURGUNDY** God save your majesty! My royal cousin,
teach you our princess English?

KING HENRY V I would have her learn, my fair cousin,
how perfectly I love her, and that is good English.

BURGUNDY Is she not apt?

290 **KING HENRY V** Our tongue is rough, coz, and my
condition is not smooth, so that, having neither the
voice nor the heart of flattery about me, I cannot so
conjure up the spirit of love in her that he will appear
in his true likeness.

295 **BURGUNDY** Pardon the frankness of my mirth, if I
answer you for that. If you would conjure in her,
you must make a circle: if conjure up love in her in
his true likeness, he must appear naked and blind.
Can you blame her then, being a maid yet rosed over
300 with the virgin crimson of modesty, if she deny the
appearance of a naked blind boy in her naked seeing

---

269 *entendre...moi* 'understands' better 'than me'   **272** *Oui, vraiment* 'Yes, truly'   **273 nice** fastidious/
coy/trivial   **275 list** boundary (literally, barrier enclosing a jousting or duelling area)   **276 follows our**
places goes with our high rank   **277 find-faults** people who seek to criticize   **289 apt** ready, quick to
learn   **291 condition** disposition   **296 conjure** i.e. raise up (spirits, but here a penis)   **297 make a circle**
magic circle for conjuring/open her vagina   **298 naked and blind** like Cupid (Roman god of love,
traditionally depicted thus)/in the form of a penis (with its 'blind eye')   **299 maid** virgin   **rosed...**
modesty i.e. blushing in modesty/flushed in sexual excitement   **301 in** within (emotionally)/inside
(sexually)   **naked seeing** emotionally exposed/aware of her physical nakedness

self? It were, my lord, a hard condition for a maid to consign to.

KING HENRY V Yet they do wink and yield, as love is
305 blind and enforces.

BURGUNDY They are then excused, my lord, when they see not what they do.

KING HENRY V Then, good my lord, teach your cousin to consent winking.

310 **BURGUNDY** I will wink on her to consent, my lord, if you will teach her to know my meaning, for maids, well summered and warm kept, are like flies at Bartholomew-tide: blind, though they have their eyes, and then they will endure handling, which
315 before would not abide looking on.

KING HENRY V This moral ties me over to time and a hot summer; and so I shall catch the fly, your cousin, in the latter end and she must be blind too.

BURGUNDY As love is, my lord, before it loves.

320 **KING HENRY V** It is so: and you may, some of you, thank love for my blindness, who cannot see many a fair French city for one fair French maid that stands in my way.

FRENCH KING Yes, my lord, you see them perspectively,
325 the cities turned into a maid; for they are all girdled with maiden walls that war hath never entered.

KING HENRY V Shall Kate be my wife?

FRENCH KING So please you.

KING HENRY V I am content, so the maiden cities you
330 talk of may wait on her. So the maid that stood in the way for my wish shall show me the way to my will.

FRENCH KING We have consented to all terms of reason.

KING HENRY V Is't so, my lords of England?

---

302 hard plays on the idea of penile hardness **303 consign** assent **304 wink and yield** close their eyes and give in **305 enforces** (love/the penis) pushes his way in **307 do** plays on the sense of 'have sex with' **309 consent winking** agree to **wink and yield** **310 on** at **311 know** understand (with sexual connotations) **312 summered** tended, nurtured **warm** comfortably, well off/sexually aroused **313 Bartholomew-tide** Saint Bartholomew's day, 24 August **blind . . . eyes** sluggish, unaware (from the summer heat) **314 handling** with sexual connotations **316 moral** lesson **ties me over** confines me to **318 latter end** late summer/lower body **319 before it loves** i.e. until it sees the object of its love/ before sexual consummation **324 perspectively** obliquely, distortedly (through a perspective: either a lens that distorts objects or a painting that only becomes clear when viewed from an angle) **326 maiden** unbreached by military/sexual force **entered** invaded in war/penetrated sexually **329 so** so long as **330 wait on her** follow her (as a dowry) **331 will** political, military desire/sexual desire/penis **332 terms of reason** reasonable terms

WESTMORLAND The king hath granted every article:
335 His daughter first, and then in sequel all,
According to their firm proposèd natures.

EXETER Only he hath not yet subscribed this: where your
majesty demands, that the King of France, having
any occasion to write for matter of grant, shall name
340 your highness in this form and with this addition in
French, *Notre très cher fils Henri, Roi d'Angleterre,*
Héritier de France: and thus in Latin, *Praeclarissimus*
filius noster Henricus, Rex Angliae, et Haeres Franciae.

FRENCH KING Nor this I have not, brother, so denied,
345 But your request shall make me let it pass.

KING HENRY V I pray you then, in love and dear alliance,
Let that one article rank with the rest,
And thereupon give me your daughter.

FRENCH KING Take her, fair son, and from her blood
raise up
350 Issue to me, that the contending kingdoms
Of France and England, whose very shores look pale
With envy of each other's happiness,
May cease their hatred, and this dear conjunction
Plant neighbourhood and Christian-like accord
355 In their sweet bosoms, that never war advance
His bleeding sword 'twixt England and fair France.

LORDS Amen!

KING HENRY V Now, welcome, Kate: and bear me witness
all,
That here I kiss her as my sovereign queen.   *Kisses her*
Flourish

360 **QUEEN ISABEL** God, the best maker of all marriages,
Combine your hearts in one, your realms in one!
As man and wife, being two, are one in love,
So be there 'twixt your kingdoms such a spousal,
That never may ill office, or fell jealousy,
365 Which troubles oft the bed of blessèd marriage,
Thrust in between the paction of these kingdoms,
To make divorce of their incorporate league,

---

335 in sequel succession **337 subscribed** signed, agreed to **339 matter of grant** official conferment of
lands or titles **340 addition** title **341 Notre...France** 'Our very dear son Henry, King of England, heir of
France' **342 Praeclarissimus...Franciae** 'Our very dear son Henry, King of England, heir of France'
345 request i.e. to marry Katherine **350 Issue** descendants **351 pale** due to the chalk cliffs **353 dear**
tender/costly **354 neighbourhood** friendly, neighbourly **355 bosoms** hearts **advance** raise
363 spousal marriage, union **364 ill office** disservice, poor dealings **fell** fierce **366 paction** pact,
contract **367 incorporate** united in one body, indivisible

That English may as French, French Englishmen,
Receive each other. God speak this Amen!
370 **ALL** Amen!
KING HENRY V Prepare we for our marriage, on which
day,
My lord of Burgundy, we'll take your oath,
And all the peers', for surety of our leagues.
Then shall I swear to Kate, and you to me,
375 And may our oaths well kept and prosp'rous be!

Sennet.   Exeunt

[Epilogue]

Enter Chorus

CHORUS Thus far, with rough and all-unable pen,
Our bending author hath pursued the story,
In little room confining mighty men,
Mangling by starts the full course of their glory.
5 Small time, but in that small most greatly lived
This star of England. Fortune made his sword;
By which the world's best garden be achieved,
And of it left his son imperial lord.
Henry the Sixth, in infant bands crowned King
10 Of France and England, did this king succeed,
Whose state so many had the managing,
That they lost France and made his England bleed,
Which oft our stage hath shown; and, for their sake,
In your fair minds let this acceptance take.   [*Exit*]

---

373 **surety . . . leagues** security of our alliance   *Sennet* trumpet signalling a procession
Epilogue   1 rough imperfect, coarse   **all-unable** inadequate   **2 bending** i.e. over his work/bowing
4 by starts in fits and starts, intermittently   **5 Small time** Henry died aged thirty-five, after a nine-year
reign   **7 world's best garden** i.e. France   **9 infant bands** strips of linen babies were wrapped in
11 Whose of whose   **13 their** i.e. Shakespeare's plays concerning Henry VI   **14 this acceptance take**
this play find favour

TEXTUAL NOTES

Q = First Quarto text of 1600
F = First Folio text of 1623
F2 = a correction introduced in the Second Folio text of 1632
F4 = a correction introduced in the Fourth Folio text of 1685
Ed = a correction introduced by a later editor
SD = stage direction
SH = speech heading (i.e. speaker's name)

List of parts = Ed

Prologue SH CHORUS = Ed. *Not in* F
1.2.40 *succedant* = F2. F = *succedaul* **47, 54 Elbe** = Ed. F = *Elue* **200 majesty** = Ed. F = Maiesties **215 End** = Q. F = And **224 dauphin** *spelled* Dolphin *throughout* F **246 are** = Q. F = is **315 SD *Flourish*** = *Ed.* F *places after* Exeunt
2.0.1 SH CHORUS = Ed. *Not in* F
2.1.22 mare = Q. F = name **30 SH HOSTESS QUICKLY** = Ed. F = *Host.* **35 drawn** = Ed. F = hewne **40 Iceland** *spelled* Island *in* F **77 enough. Go to** = Ed. F = enough to go to **80 you, hostess** = Ed. F = your Hostesse **110 that's** = F2. F = that
2.2.29 SH GREY = Ed. F = *Kni.* **88 furnish him** = F2. F = furnish **108 a** = F2. F = an **109 whoop** = Ed. F = hoope **115 All** = Ed. F = And **140 mark the** = Ed. F = make thee **148 Henry** = Q. F = *Thomas* **159 Which I** = F2. F = Which **176 you have** = Q. F = you
2.3.17 on a table = Ed. F = and a Table **31 SH HOSTESS QUICKLY** = Ed. F = *Woman.*
2.4.111 pining = Q. F = priuy **137 Louvre** *spelled* Louer *in* F **152 SD *Flourish*** = Ed. *After act break in* F
3.0 Act 3 = Ed. F = *Actus Secundus* **1 SH CHORUS** = Ed. *Not in* F **6 fanning** = Ed. F = fayning **17 Harfleur** *spelled* Harflew *in* F
3.1.7 conjure = Ed. F = commune **17 noblest** = F2. F = Noblish **24 men** = F4. F = me **32 Straining** = Ed. F = Straying
3.2.47 Calais *spelled* Callice *in* F **70 SH FLUELLEN** = Ed. F = *Welch.* **85 SH JAMY** = Ed. F = *Scot.* **89 SH MACMORRIS** = Ed. F = *Irish.*
3.3.32 heady = F2. F = headly **35 Defile** = Ed. F = Desire
3.4.1 *parles* = F2. F = *parlas. Textual notes for the French-language scenes are selective, since the distinction between modernization and emendation is hard to maintain* **7 *Et les doigts*?** *assigned to Alice in* F **8 SH ALICE** = Ed. F = *Kat.* **11 SH KATHERINE** = Ed. F = *Alice* **14 *Nous*** = Ed. *Not in* F **20 *le*** = F2. F = *de* **46 coun** = Q. F = *Count* **47 *Ce*** = F2. F = *il*
3.5.7 scions *spelled* Syens *in* F **11 *de*** = F2. F = *du* **43 Vaudemont** = F2. F = *Vandemint* **45 Foix** = Ed. F = *Loys* **46 knights** = Ed. F = Kings
3.6.8 life = Q. F = liue **31 her** = Q. F = his **70 perfect** *spelled* perfit *in* F **112 lenity** = Q. F = Leuitie
3.7.12 pasterns = F2. F = postures **60 lief** *spelled* liue *in* F **66 *truie*** = Ed. F = *leuye*
4.0 Act 4 = Ed. F = *Actus Tertius* **1 SH CHORUS** = Ed. *Not in* F **16 name** = Ed. F = nam'd **20 cripple** *spelled* creeple *in* F

4.1.3 Good *spelled* God *in* F   **94 Thomas** = Ed. F = *Iohn*   **246 adoration** = F2. F = Odoration   **254 Think'st** *spelled* Thinks *in* F   **276 Hyperion** = F2. F = *Hiperio*   **294 ere** = Ed. F = of   **312 friends** = Q. F = friend

4.2.2 *Monte à* = Ed. F = *Monte*   **6 *Cieux*** = Ed. F = *Cein*   **25 gainst** = F2. F = against   **49 gimmaled** = Ed. F = Iymold   **50 chewed** *spelled* chaw'd *in* F   **60 guidon** = Ed. F = Guard: on

4.3.12 Farewell . . . today *printed after line 14 in* F   **13 And . . . valour** *assigned to Bedford in* F   **50 And . . . day.'** = Q. *Not in* F   **133 vanguard** = F *(spelled* Vaward)

4.4.12 *miséricorde* = F2. F = *miserecordie*   ***pitié*** = F2. F = *pitez*   **34 *à cette heure*** = Ed. F = *asture*   **54 *j'ai tombé*** = Ed. F = *Ie intombe*   **64 *Suivez-vous*** = Ed. F = *Saaue vous*

4.5.3 *Mort de* = Q. F = *Mor Dieu*   **16 by a** = Q. F = a

Act 4 Scene 7 = Ed. F = *Actus Quartus*   **79 our** = Ed. F = with   **118 God** = Q. F = Good

4.8.113 we = Ed. F = me

5.0.1 SH CHORUS = Ed. *Not in* F

5.1.68 begun = Ed. F = began   **78 hussy** = F *(*huswife*)*   **87 swear** = Q. F = swore

5.2.12 England = F2. F = Ireland   **21 SH KING HENRY V** = Ed. F = *Eng.* or *England* in lines 21, 68, 76, 84, 96   **45 fumitory** *spelled* Femetary *in* F   **78 cursitory** = Ed. F = curselarie   **110 vat** = Ed. F = wat   **133 vell** = Ed. F = well   **251 sall** = Ed. F = shall   **267 *baiser*** = Ed. F = buisse   **326 hath never** = Ed. F = hath   **335 then in** F2. F = in   **366 paction** = Ed. F = Pation

Epilogue SH CHORUS = Ed. *Not in* F

SYNOPSES OF THE TWO PARTS OF *HENRY IV*

PART I

After deposing King Richard II, Henry Bullingbrook has ascended the throne as Henry IV. Guilt about the deposition troubles his conscience, and the stability of his reign is threatened by growing opposition from some of the nobles who helped him to the throne. His son, Prince Henry (also known as Harry and, by Falstaff, as Hal), is living a dissolute life, frequenting the taverns of Eastcheap in the company of Sir John Falstaff and other disreputable characters with whom he participates in a highway robbery. Opposition to the king becomes open rebellion, led by the Earl of Northumberland's son Henry Percy, known for his courage and impetuous nature as 'Hotspur'. The Percy family support the claim to the throne of Hotspur's brother-in-law, Edmund Mortimer. The rebellion brings Hal back to his father's side, while Falstaff musters a ragged troop of soldiers. The king's army defeats the rebels at the battle of Shrewsbury, where Hal kills Hotspur. Falstaff lives to die another day.

PART II

In despair at the death of his son Hotspur, the Earl of Northumberland lends his support to a second rebellion, led by the Archbishop of York. As the threat of civil war looms over the country, King Henry IV grows sick, while also fearing that his son Prince Henry (or Harry/Hal) has returned to his old life with Falstaff and the other disreputable denizens of the Eastcheap tavern. Falstaff is sent on a recruiting expedition and renews old acquaintances in

Gloucestershire. The rebel army is met by the king's forces, led this time by Hal's younger brother, Prince John of Lancaster. On his death-bed, King Henry is reconciled with his son, who has begun to distance himself from his former companions. A new, mature Hal accepts the crown as Henry V.

SCENE-BY-SCENE ANALYSIS

PROLOGUE

In a prologue full of meta-theatrical devices the Chorus calls for a 'muse of fire' to enable it to truly represent the play's historical characters and events and apologises to the audience for the limitations of the playhouse, the 'wooden O' in which they perform, and the 'flat unraisèd spirits' of those who are to act. The audience are asked to make up for these deficiencies with their own imaginations, stimulated by vivid imagery of the 'perilous narrow ocean' separating England and France, asking that for each man represented, a thousand should be imagined, and when they talk of horses, to picture them trampling the earth, emphasizing the power of language and importance of the mental collaboration with the audience in production of the play.

ACT 1 SCENE 1

The opening scene establishes the play's concerns with politics and religion. The Bishops of Canterbury and Ely are discussing a bill that would have been passed under the previous king (Henry IV) if it had not been for the 'scambling and unquiet time' during his reign, which would have required the Church to surrender much of their money and land to the crown. Now that Henry V has achieved civil peace, the bill is under question again and the bishops are worried. They discuss the change in Henry since he has become king: his transformation from the 'wildness' of his youth (see *Henry IV Part I* and *Part II*) to being 'full of grace and fair regard'. Canterbury marvels at the king's ability to 'reason in divinity' and 'debate of commonwealth affairs', emphasizing Henry's skill with language. Canterbury has suggested to the king that the Church will make a contribution to funds should England go to war with France, a tactic designed to divert Henry's attention away from the bill. He adds that Henry is interested in his potential right to inherit 'the crown and seat of France' through the line of his grandfather, Edward III, raising the theme of lineage and inheritance, and ideas about 'rights' to kingship. They leave to attend Henry's meeting with the French ambassadors.

ACT 1 SCENE 2

Lines 1–236: King Henry and his court are waiting for Canterbury and Ely before they admit the French ambassador. When the bishops arrive, Henry asks Canterbury to 'justly and religiously unfold' the arguments supporting his claim to the French throne. He urges the bishop to answer honestly, reminding him that if they go to war with France, many 'Shall drop their blood', the motif of blood playing on the relationship between lineage and conflict. Canterbury's response is long and complicated, based on the argument that the Salic law that prevails in France preventing inheritance through the female line is invalid. He argues, therefore, that Henry's right to the French throne is 'as clear as is the summer's sun' in contrast to the French, who have 'Usurped' Henry to retain their 'crooked titles', establishing the ongoing opposition of the two nations. Again Henry demands to be assured that he may 'with right and conscience' make his claim; his directness contrasts with Canterbury's lengthy, carefully-contrived speeches, suggesting that for the king at least, the need for the war to be 'just' is genuine. Canterbury and Ely, assisted by Exeter and Westmorland, urge Henry to go to war with France. Reinforcing the patriotism that characterizes descriptions of England throughout, they present him with glorified images of his warrior ancestry: 'the former lions of your blood', placing the events of the play within their wider historical context. Despite their stirring language, Henry shows himself to be shrewd and practical as he observes that his armies must defend England against the Scots as well as engaging in war with France. His followers reassure him that 'the eagle England' can easily deal with 'the weasel Scot', as their army is big enough even if they only take 'one quarter into France'. Henry resolves to invade France with 'God's help', and sends for the French ambassadors.

Lines 237–315: The ambassadors come from the dauphin, rather than the French king. Henry greets them graciously, describing himself as 'no tyrant, but a Christian king', and urges them to deliver their message. Henry has recently made claims on 'certain dukedoms' of France, which the dauphin dismisses as foolish, attributing it to the reckless character of Henry's youth. To reinforce his point, he has sent Henry an insulting gift: a box of tennis balls. Henry remains polite, showing his capacity for self-control, although his anger is evident in his language as he tells the ambassadors they will 'play a set' that will 'strike' the crown of France 'into the hazard'. His use of sporting imagery shows his wit and verbal dexterity, which compares favourably with the dauphin's blatant mockery, establishing the ongoing paralleling and comparison of these two characters. Henry describes the violent and tragic consequences of this insult: the tennis balls will be returned to France as 'gun-stones'. He concludes by appealing to God to help him in his 'well-hallowed cause' and sends the ambassadors back to the dauphin.

ACT 2 CHORUS

The Chorus moves the focus away from the court to encompass a wider England as it describes how 'all the youth' are 'on fire' to be at war with France and 'every man' thinks of honour. The speech emphasizes the unity of the English people and creates a stirring, patriotic image of the country: a 'little body with a mighty heart'. The Chorus warns, however, that not all of England's children are 'kind and natural': the Earl of Cambridge, Lord Scroop of Masham, and Sir Thomas Grey are traitors to King Henry and have been bought by 'the gilt of France' to kill him. The Chorus urges the audience to 'Linger [their] patience' while the action moves from

London to Southampton, reinforcing both the play's meta-theatrical framework, its geographical movement and the recurring emphasis on the audience's involvement.

ACT 2 SCENE 1

In contrast with the action so far, the focus is on low-status characters (all comrades of Henry in his disreputable youth) who provide humour as well as reflecting the wider concerns of the play. In a bawdy exchange, Bardolph and Nym discuss Pistol, who has married Hostess Nell Quickly despite the fact that she was 'troth-plight' to Nym. Bardolph urges Nym to make friends with Pistol, so they can 'be all three sworn brothers to France'. Pistol arrives with Hostess Quickly, and the bawdy humour continues as Nym and Pistol argue, their quarrel echoing the more serious conflicts in the play. The hostess is called away to her tavern, where Sir John Falstaff (a former companion of the youthful Henry: see *Henry IV Part I* and *Part II)* is very ill. Bardolph encourages Pistol and Nym to be friends, and Hostess Quickly returns to call them to Falstaff. They leave, commenting that although 'a good king', Henry has treated Falstaff badly by banishing him, hinting at a more ruthless side to the king's character.

ACT 2 SCENE 2

Bedford, Exeter and Westmorland discuss the traitors revealing that Henry has known of their plans for some time. Trumpets are sounded and the king enters with his train (including Cambridge, Scroop and Grey), emphasizing the public nature of this scene. Henry discusses the forthcoming invasion with the unsuspecting traitors, feigning friendliness and ignorance in a conversation that generates tension and dramatic irony.

Henry instructs Exeter to free a man who has been imprisoned for insulting him while drunk. Scroop and Grey suggest that the king is too lenient, and that the man should be punished, advising Henry against showing mercy (a recurring motif). Henry comments that if he does not 'wink' at small crimes, he will not be able to deal harshly enough when faced 'with capital crimes'. Pretending to hand Cambridge, Scroop and Grey their commission papers, he gives each of them written evidence of their treachery. When they ask for his mercy, he reminds them that they have just advised him against showing leniency. In a passionate but restrained speech that reminds us of his self-control and linguistic skill, he addresses the traitors, focusing chiefly on 'Ingrateful, savage and inhuman' Scroop, his close friend. He orders their arrest and execution, pointing out that they have betrayed not just their king, but the 'whole kingdom', emphasizing the inextricable link between king and country. The traitors are led away. Henry sees the revelation of the conspiracy as God's work and considers it bodes well for 'a fair and lucky war'. He announces they will sail for France straight away.

ACT 2 SCENE 3

The previous scene of highly-charged court politics is once again contrasted with the narrative of the lower-status characters. The mood is more sombre, however. Falstaff is dead and Hostess Quickly describes his death in moving terms. Falstaff's death is a precursor of the many deaths to come in battle: Pistol, Bardolph and Nym must leave for France, reminding us of the country-wide impact of the war.

ACT 2 SCENE 4

Lines 1–78: The action moves to the French court where the king is preparing for the English invasion. He sends his noblemen and the dauphin to reinforce the coastal towns, reminding them of the cost of underestimating the English. The dauphin does not believe that France is in danger; he still sees Henry as 'a vain, giddy shallow, humorous youth'. The Constable reminds him of the ambassadors' report: Henry was moderate, noble, and 'terrible in constant resolution'. The dauphin remains unconvinced, but the king urges his court to 'strongly arm to meet' Henry, reminding them again of previous defeats by the English, a device which reinforces the wider historical context of the play and appeals to an English audience. A Messenger announces the arrival of ambassadors from Henry.

Lines 79–151: Exeter, Henry's ambassador, urges the French king to 'lay apart / The borrowed glories' of his kingship. He argues that Henry is King of France 'by gift of heaven', clearly establishing the concept of the 'divine right of kings', which is fundamental to the action of the play. Exeter gives the king a paper detailing Henry's claim as 'the native and true challenger' to the French throne. He warns the king of what will happen if France resists, vividly describing the power of Henry who is 'coming, / In thunder and in earthquake, like a Jove'. He points out that the French king will be responsible for many deaths if he does not surrender now. The king promises a response by the next day. Exeter delivers a separate message to the dauphin from Henry informing him that he regards him with 'Scorn and defiance, slight regard, [and] contempt', establishing an individual enmity between the two men in addition to the national conflict. He urges the French king to respond quickly; Henry has already landed in France.

ACT 3 CHORUS

The Chorus provides a vivid description of the English fleet crossing the Channel, appealing to the audience's senses as they are asked to imagine 'silken streamers' and 'hempen tackle', to hear the noise of the 'shrill whistle' and to feel the hot sun and 'th'invisible and creeping wind'. We learn that the French king has replied to Henry, offering him marriage to his daughter, Katherine, with some 'petty and unprofitable dukedoms' as a dowry, that Henry has refused, and the English cannon have begun to bombard France.

ACT 3 SCENE 1

In a speech famous for its stirring patriotism, Henry urges his troops into battle: 'Once more unto the breach, dear friends, once more', which suggests that the battle is not going England's way at this point. He shows his command over language with his powerful rhetoric, characterizing England's 'modest stillness and humility' during peacetime in contrast to the 'hard-favoured rage' required when at war. His language is subtly inclusive: using the royal plurals, 'our' and 'us', he addresses himself to his 'dear friends', then to the 'noblest English' and finally to the 'good yeoman', and concluding with the rousing cry, 'God for Harry, England, and Saint George!'

ACT 3 SCENE 2

Lines 1–55: The effects of Henry's speech are immediately apparent as Bardolph urges his friends, 'On, on, on, on, on! To the breach, to the breach!' Nym's response creates bathos, however, as he urges Bardolph to wait: the battle is 'too hot' and he doesn't want to die. Pistol agrees: he would rather be 'in an ale-house in London'. The Welsh Captain Fluellen arrives and drives them on into the breach, leaving the Boy alone on the stage. Unusually for a minor character, the boy delivers a soliloquy, a device which shows the far-reaching impact of the conflict and illustrates the potential nobility in the 'lowest' of characters. He comments on the dishonest, cowardly nature of Bardolph, Pistol and Nym, and announces his intention to leave them.

Lines 56–141: Gower and Fluellen discuss the plan to dig 'mines', or tunnels, under the walls of Harfleur. Fluellen is not convinced, particularly when he learns that the Irish Captain MacMorris is in charge. MacMorris arrives, accompanied by the Scottish Captain Jamy, and Fluellen tries to convince MacMorris that mining the walls was a mistake. His long-winded, pedantic opinions on Roman military discipline make him a gentle figure of fun, as does his exaggerated and unlikely 'Welsh' pronunciation. All of the English allies have marked 'accents' and display stereotypical national traits and prejudices against each other. This might have appealed to an English audience, often in conflict with neighbouring countries during the early modern period, but it also suggests Henry's ability to unite habitual enemies in a common cause against a 'foreign' enemy. As Fluellen and MacMorris argue and Gower tries to pacify them, a parley is sounded.

ACT 3 SCENE 3

Henry is at the gates of Harfleur, where he calls upon the governor to surrender. He describes himself as 'a soldier', once again identifying himself with his men, but also emphasizing the more ruthless, tactical side to his character. He declares that there will be no 'mercy' if the English are forced to attack, and threatens that the English soldiers, 'rough and hard of heart' will mow 'like grass' the 'fresh fair virgins' and 'flow'ring infants' of Harfleur: brutal images that counter the glorious representation of war elsewhere in the play. The Governor announces that they have been failed by the dauphin who was not ready in time to defend them. He surrenders Harfleur to Henry, who orders Exeter to secure the town and to 'use mercy' towards the French; a contrast to his recent threatened violence.

ACT 3 SCENE 4

The action shifts to a private, female exchange that contrasts with the male-orientated public scenes, and provides a counterpoint and humorous relief from the tensions of the political and military events. The French princess, Katherine, asks her maid, Alice, to help her learn English, suggesting that she is not unwilling to marry Henry, or is perhaps reconciled to her role in forging a political alliance. Comedy is generated through the misunderstanding and misuse of English words, ('bilbow' for 'elbow', for example), as well as the potential for obscene double entendres as they practise the names for parts of the body.

ACT 3 SCENE 5

The King of France and his court discuss Henry's progress. Showing little interest in military matters, the noblemen insult the 'barbarous' English, who inhabit a 'slobb'ry' and 'dirty' country, but admire their 'mettle', particularly as it seems to have been generated in a 'foggy, raw and dull' climate. The French king urges his noblemen into battle, ordering them to bring in 'Harry England' as a prisoner. The Constable approves of this plan, pointing out that the English armies are depleted, and 'sick and famished in their march'.

ACT 3 SCENE 6

Lines 1–87: Gower and Fluellen discuss the recent fighting, and Fluellen comments on the bravery of 'Aunchient Pistol'. Pistol himself enters and tells them that Bardolph is due to be hanged for stealing. He asks Fluellen to intercede with Exeter on Bardolph's behalf, but Fluellen refuses, saying that 'discipline ought to be used', whereupon Pistol tells him to 'Die and be damned' and leaves. Gower now remembers Pistol as 'a bawd, [and] a cutpurse'. Fluellen says that Pistol spoke bravely before, but Gower tells him this was an act, Pistol is not the man that he 'make[s] show' to be. They are interrupted by the arrival of King Henry.

Lines 88–174: The king questions Fluellen about the recent action, and he gives his report, including the fact that Bardolph is to be executed. Henry shows no reaction to this news about his former companion other than to observe that he would have 'all such offenders so cut off', demonstrating his strict moral code and absolute break with his former life. Montjoy, the French herald, brings a message. The French king claims that his armies have merely been waiting and are now going to make England 'repent'. He asks Henry to consider his own ransom which should be substantial. Henry sends Montjoy back with the message that, although the English army are 'much enfeebled', they will fight on. Placing their fortunes 'in God's hand', he marches with his army.

ACT 3 SCENE 7

In a scene that reveals the French as foolish and frivolous, the Constable and Orléans compare armour and horses while waiting for morning. They are interrupted by the dauphin who praises his own horse, comparing it to 'Pegasus' and himself to 'a hawk'. Further humour is generated as he compares his horse to his mistress. A Messenger brings the news that the English 'lie within fifteen hundred paces' of the French camp. The French are unconcerned, mocking Henry and his 'fat-brained followers' and boasting that they will easily win.

ACT 4 CHORUS

The Chorus evokes the English camp the night before the battle. The language conjures the bleak conditions of the outnumbered and 'war-worn' English. The Chorus describes how Henry, 'The royal captain of this ruined band', visits all of his soldiers, calling them 'brothers, friends and countrymen', giving them courage for the coming conflict. The emphasis is on Henry as a man, able to connect with all his people rather than as a remote and distant figure, his nobility evident as he is described as giving comfort 'like the sun', bringing 'A little touch of Harry in the night'.

ACT 4 SCENE 1

Lines 1–225: Henry and Gloucester discuss the 'great danger' facing the English. The King borrows Sir Thomas Erpingham's cloak before sending his noblemen away, explaining he wishes to be alone. In this 'disguise' Henry wanders through the English camp and talks to his men, who are unaware of his true identity. He meets Pistol, who praises the king in his usual, rough language: he describes him as 'a bawcock', 'a heart of gold' and a 'lovely bully'. When questioned, Henry pretends he is a kinsman of Fluellen's, whereupon Pistol insults him and leaves. Fluellen and Gower enter and Henry stands aside to overhear their conversation. Fluellen admonishes Gower for speaking so loudly near the enemy, and, despite Fluellen's verboseness, Henry admires his 'care and valour'.

Finally, he meets with three common soldiers, Bates, Court, and Williams, who are pessimistic about their chances in the forthcoming battle. They discuss the role and responsibilities of the king. Henry argues that 'the king is but a man' and says they should be proud to fight with him because his cause is 'just' and 'honourable', but this claim is met with cynicism and Williams argues that 'few die well that die in a battle'. Henry and Williams continue to dispute the case and Henry says that 'if the time were convenient', he would fight Williams. They agree to suspend their 'quarrel' until they meet again, and exchange gloves in token of the challenge.

Lines 226–312: Henry's soliloquy focuses on the responsibilities of kingship and the conflict between his public and private selves. To be king is a 'hard condition': he cannot feel the 'heart's-ease' of 'private men'. Despite all of the trappings, 'The sword, the mace, the crown imperial', he has none of the peace of mind felt by the common man with no responsibilities. He is interrupted by Erpingham, who tells him his nobles are searching for him. Henry sends him to assemble them at his tent. He makes a prayer for his 'soldiers' hearts', and dwells on the penance he has done for his father's fault in usurping Richard II, again emphasizing his concern with the 'just' nature of his own kingship. Gloucester calls and Henry leaves for the battle.

ACT 4 SCENE 2

The French also prepare for the coming battle, showing their confidence as the Constable claims that they have 'A very little little' to do before 'all is done'. Their self-assurance is increased by Grandpré, who reports the pitiful state of the English army. The dauphin jokes that maybe they should feed and clothe the English before fighting with them and they set off.

ACT 4 SCENE 3

The English noblemen discuss the strength of the French army: 'they have full threescore thousand' of 'fresh' soldiers. Westmorland wishes that some of the men that they left in England were there, and Henry overhears him. He delivers another rousing speech, arguing that the fewer of them there are, the greater the share of honour. He foresees a time when men will be proud to say that they fought 'on Crispin's day' (25 October), alongside 'Harry the king'. He says that those that remain 'abed' in England will be sorry that they were not part of the 'band of brothers' that fought. Salisbury brings news that the French are ready to charge, and Westmorland is now eager to fight, showing the power of Henry's speech to inspire others. As the English nobles are about to leave, Montjoy returns with another request from the French Constable that Henry name his ransom. Henry refuses and leads his men into battle.

ACT 4 SCENE 4

Pistol fights a French soldier, and the serious nature of the violence is juxtaposed with the humour derived from their miscommunications and the Boy's attempts to translate Pistol's insults. Mistaking Pistol for a 'brave' and 'valorous' nobleman, the Frenchman offers him two hundred crowns' ransom, which Pistol accepts, saying that he will 'some mercy show'. Alone, the Boy comments on Pistol's 'empty' heart, observing that both Bardolph and Nym had 'more valour', although he reports that Nym has also been hanged. He returns to the camp, noting that it is unguarded except for servants and boys.

ACT 4 SCENE 5

The French are amazed and ashamed: against the odds, the English are winning. They contemplate suicide, but Bourbon rouses them to fight back.

ACT 4 SCENE 6

Henry and Exeter discuss the recent fighting, moved by the bravery and nobility of the English. An alarum sounds as the French return to the battle and Henry gives the order that all the prisoners are to be killed; a practical but brutal tactic that shows his ruthless leadership.

ACT 4 SCENE 7

Lines 1–120: The French have attacked the camp and killed the boys, another reminder of the brutality of war. Fluellen and Gower are outraged at this violation of 'the law of arms' and feel that Henry's order to kill the prisoners was justified. As Fluellen rather ponderously compares Henry to Alexander the Great, the king arrives. Henry is furious about the deaths of the boys and urges his men back into battle, promising that there will be no mercy for the French. He is interrupted by the arrival of Montjoy requesting that the French be allowed to recover their dead. Henry demands to know if it means that the English have won the day, and Montjoy confirms that they have. Henry praises God. As he sends out to find out 'the numbers dead' in the battle, he sees Williams wearing the glove that he gave as a challenge while in disguise.

Lines 121–186: The mood of the scene shifts from the brutal realities of war to comedy. Henry questions Williams, who tells him that the glove belongs to 'a rascal' he intends to fight, failing to recognize the king as the man he challenged. Henry sends Williams to find Gower and then gives Fluellen the glove he accepted from Williams. He tells Fluellen he 'plucked' it from the French nobleman, Alençon, and that anyone who challenges him for wearing it must be a friend of Alençon and an enemy of the king. Henry sends Fluellen to find Gower as well, and reveals his joke to the others: the glove he has given Fluellen 'May haply purchase him a box o'th'ear'. They follow to watch.

ACT 4 SCENE 8

Fluellen meets Gower and Williams. Williams sees the glove in Fluellen's cap and strikes him. Remembering what he has been told, Fluellen accuses Williams of treachery and tries to apprehend him. As they argue, Warwick and Gloucester arrive, followed by the king. Henry reveals the truth about the exchanged gloves, telling Williams that he was the man he 'promisèd'st to strike'. Williams defends himself, claiming he would not have spoken as he did if he had known who Henry was, and Henry shows his just side, filling Williams' glove with money and urging him and Fluellen to be friends. The mood changes again as the Herald brings news of those killed in battle. The French losses are massive, 'Full fifteen hundred, besides common men', but the English have lost only twenty-nine. Henry sees this as God's work, and leads his men to process through the village before returning to England.

ACT 5 CHORUS

The Chorus tells the story of Henry's return to England which cannot be presented in 'huge and proper life' on the stage, describing the numbers of people who waited on 'the English beach' to greet the armies. We learn of Henry's refusal to process through the streets of London, 'Being free from vainness and self-glorious pride', and of his popularity with his people. The Chorus concludes by reminding us that time has passed and taking our thoughts 'straight back again to France'.

ACT 5 SCENE 1

Gower wonders why Fluellen is still wearing a leek, as 'Saint Davy's day is past', emphasizing the Chorus' point about time passing. Fluellen explains that Pistol insulted him in public, offering him 'pread and salt' to eat his leek with and that he is waiting to have his revenge. Pistol enters and Fluellen tells him that *he* must eat the leek. Pistol refuses and they fight until he gives in. Once Pistol has eaten the leek, he swears that he will have revenge, but Gower tells him that he should not have assumed that because Fluellen 'could not speak English in the native garb, he could not therefore handle an English cudgel'. The scene generates humour, but once Pistol is alone he reveals that Hostess Quickly has died of venereal disease, leaving him as the last of the Eastcheap tavern group. He resolves to return to England and become a 'bawd' and a 'cutpurse'.

ACT 5 SCENE 2

Lines 1–99: The French and English negotiate peace. The Duke of Burgundy expresses his hope that English rule will return France to her former 'beauty and utility' after years of neglect, but Henry says that peace must be bought by France agreeing to England's 'just demands'. He sends his noblemen to discuss terms with the French king, accompanied by Queen Isabel of France, who suggests that 'a woman's voice may do some good'. Henry asks that Princess Katherine remain with him, however, as she is the 'capital demand' of his terms.

Lines 100–284: Assisted by Alice, Henry speaks to Katherine. Although he claims that his French is poor and his 'wooing' plain, he shows his mastery of both languages as he tells 'Kate' of his love for her, and asks if she can love him. The scene provides a light-hearted, comedic resolution to the play's brutal conflicts.

Lines 285–375: The French court and English nobility return and the terms of the treaty are established: Henry is to marry Katherine, and is named as the French king's son, and heir to the throne of France. Queen Isabel blesses the 'marriage' of the two countries and hopes are expressed for future peace.

EPILOGUE

The optimism of the final scene is tempered by the Chorus who places events in their historical context: Henry and Katherine's son, Henry VI, eventually 'lost France and made his England bleed'. The play ends with a meta-theatrical appeal hoping the play has found favour with the audience.

HENRY V
IN PERFORMANCE:
THE RSC AND BEYOND

The best way to understand a Shakespeare play is to see it or ideally to participate in it. By examining a range of productions, we may gain a sense of the extraordinary variety of approaches and interpretations that are possible – a variety that gives Shakespeare his unique capacity to be reinvented and made 'our contemporary' four centuries after his death.

We begin with a brief overview of the play's theatrical and cinematic life, offering historical perspectives on how it has been performed. We then analyse in more detail a series of productions staged over the last half-century by the Royal Shakespeare Company. The sense of dialogue between productions that can only occur when a company is dedicated to the revival and investigation of the Shakespeare canon over a long period, together with the uniquely comprehensive archival resource of promptbooks, programme notes, reviews and interviews held on behalf of the RSC at the Shakespeare Birthplace Trust in Stratford-upon-Avon, allows an 'RSC stage history' to become a crucible in which the chemistry of the play can be explored.

We then go to the horse's mouth. Modern theatre is dominated by the figure of the director. He or she must hold together the whole play, whereas the actor must concentrate on his or her part. The director's viewpoint is therefore especially valuable. Shakespeare's plasticity is wonderfully revealed when we hear the directors of several different highly successful productions answering the same questions in very different ways.

FOUR CENTURIES OF *HENRY V*: AN OVERVIEW

The unauthorized 1600 quarto edition of the play claims 'it hath been sundry times played by the Right Honourable the Lord Chamberlain his servants'. By tradition *Henry V* is regarded as the first play performed by Shakespeare's company in the newly built Globe in the summer of 1599. The first recorded performance, however, was on 7 January 1605 at the court of James I. Richard Burbage, the company's leading actor, is thought to have played Henry, and it is surmised that Shakespeare himself may have spoken the lines of the Chorus.

The play did not appeal to Restoration audiences after the reopening of the theatres in 1660, perhaps because of its emphasis on war with France and lack of female parts, and so was adapted in a variety of ways. Samuel Pepys saw a production of Roger Boyle, Earl of Orrery's play in rhyming couplets in 1668 about the rivalry of Henry V and Owen Tudor for the hand of Katherine. Thomas Betterton played Owen Tudor, and in the first performance wore the actual coronation suit of Charles II while Henry Harris as Henry borrowed the Duke of York's. In 1720 Charles Molloy produced *The Half-Pay Officers,* which combined elements of *Henry V* and *Much Ado about Nothing* with William Davenant's *Love and Honour* and James Shirley's *The Wedding.* Aaron Hill's 1723 adaptation turned Shakespeare's play into a tragic drama set in France, eliminated the low comedy and cut and redistributed many of the lines. It introduced a new character, Scroop's niece, 'gentle Harriet', played as a breeches part (i.e. a female actor in a male role). She is a cast-off mistress of Henry's and tries to enlist Katherine and the dauphin in the plot against Henry in revenge, but, overcome with remorse, kills herself. The Genius of England rises and sings a song to celebrate the victory at Agincourt.

Shakespeare's play was performed at Drury Lane in 1747 with Spranger Barry as the king and David Garrick as the Chorus. In 1761 in celebration of the coronation of George III, a dramatic representation of the coronation procession of Henry V was enacted at Covent Garden, one of many occasions on which the play has been associated with celebrations of national pride. John Philip Kemble's production at Covent Garden in 1789, on the eve of the French Revolution, was the first to achieve wide popular success, although the text was heavily cut, eliminating the Choruses as well as anything which showed Henry in a negative light or the French in a positive one. It was enthusiastically received:

> The entire receipts of yesterday evening were appropriated by the Proprietors to the Patriotic Fund at Lloyd's Coffee-house. The play chosen for the occasion was happily suited to the purpose. A more congenial subject to the feelings of Britons, at the present crisis, could not well be selected than the *Henry V* of our immortal Bard. The noble and animating passages with which it abounds, produced the most enthusiastic plaudits, and the antient [*sic*] valour and spirit of our forefathers were revived with all their glowing energies in the breasts of the audience.[1]

Kemble's performance won special praise:

> The hero of his country was admirably delineated by Mr Kemble. In the 'words that breathe and thoughts that burn' of his inspired author, his soul was up in arms; and to the pious effusions and benevolent sentiments of the character, he gave every possible embellishment.[2]

In his lavish 1839 Covent Garden production, William Charles Macready restored the Chorus in the character of Time, 'a russet, bearded figure carrying scythe and hourglass':

> In the Prologue Time appeared on a circular platform surrounded by clouds which then dissolved to reveal an allegorical scene of warlike Harry with famine, sword and fire at his heels. Dioramas were used for the other four choruses. In the second one the conspirators were shown receiving bribes of gold from the French. In the third one the course of the English fleet to France was traced and gave place to the siege of Harfleur, an elaborate set-piece which required over a hundred performers.[3]

Samuel Phelps' productions at Sadler's Wells from 1852 to 1858 retained Time as the Chorus and restored more of the text. A three-dimensional set for the siege of Harfleur was used together with a 'medieval war machine, a ramp-like bridge, up which Henry led his army, was used in the assault'.[4] Agincourt was staged using forty actors, each with a dummy with a waxwork head made by Madame Tussaud strapped on either side. The acting took second place to the highly praised sets and costumes.

Charles Kean's productions at the Princess' Theatre were noted for their historical accuracy and spectacular staging and effects. *Henry V* was his final production there in 1859. His wife, Ellen Tree, played the part of the Chorus in the persona of Clio, the Muse of History; Kate Terry played the Boy. The scenery was 'accurate and beautiful', but the dramatic highlight was the siege of Harfleur – 'in sooth, a stirring spectacle, full of the terror and noise of battle'[5] – employing 212 people.[6] The performances were generally praised:

> One great charm of the performance was . . . the really grand manner in which Mrs Kean declaimed the choruses. The part of King Henry V was exquisitely acted by Mr Kean. His elocution in the war orations, and his familiar delivery in the less heroic scenes, were governed by the most correct taste and judgement.[7]

Charles Calvert's production at the Theatre Royal, Manchester, in 1872 successfully toured America before finally going to London in 1879. Theatre historians regard this as the first production to acknowledge the anti-war aspects of the play.[8] Calvert himself had raised funds for the victims of the Franco-Prussian war and sympathy for the French became permissible, hence Henry's threats before the walls of Harfleur were restored and the executions of the traitors, Bardolph and the French prisoners. He retained Kean's dramatic representation of Henry's return to London, but, '[i]n contrast to Kean's heroic pageant, Calvert's production was informed by a realistic attitude to war shaped by contemporary events'.[9] The part of Henry was played by the exceptionally handsome English actor, George Rignold, of whom one critic claimed: 'Every susceptible girl in those days bought a photograph.'[10] He rode onstage on a white horse called Crispin in the battle scenes. Henry James thought Rignold made 'a very charming impression', but goes on to criticize the contemporary fashion for theatrical spectacle believing it to be 'founded on a fallacy. Illusion, as such an enterprise proposes to produce it, is absolutely beyond the compass of the stage.'[11]

Despite this, the first all-American production directed by Richard Mansfield, who also played Henry, at the Garden Theater in 1900 was an equally spectacular affair in which, following Kean's example, Mansfield trusted,

> not to the quick forge and working-house of thought, but to the improvement in stage machinery and the love of visible motion which dwells within the human breast. The whole fourth act, in this arrangement, was a scene in a London street, where the populace hailed the arriving troops, marching in battalions, with crossbows, pikes, and lances, passing rapidly forward through an arch in the rear and off through the crowd to the side. Now and again a soldier was joined by his wife or by a waiting maiden, and amidst the excitement of it all the harder side of war was suggested by one woman's fate; she rushed among the soldiers to ask one question, and then was carried senseless from the ranks. A dance of girls with flowers was one feature of the pageant, which ended with the entrance on the stage of King Henry on his battle horse.[12]

Frank Benson produced the play at Stratford with himself as Henry sixteen times between 1897 and 1916 (Lewis Waller played the part in 1908), in a production which, against the background of the Boer Wars and First World War, emphasized the play's patriotism; indeed, it is argued that presentation of the play acted 'as a recruiting poster'.[13] It provided 'many 'fine and thrilling moments...though some considered a dance of the two scantily attired young ladies in the French camp to be in bad taste'.[14] The 'fine and thrilling moments' included Benson's 'pole-vault in complete armour on to the walls of Harfleur', a feat which he enjoyed performing into 'late middle age'.[15] Between 1901 and

1906 the play formed the centrepiece in Benson's cycle of history plays which included *King John, Richard II, Henry IV Part I, Henry V, Henry VI Part II* and *Richard III*.

William Poel's production in 1901 with the Elizabethan Society in Burlington Gardens was the first to use the full text of Shakespeare's play since the seventeenth century and attempt to reproduce Elizabethan staging conditions. Playing a fuller text revealed the play's complexity and allowed its ambiguities to emerge. Poel went on to direct a performance with Ben Greet's company at Stratford. Both William Bridges-Adams at Stratford and Robert Atkins at the Old Vic directed the play in 1920 with a female Chorus, an uncut text and minimal scenery. There were regular revivals throughout the 1920s and 1930s: at the Old Vic in 1926 with Baliol Holloway as Henry, the Lyric Hammersmith in 1928 with Lewis Casson, Ralph Richardson at the Old Vic in 1931, Godfrey Tearle at the Alhambra in 1934, Hubert Gregg at the Ring, Blackfriars in 1936, Laurence Olivier at the Old Vic in 1937, and Ivor Novello at Drury Lane in 1938 in a production in which Henry 'and his staff at Southampton . . . were in a ship that moved offstage from the quayside, very much in the Charles Kean style'.[16]

Despite the continuing sense of the play as a 'recruiting poster', Henry became less heroic and more human, as the critic James Agate recognized in his review of Ralph Richardson's Henry at the Old Vic: 'one saw the actor's intention, which was to present Harry as a human being and not as a mailed fist, eating and sleeping and thinking in armour'.[17] In his autobiography Laurence Olivier records how, when he took on the role in Tyrone Guthrie's 1937 production, he tried to find ways of deliberately undercutting the heroic tradition of the part but felt he was only partially successful.[18] Reviews were mixed; one critic describing it as 'a pacifist tract' in which the archbishop 'became an unprincipled cleric driving a well-meaning young man into a course which his conscience disapproved'.[19] He 'objected to Olivier's display of troubled thoughtfulness' on the grounds that 'what is needed "is straightforward, dashing rhetoric, and no nonsense about the ethics of war"'.[20] This production was to form the basis of his popular, influential 1944 film.

1. Stratford 1946: a young Paul Scofield, with Ruth Lodge as Katherine, in the wooing scene.

Paul Scofield's deliberately underplayed Henry in the 1946 Stratford production that was considered 'lacking in fire and better in the quieter moments'.[21] In 1951 Anthony Quayle, Michael Redgrave and John Kidd staged a cycle of the four plays of the second tetralogy, comprised of *Richard II* with both parts of

Henry IV and concluding with *Henry V*. This decisively influenced response to the plays as an exploration of the politics of kingship. As one critic suggested, 'One will never again think of these plays as single entities, and when they are played as such we shall feel them to have been lopped.'[22] Not all critics were convinced by the strategy, though, and Richard Burton's Henry was compared unfavourably with Alec Clunes' performance at the Old Vic earlier that same year:

> At almost every point – the most notable exception being the scene of the three conspirators, presented at Stratford with rare concentration – the Old Vic led, for the simple reason that the play had there no strings to it and could be left to unroll without constraint its extraordinary variety of turns – romance and philosophy, high comedy and slapstick, melodrama, music-hall, epic. Thus unbuttoned it has a size and an immediacy that as the peroration to a political treatise it must forgo, a sparkle and verve that are lost when it is trimmed to fit a tetralogy.[23]

The majority of RSC productions since then (discussed in detail below) have continued to stage *Henry V* as part of a grand historical cycle, frequently staging the second tetralogy in conjunction with the three *Henry VI* plays and *Richard III* of the first. Critics, however, continued to resist 'this fresh approach', feeling 'cheated that they had not been offered a noble, tall, martial, uncomplicated, clarion-voiced ideal king – the figure that Lewis Waller and Olivier stamped on the first half of the century'.[24]

Michael Langham directed *Henry V* in his first season at the Stratford Ontario Festival in 1956 in a production which focused on Henry's development as king. It was praised for the way in which 'The pageantry and elaborate action were finely subordinated to this main concept, and it was a pleasant change after the Henry made familiar through Sir Laurence Olivier's film who, in moments of crisis, ceased to be a man and became an embodiment of heroic kingship.'[25] Not all the critics were so convinced by Christopher Plummer's Henry, and Olivier was again the yardstick: 'Christopher Plummer, as the King, gave a convincing imitation of Lawrence [*sic*]

Olivier, which occasionally became an interpretation in its own right.'[26] Critics were also divided over the decision to cast French Canadians as the French, and their views reflect how the play's patriotic appeal can easily be co-opted. While one thought it a 'serious blunder . . . to entrust the French parts to French Canadians with thick accents' which 'destroyed all the Dauphin's superb poetry and made the elegant French nobles sound like a collection of recently arrived refugees, strenuously talking English – the last thing such proud peacocks would dream of being or doing',[27] another considered it

> a masterly stroke on the part of Mr Langham to cast our French-speaking actors in the French parts in this play. Their physique, their very bones, spoke of a heritage different from that of the English nobles; their elegance came from within . . . In this production something exclusively Canadian was brought to the service of that national culture which we are so often assured we lack, and in the final scene of French and English reconciliation a Canadian audience may be excused for wiping its eyes.[28]

There were two English productions in 1960, both of which focused on the grim realities of war. John Neville's at the Old Vic was noted for its Mother Courage wagon and 'crude, tub-thumping patriotism',[29] while Julius Gellner's at the Mermaid featured:

> Battledress and boots, 15-pounders and barbed wire, interpolations of 'Get fell in, you 'orrible men,' revolvers and sandbags, films of the Eighth Army advancing through the Alamein minefields, and more film of the VE-Day celebrations, bangs and screams and whistling shells.[30]

A radical German 1964 production in Bremen entitled *Henry Hero* and played in First World War costumes portrayed the king as 'a cynical, bullet-headed thug who delivered the exhortation on the eve of Agincourt not to his generals but to a French whore with whom he is in bed . . . To ensure that the audience made no mistake in its attitude to Henry there was a backcloth adorned with painted heads of leaders from Attila the Hun to Elvis Presley.'[31] Langham's 1966 production at Stratford Ontario was more sceptical than his earlier production, with a less charming Henry played by Douglas Rain as 'a hard man always on the verge of failure, shouldering his burden of kingship with reluctance, a plodding man so troubled by growing worries as to move almost into paranoid isolation'.[32] Most critics found Michael Kahn's 1969 production at Stratford, Connecticut 'a crude anti-war tract' in which the 'Brechtian devices of using titles to announce segments of the action...worked all too effectively in alienating the audience'.[33] The reaction against the conventional view of the play as a patriotic pageant seemed to many to have gone too far in the opposite direction.

Joseph Papp's 1976 production at the New York Shakespeare Festival, however, provided a

> splendidly handsome military spectacle with banners that flutter, torches that flare, and guns that go boom...The Battle of Agincourt, 'choreography be Lee Breuer' and 'combat by Erik Fredericksen' is the biggest production number since 'Shanghai Lil,' with processions before and after, mass combat, single combat, one of those moments where everyone freezes, a slow-motion sequence, broadsword fighting, pike work, a brilliant flight of arrows, and God knows what more.[34]

Paul Rudd's Henry was seen as solid and conventional rather than inspiring, but one critic confessed that Meryl Streep (playing Katherine) 'finds more in the part than I had ever known was there'.[35] Michael Bogdanov's English Shakespeare Company's 1986 production presented the play in the light of 1980s English culture: 'Michael Pennington's king was a cold, conniving unappealing Tory patronising a rag-tag army of public school chaps barely in control of a lower order of yobs and petty crooks.'[36]

Directors since then have struggled to find ways to combine contemporary views of war with the historical view of the play as a celebration of patriotism and national pride; of a sympathetic Henry, 'the mirror of all Christian kings', with the ruthless politician.

John Wood's 1989 production at Stratford Ontario was set just pre-First World War and recapitulated the experience of a nation which went naively into a war in which youthful optimism was rapidly overcome by grim reality, embodied in the king's personal journey from boyish enthusiasm to hard-won maturity.

The first French production of the play was Jean-Louis Benoit's triumphant French-language version in 2000 in which

> a Chorus in a bright orange wig and twentieth-century gamin costume (Laure Bonnet) emphasizes the use of a wooden wheel lying flat stage centre, a literal 'Wooden O' on to which characters step out of the action to address us directly . . . Not only the Chorus, but the Heralds, are women, cross-dressed . . . The playing style is broad, making cartoon characters of the old English enemy.[37]

Against this the English king 'is in a different play, and remains there through five acts'. The languages were reversed for the language lesson, and in the final act Philippe Torreton as Henry and Marie Vialle as Katherine moved so rapidly between English and French that the audience were 'whirled from one pretence to another', turning the romantic interlude into 'an ironic send-up of romantic interludes' in which 'only the Dauphin's disappointment spoils the fun'.[38]

The National Theatre's first production of the play in 2003 was Nicholas Hytner's first as Artistic Director, as discussed in his interview below. It was updated to suggest contemporary parallels with the war in Iraq:

> Hytner's battle-dress production is not only much darker, but also more divided, with different versions of events fighting for the upper hand. Penny Downie's Chorus – an insinuating spin-doctor in high heels – announces 'All the youth of England are on fire' as the poor old low-lifes appear, staring gloomily at their pints and the telly.[39]

Adrian Lester's Henry – the first black actor to play the part – was seen as 'a triumph of colour-blind casting'.[40] Hytner's politicized version was frequently compared with Mark Wing-Davey's Delacorte Theater production in New York's Central Park of the same year:

> The current National Theater production of *Henry V* in London, directed by Nicholas Hytner, coolly and critically suggests parallels between Henry's war against the French and the war in Iraq. Whatever his intentions, Mr Wing-Davey has devised a *Henry V* that shirks from seriousness on the unavoidable subjects of war and patriotism.[41]

Henry James' remark that the 'Illusion' required to mount a realist production was 'absolutely beyond the compass of the stage'[42] does not apply to cinema, and there have been two remarkable and successful films. Laurence Olivier's 1944 version, set against the background of the Second World War and dedicated 'To the Commandos and Airborne Troops of Great Britain the spirit of whose ancestors it has been humbly attempted to recapture in some ensuing scenes', was enthusiastically received, winning four Oscars:

> Laurence Olivier's screen version of *Henry V* represents a memorable cinema event. It is not the dramatic quality of the play nor the high standard of the acting which makes a deep impression so much as the rare pleasure of hearing in the cinema beautiful lines beautifully spoken. The stylised sets, the painted landscapes, the technical devices which transport us from the boisterous intimacies of the Globe Theatre to Harfleur and the Field of Agincourt, all these have aesthetic and dramatic justification, yet it is such lines as those spoken before Agincourt which leave us feeling that something new has happened in the cinema.[43]

The film's 'continuing appeal' has been defined as 'its capacity to activate a kind of double nostalgia: for the fairy-tale feudalism it celebrates, but also for the wartime history which permeates the film, from the opening dedication to the troops onwards'.[44] Kenneth Branagh's 1989 adaptation was by contrast 'pictorially low-key' and 'made for a generation that has the Indo-China war and the Falklands campaign just behind it and is wary of calls to arms'.[45] Olivier's film represented a constant critical touchstone, and comparisons were inevitable:

> Olivier's Chorus, clad in doublet and hose, leads his audience from the Wooden O of the Thameside Globe into an attractively colourful England and France...Branagh's Chorus (Derek Jacobi), dressed in black overcoat and muffler, takes us from a movie studio into a murky palace where the courtiers look as if they've been painted by Holbein at his cruellest, or photographed in unflinching close-ups by Richard Avedon.[46]

Much grittier than Olivier's film, nevertheless film historian Kenneth Rothwell argues that 'Kenneth Branagh's *Henry V* is, and will be recognized as, one of the outstanding Shakespeare movies of the century.'[47]

AT THE RSC

Reality and Myth

> Largely through Shakespeare, a King who was an unpleasantly ruthless fanatic who liked nothing better than burning heretics became what Hazlitt called 'the favourite monarch of the English nation', much cited whenever England was under attack.[48]

Henry V is a play at the mercy of the society and time in which it is produced. This is strongly evidenced by the 'swing of 180 degrees, from patriotic heroism to bitter irony'[49] after the Second World War:

> As the dramatist John Arden once pointed out, it is as if there is a sceptical unofficial play beneath the patriotic official one. We get to know the braggarts and the victims, the would-be war-profiteers and the common soldiers who suspect they will die in an unjust cause. We also hear a great deal of questioning and self-questioning.[50]

It is only in the last fifty years that we have seen this emphasis on the 'unofficial play', prompted by a radical shift in the way people think about national identity, politics and ideas of heroism:

> We see more productions of *Titus Andronicus* than of *Henry V* these days, as if we are embarrassed by the latter's undeniable patriotism. But directors ... have shown that it is an emotionally complex play as much about the pain of war and the cost of kingship as it is about military triumph.[51]

The programme to the 1964 Peter Hall production used a sixteenth-century quote about war to emphasize the anti-war stance and provide evidence that nothing is learned from history:

> War is sown from war. The prince is compelled to expose his young men to so many dangers, and often in a single hour to make many an orphan, widow, childless old man, beggar, and unhappy wretch. The wisdom of princes will be too costly for the world if they persist in learning from experience how dreadful war is.[52]

In an age in which mankind was supposed to be more reasoned, aware and humane, there were more deaths by war in the twentieth century than in all the centuries preceding in the Christian calendar put together. An awareness of this depressing fact on twentieth-century warfare has had an indelible effect on performances of Shakespeare's history plays, and more so with *Henry V* than any other. Terry Hands referred to Peter Hall's 1964 production as 'the Vietnam anti-war version';[53] Adrian Noble's 1984 version 'powerfully and effectively ... responded to the recent Falklands conflict by stressing the awful realities of war'.[54]

Many of the RSC's productions have brought together an amalgam of recognizable and iconic images from film, television and newspapers to make a direct connection to a twentieth-century audience. The physical remembrances of war, including memorials, litter the scenic design. The social impact has also played a part, especially with regards to the democratization that happens in war – the bringing together of all classes, the dropping of social pretensions. This was emphasized in Edward Hall's 2000 production which dispensed with the Chorus as a single identifiable figure, giving his lines to the cast of men and women in army fatigues: 'The Chorus's text is chopped up so that everyone can have his – or her – own little piece . . . expressions of relevance and democratic individualism.'[55]

Soldiers are no longer nameless faceless casualties; we see their families' grief on television, read about their suicides in the newspapers. At the start of the twenty-first century each soldier has a voice in a way they never had before. The common soldiers' domination of this production was emphasized by the use of striking songs by the political songwriter Billy Bragg:

> The entire cast wear military fatigues, and the low-life scenes, set in a boozed-up Naafi, are superbly played, with fights breaking out and the entire cast singing an 'Ere-we-go, ere we go' – style anthem especially written for the occasion . . . with repeated cries of 'Eng-er-land'.[56]

The setting, predominantly Second World War, with references to other modern conflicts, also emphasized an anti-heroic stance by removing the king from centre stage:

> For a play that is so closely identified with its charismatic leader, this is not a production in which all hearts and minds are bent on good King Harry. On the contrary, Henry here blends into a busy, populous world and a stage that is as permanently crowded as a musical.[57]

Similarly, in the RSC's 1964 production the costumes of the soldiers were indistinguishable with regards to rank. In this army a man's worth was gauged by his valour. The 'band of brothers' motif extended to the king and there was 'no perceptible difference between officers and men'.[58] The battles were

> presented as bloody, clobbering and unpleasant [with] no traditional heroics in the speeches of the king to his troops. This

2. Ian Holm addressing his ragged army before Harfleur in the Brechtian 1964 production directed by Peter Hall and John Barton.

is a ragged army led by a leader at times almost desperate with fatigue. The heroism, where is exists, is found almost entirely in the sheer dogged pugnaciousness. It is the heroism of the First World War trenches, of attrition...and of men following a leader, not because he is a king, but because he is as tired and stubbornly determined as they are. It is, in short, democratic twentieth-century heroism.[59]

The brutal realities of war are not something that can be shirked in production. Adrian Noble's 1984 production underlined the conflict between soldiers' emotional life and the hardships of the battlefield:

the cruelty, pain, and pathos of the ensuing war as well as its moments of professional exhilaration...the most touching is the sight of the impoverished English soldiery...huddled together under tarpaulin sheets as the rain pelts down. This is what war means – getting soaked in some foreign field...What this humane and thoughtful production offers is the soldier's view of war; and their feelings about conflict are summed up in...the memorable sound of the clang of swords hurled to the ground as the battle is finally won.[60]

By use of war memorials, designers have dominated productions with a sense of death – the greatest leveller of all. In an eerie opening, the 1997 production, directed by Ron Daniels, saw the ghosts of the dead, names from a memorial, coming to life to relive and tell their story in the eternal field of conflict. Henry and the others entered, 'a phalanx of officers in gold-and-blue uniforms slow-marching to a drum':[61]

[This was a]...sustained critique of the horrors of war. The set is part American Vietnam memorial, part Menin Gate. Well over 2,000 names cover every wall, an ever-present reminder of the fellowship of death. King Henry is first seen watching with appalled fascination a flickering film of the carnage of 1914–18 trench warfare...the production portrays remorselessly how soldiers on both sides die brutally in war.[62]

Likewise, in Matthew Warchus' 1994 production there was an added sense of mortality and futility as Henry battled across the stage at Agincourt:

> with a fiercely rising spotlight of the sun capturing Orléans's 'The sun doth gild our armour' [4.2.1], the stage floor tipped to a steep rake, revealing that the rake carried the dates '1387–1422', the limits of Henry's life, so that the battle was fought across his tomb.[63]

Warchus emphasized the brutality of war by choosing to show the killing of the French prisoners – a moment which is often left offstage, cut, or moved to after the discovery of the murdered boys to maintain sympathy for Henry. Again the effect on the ordinary soldier was marked:

> ... having the prisoners killed on stage brilliantly produced a reaction of protest and horror from Clive Wood's Pistol, a coward forced to kill and loathing it, nearly vomiting after the killing, an unwilling participant in the actuality of the war off which he has been freeloading.[64]

In the words of the critic and academic, Jan Kott, 'The greatness of Shakespeare's realism consists in his awareness of the extent to which people are involved in history'[65] – the common citizen as much as the king.

Nationalism

In a time of war Shakespeare brings together the different nations of Britain. The ordinary soldiers represent the forced unity of war behind which lies national antagonism. Ron Daniels, who staged the play in 1997, hoped that his use of twentieth-century references would express:

> ... his fear of the dangers of nationalism, of the 'flaring up of genocidal tendencies and religious ethnicities' to be observed around the world in the 20th century ... There is an unashamed xenophobia in the play: 'It's quite clear that Henry's army is an

army of invasion. It is not defensive and it practically destroys another culture.'[66]

When tackling the play at the start of a new millennium, Edward Hall commented:

Now is a more important time in terms of national identity than ever before … We don't quite know how to think about nationalism because of the echoes it has with football hooligans and far-right politics. It belongs to them, that's what we feel. So it's quite difficult for us to think about … its positive aspects, particularly when England is a multicultural, multiracial society and has been since the Romans … This play deals with a moment in time … where a great national unity is achieved through the coming together of disparate parts of what is now Britain. For a moment they gained the world, but then lost it in the end.[67]

The programme to Hall's production included iconic English national images: the Union Jack, a pint of beer, a bull dog, a red rose, a tennis ball, alongside definitions of individual nations and nationalist feelings. Echoing back to earlier in the series of histories, the words of Richard II came to mind with the image of a 'To Let' sign stuck in an outline of Britain, filled with an image of a 'green and pleasant land'. Hall obviously took *Henry V*'s part in the *This England* series of history plays as ironic and post-modern. This irony flowed through the production with uneasy but comic effect, which seemed at odds, almost conflicting, with the original play by not taking it seriously:

In working to re-create the experience of patriotism, this production shows it to be a mixed and composite thing: beautiful, confused, self-contradictory, stupid, fleeting and circumstantial at the same time. Moreover, this experience is shown to be primarily a cultural one, and as such it is constituted by bits and pieces – a random assortment of, more often than not, visual icons and motifs. The arrival of the English soldiers in France at the beginning of Act Three, for example, is instantly recognized as our visual shorthand for the Normandy landings. Fluellen's first appearance on the stage as the solitary soldier, last in line, with his flag (here a Welsh one, of course) sticking jauntily from his pack is the nation's collective signifier for the Falklands war. If patriotism or national identity exist at all, they seem to be made up of such images – images drawn from war photography, documentary and film, and processed in turn by comedy, musical and soap... [it suggests] our sense of national character... if it exists at all, seems to lie in the shallows of the national consciousness from where it can so easily, so effortlessly be whipped up into a storm.[68]

Many productions have been criticized for making the French seem weak or corrupt in order to accentuate English superiority. Of the RSC's 1994 production one critic noted: 'Warchus falls into the trap... of presenting the French court as ineffectual fops. It makes for some gorgeous costumes but detracts from Henry's achievement.'[69] However, in an interesting move Warchus emphasized the horror of Henry's speech before Harfleur by casting a female as Governor of Harfleur, and so 'feminised the city and provided a direct response to the horrendous threat of rape and murder that Henry had offered, his language and her body directly connected'.

In 1997 the French were

at something of a disadvantage, having not caught up, by some margin with the modern techniques of destruction espoused by the English. They totter medievally – not to say suicidally – around on high, two-legged silver horses that look more like the weirdo frocks of some post-Vivienne Westwood designer than animals you'd take anywhere near a battlefield.[70]

Likewise, in 1984 the costuming indicated the difference between the democratic, down-to-earth nature of the English army, the 'band of brothers', as opposed to the French who held on to an outmoded chivalry and hierarchy: 'the Chorus prowls over the squalid downstage area shining a torch over Henry's followers while in the farthest depths of the stage the French are seen lolling in golden luxury languidly passing the night in games of chess before their supposedly certain victory'.[71]

In 1975 Terry Hands commented:

> Theatrically, period costume is an outmoded convention. Used here it helps to accentuate the fact that the French are frozen in an era that has already passed. The French, all in golden armour, were fifteenth century; the English, in greys and brown, appeared in a timeless ambience suggestive of world war combat... Throughout, the English scenes emphasized the realities and human costs of war, while the French still inhabited a beautifully illuminated Book of Hours.[72]

The Chorus

The fictional nature of theatre (and therefore also the story Shakespeare presents to us) is emphasized by the role of the Chorus.

Matthew Warchus' 1994 *Henry V* was an interactive museum piece with Chorus as guide to history. Rather like a modern history programme with reconstructions based around iconic objects – a robe, broken bits of armour, poppies; and the actors often placed to create stage pictures or tableaux – frozen moments in history like old photographs or war paintings:

> Warchus investigated the play as a series of overlays of history. Its opening and closing image, with Henry's red regal gown with a gold collar placed on a dummy, roped off like an exhibit in the Imperial War Museum, established a sense of royal myth. But the robe was surrounded by tall red poppies, the strongest modern symbol of the cost of war. Tony Britton's Chorus was an old soldier, in military camel-coloured overcoat and campaign ribbons; the poppy in his buttonhole and his rich theatrical voice summoned up past wars. With the house lights still up he strode to an electrical box on stage, turned the handle and put out the house lights, taking the audience from his contemporary perspective on the history of war into the play's sense of its own history.
>
> ...But Britton's Chorus was also a reminder of what will happen to the myth of Agincourt, so that in the middle of the battle, at Henry's lowest ebb, he could come forward and help the

King to his feet, reassuring him of the outcome that the Chorus, the military historian of the future, already knew.

The Chorus's perspective...was set against the frequent appearances of a crowd of English non-combatants, principally women and children, dressed in 1940s costumes, both visitors to the 'museum' and a reminder of the civil cost of war.[73]

It seemed to indicate that 'Shakespeare's play is not just a celebration of our unlikely success at Agincourt but the case-study of a

3. Ian McDiarmid as Chorus in Adrian Noble's 1984 production.

campaign. Listen and watch, and we may learn something about how men feel when they go to war and why they continue to do so.'[74]

Ian McDiarmid's Chorus in 1984 was a sceptical commentator, the cynical manipulator of events, conjuring and revealing the story through the will of his imagination:

> He ridicules the brawls he is to present then draws back the white traverse curtain to reveal a breathtaking ballet of flags, lights and smoke. He watches and he goads. He even appears to be enjoying the performance before quickly resuming a bitchily jocose manner with a swirl of his mephistophelian black cloak. At Harfleur the traverse is suddenly one of shining steel and three long ladders reach to the sky ... Mr McDiarmid not so much imagines as dreams this scene, pounding on the walls and willing them to rise on English soldiers, ablaze in spotlights, slithering through the gaping scenic wound. This most original and creative playing of the Chorus is at one with a production of which it is a corporate element.[75]

In a timeless black costume, he remained

> on stage throughout, reflecting every queasy shift of emotion with which modern audiences view this discordant work ... [The] main importance is structural. It invites the spectator not only to share the task of imagination but also to acknowledge complicity in the play's nationalistic prejudices.[76]

Eric Porter in 1964 deliberately appeared as if he was in a different production. His costuming was elaborate and Elizabethan, and his rhetoric appeared at odds with the depiction of the play. This emphasized the difference between the theatricality of the play and the realities of war:

> The Chorus ... has a romantic, heroic, theatrical view of events. But the events are often handled by Shakespeare in an unromantic, unheroic way. We see what it was actually like to be in the field with Harry, cold and wet, in fever and fear, boredom and pain. These are the real elements of a campaign ... the

play ... is a criticism of the Chorus's view of the story, as the Chorus is meant to tell us how to respond to the action.[77]

The simplicity of the staging for the 1975 production put the emphasis on the Chorus's plea for the audience to imagine the setting. The actors arrived on stage in their rehearsal clothes, and, as if to mirror the audience's engagement and immersion in the world of the play, the characters gradually assumed their costumes in the opening scenes. Farrah, the designer, felt that:

> What we wanted to create was not a box of illusions, but something that freed the audience's imaginations and made them conjure their own illusions ... So we stripped the stage; we cleared it of everything extraneous, to make it as austere and as bare as possible ... we built a new stage-platform with one-in-twelve rake. It was a stage designed to launch the actors into the audience.[78]

> The audience discovered [the actors] in workshop gear, jogging, improvising, lying down, studying. One of the actors detached himself from the others, and came forward: 'Oh for a Muse of fire ...' and Chorus (Emrys James) indicated, as he spoke, the 'flat unraised spirits' lying around the stage. The drab, modern garb – inviting a detached and sceptical response – was retained into the clerics' scene, and the Council. Thereafter the action reverted to period costume.[79]

Henry

If you have to be a king and do your job, you become a pattern of contradictions. Henry is therefore both a devious politician and a man of sincerity; a hypocrite and an idealist ... Henry is no shining Sir Galahad: he executes men when it is needful ... The Church's role in *Henry V* is totally political. Henry's prayers are, like most things about him ambiguous. They are both sincere and expedient. God is on the English side ... Henry dies young, leaving the country bankrupt because of his glorious wars, and leaving government to his baby son ... It is a celebration of war and a criticism of war. An ambiguous document: Shakespeare usually is.[80]

In 2000, Edward Hall's revival was the third in a row 'in which the RSC have put English war-mongering and the medieval war hero under the severest scrutiny'.[81] Shakespeare faces us with the fact that what makes a great king and leader is often at odds with what makes a great human being. Henry's outburst of rage, the hanging of Bardolph, the speech before Harfleur, the killing of the French prisoners, the domination of a land and culture that don't belong to you, are all expedient tactics and necessary steps in Henry's development as a king, but their morality is in doubt.

When *Henry V* is played in conjunction with *Henry IV* we can trace the development, the education of Henry from wayward child to determined monarch. When performed on its own the actor has to reconcile the emotional, psychological and moral turmoil brought about by conflicting personal and public interests – between the man and his role as king.

Alan Howard, who tackled all three plays in 1975, saw no

discrepancy between Hal and Henry V, between Prince and King. It is an extraordinary progression straight through. At the beginning of Henry V he has still not established himself as a person or a King . . . Almost immediately he begins questioning his position . . . His self-questioning is extraordinary right through the play. He questions what his responsibilities are and, indeed, what the place of the King should be.[82]

Theatre historian Ralph Berry thought that,

On the one hand, Howard demonstrated the traditional qualities that the part calls for – a commanding stage presence, good looks, a voice that has to deliver the battlefield goods . . . on the other hand, he displayed a moral awareness of the drama, a continually surprising inventiveness, and an intelligence directed always towards exploring the self-doubt and pain in the role.[83]

The critic Irving Wardle detailed some of these moments:

Howard grapples on the floor with the treacherous Scroop, as a father who has let him down. He practically vomits after hurling the barbarous threats at Harfleur; and again half way through reading the roll call of the French dead. His stainless adventure is haunted by the Eastcheap ghosts; and when Bardolph is caught robbing the church Howard has to stand and give the execution order with Pistol looking him straight in the eye; an ordeal that shakes his nerve with the French herald. Then, in a wonderful transition, he begins a halting speech, hits by accident on a joke and a smile of surprised delight steals across his face at his own powers of recovery, and his capacity to keep on acting.[84]

Another thought that 'Ghosts haunt his queasy mind, principal among them his own father, usurper of Richard II's throne – witness the hoarse panic of Mr Howard's prayer that this crime should be remembered: "Not today, O Lord, O, not today" [4.1.295–6]'.[85]

The agonizing self-doubt of Howard's performance gave Henry an emotional depth which most of the actors following have also made much of. William Houston, in 2000, however, played a far more enigmatic character, more ambitious, calculating and

4. Alan Howard reading the list of the dead in Terry Hands' 1975 production.

controlled than most Henrys – a portrayal that carried through from his rather cold-hearted performance as Hal:

> You can also see . . . what makes him such an effective ruler and leader of men. Houston is cold, watchful, efficiently insincere, adept at presenting his actions in a generous light, buoyed up by an enormous belief in himself. He keeps his feelings under tight control when he has to, but an almost feral quality peeps through. He is not particularly impressive physically, but he has acquired charisma through sheer force of will.[86]

> The coldness and the cruelty [demonstrated as Hal] continue here, the feeling that Henry has a pocket calculator where his heart ought to be. But Houston finds a touching vulnerability on the eve of Agincourt which suddenly persuades you that this is a character worth caring about, and his sense of kinship with his fellow soldiers is genuinely moving.[87]

In 1997 Ron Daniels picked Michael Sheen to play Henry 'for his youth, his gentleness, his mixture of innocence and maturity'.[88] Coming to terms with his role as king, Sheen demonstrated an almost psychotic instability prompted by a lack of confidence:

> Confronting the friend who had plotted to assassinate him, this Henry reacts with an embarrassing neurotic intensity, first putting a pistol in the man's hand and daring him to shoot, then snatching it back and holding it to the ex-friend's temples in a frenzied, near-murderous scuffle.[89]

'The gruesome threats directed at Harfleur become genuinely terrifying, a near-psychotic outburst rather than a simple piece of strategy.'[90] To counterbalance his volatile king, Daniels

> equips Henry with a tearful, conscience stricken colleague in the shape of the young Earl of Warwick. This expanded figure is so appalled by the King's speech threatening the besieged town of Harfleur with hair-raising horrors – a speech made all the more unpleasant here by the squeezed sound of the loudspeakers

through which it is relayed – that he tries to snatch the mike from the crazed monarch's hand.[91]

Michael Sheen's laddish portrayal lessens none of the growth of the character; powerfully it never lets us forget the importance of the lessons he has learnt about the real world from his time with Falstaff and his retinue. In the moments of indecision, of his changes of heart, you can see the tension between what he would have done (maybe what, in part, he would still like to do), and his growing knowledge of what he must actually do for the general good – for the sake of his nation. These moments are real and genuinely touching.[92]

Henry's declaration of astonishment after the Battle of Agincourt is often the first moment when we get a real sense of Henry as a religious man. In 1994 actor Iain Glen played Henry as deeply religious from the start. As critic Benedict Nightingale asked:

Is there a character in Shakespeare who invokes God so often? For Bernard Shaw, this was evidence of an enthusiastic frog-basher's hypocrisy and cynicism. For Warchus, it is an integral part of a production much concerned with the topic that is as timely as ever, the ethics of slaughter.[93]

Others may talk of the reformation of the wild Prince Harry but this King Henry was born-again in a rather modern sense. Canterbury's assessment in the first scene, 'Never was such a sudden scholar made, / Never came reformation in a flood, / With such a heady currance, scouring faults' [1.1.33–5], was entirely accurate ... he knelt to the Archbishop and kept with him throughout the rest of the play the crucifix his spiritual father had given him. The scenes the night before the battle did not here show Henry 'Walking from watch to watch, from tent to tent' [4.0.30] but instead a man who desperately wanted to find a quiet place to pray and kept being interrupted ... not the usual pretext to allow a little surreptitious wandering around in disguise. The scenes built towards the prayer itself and, later, the deeply felt tones of the culmination of this sequence, the last line before the battle, 'And how thou pleasest, God, dispose the day' [4.3.135].

Serious-minded, sincerely religious, this Henry, often seen shouldering a huge pack like his troops, took his share of the work of war. He was part of a band of brothers and was respected for it.[94]

In 1984 Kenneth Branagh's Henry highlighted Adrian Noble's theme of 'the painful cost of war to the individual . . . an angry Harry driven to personal violence by the degradation of a war he has been told is just':[95]

The . . . programme contains two parallel essays on 'Hero-King' and 'Scourge of God', both of which relate to Kenneth Branagh's performance. At his first appearance . . . a quiet, cold figure watching and listening while giving nothing away, and generally avoiding the centre of the stage. He first shows his hand in the tennis ball scene, beginning with a mild answer to the French insult, and then exploding into paroxysms of psychotic rage . . . The effect is characteristic of this actor, and it is well matched to Henry's habit of playing the sympathetic private man and then arising into violent public action . . . there is no clear cut division between the two . . . Not content with sentencing the English conspirators to death, he hurls himself on Stephen Simms's Scroop for an act of personal betrayal. And after the massacre of the boys, he similarly assaults the French herald. The performance throughout presents a poised, confident mask through which panic and savagery periodically break out. This can take the form of physical courage, as in the vertiginous fall from a ladder into the arms of his followers. More often he comes over as a haunted man pursued simultaneously by personal and dynastic history. His prayer before Agincourt is a gabbled, terrified act of bribery, fully in the spirit of his guilty father. Likewise, memories of Eastcheap come home to roost at his last encounter with Bardolph . . . who kneels fixing the king with a mute, terrifying stare as he is slowly garrotted by Brian Blessed's hulking Exeter.

This is by far the most painful moment of the evening and the one passage where Mr Branagh comes closest to public collapse.[96]

Alan Howard thought Shakespeare was trying show us that at the end of Henry's initiation through war there could emerge a king who understands human frailty as well as commanding the respect of others,

who could be strong without being authoritarian ... What is so sad is that whatever tremendous journey both Hamlet and Hal

5. Kenneth Branagh leads his men into the breach at Harfleur in Adrian Noble's 1984 production, which was to be reprised cinematically (with live horse in place of ladder) five years later.

have made into themselves, they both die so young that whatever potential is there, whatever they find out about themselves will never be realized. That . . . makes Henry's end as sad, as tragic, as Hamlet's.[97]

Henry V as a play of 'doubt' and 'uncertainty'[*] often evokes conflicting responses in modern audiences. Shakespeare encourages us to support a man who, regardless of his scruples, enters into a trumped-up war, which sustains terrible casualties, in order to maintain his kingdom. The great challenge for the modern director is 'to square anti-militarist scruples with a full-blooded treatment of the great national folk tale.'[98]

THE DIRECTOR'S CUT: INTERVIEWS WITH KENNETH BRANAGH, EDWARD HALL, NICHOLAS HYTNER AND MICHAEL BOYD

Kenneth Branagh was born in Belfast in 1960 but moved with his family to England at the age of nine. A year after graduating from RADA, where he won the prestigious Bancroft Gold Medal, he was awarded the Laurence Olivier Most Promising Newcomer Award in 1983 for his performance in Julian Mitchell's *Another Country*. He joined the RSC later that year, becoming the youngest-ever actor to play Shakespeare's Henry V, in Adrian Noble's production at Stratford. In 1987 he set up the Renaissance Theatre Company with David Parfitt, creating a company of like-minded actors and writers; their productions included *Romeo and Juliet*, *Twelfth Night*, *Much Ado about Nothing*, *As You Like It*, *Hamlet*, *King Lear*, *A Midsummer Night's Dream*, as well as John Osborne's *Look Back in Anger* and Chekhov's *Uncle Vanya*. In 1988 Branagh was awarded the London Critics' Circle Theatre Award. He returned to the RSC to play Hamlet in 1992. He played Richard III at the Sheffield Crucible in 2002, and in 2004 won the Evening Standard Best Actor Award for his performance in *Edmond* at the Royal National Theatre. In 1989 Branagh directed a much-acclaimed, Oscar-nominated film of

---

[*] Words used by the director, Terry Hands, to describe the play as well as Henry's character.

Henry V, drawing on his RSC experience of playing Henry. He went on to make more Shakespeare films including *Much Ado about Nothing* (1993), *Hamlet* (1996), *Love's Labour's Lost* (2000) and *As You Like It* (2006). He also played Iago in Oliver Parker's film of *Othello* (1995); his numerous other film roles include Professor Gilderoy Lockhart in *Harry Potter and the Chamber of Secrets* (2002). Television roles include Guy Pringle in the BBC mini-series *Fortunes of War* (1987), and he adapted and directed, as well as played the lead in, the BBC crime thriller *Wallander* (2008), which won the BAFTA for Best Drama Series. He talks here about both his film and the RSC stage production by Adrian Noble, out of which it grew.[*]

Edward Hall was born in 1967, the son of Sir Peter Hall, founder of the RSC. Educated at Leeds University and Mountview Theatre School, he began his professional career as a theatre director at the Watermill Theatre in Newbury in the early 1990s, where he directed a number of Shakespeare plays, including *Henry V* and *The Comedy of Errors.* He came to national prominence as a Shakespearean director with a highly successful touring adaptation of the three parts of *Henry VI* entitled *Rose Rage.* His all-male Shakespeare company, Propeller, has gone on to stage acclaimed versions of several of the comedies. He talks here about the modern-dress production of *Henry V* he directed for the RSC as part of its *This England* sequence of history plays in 2000.

Nicholas Hytner was appointed Director of the National Theatre in 2003. He was born in Manchester in 1956 and, after attending Manchester Grammar School, read English at Cambridge. He was Associate Director of Manchester's Royal Exchange Theatre from 1985 to 1989 and at the National from 1989 to 1997. He was a Visiting Professor of Contemporary Theatre at Oxford University in 2000–01, and is an Honorary Fellow of Trinity Hall, Cambridge. He is credited with revolutionizing the National Theatre artistically and with attracting large new audiences by producing bold, original

---

[*] His answers are based, with his kind permission, on his introduction to the film's screenplay (Chatto and Windus, 1989) and his responses to questions asked at a discussion following the US premiere of the film in Westwood, California, in November 1989.

work. He has directed many plays from the classical repertoire including *King Lear* and *The Tempest* at the RSC and *The Winter's Tale*, the two parts of *Henry IV* (with Michael Gambon as Falstaff), *The Alchemist* and *Phedre* at the National. His long-standing collaboration with the playwright Alan Bennett includes *The Madness of George III*, *The History Boys* and *The Habit of Art* at the National. His films include *The Madness of King George*, *The Crucible* and *The History Boys*. He talks here about the 2003 production of *Henry V*, his debut upon becoming Artistic Director of the National.

Michael Boyd was born in Belfast in 1955, educated in London and Edinburgh and completed his MA in English Literature at Edinburgh University. He trained as a director at the Malaya Bronnaya Theatre in Moscow. He then went on to work at the Belgrade Theatre in Coventry, joining the Sheffield Crucible as Associate Director in 1982. In 1985 Boyd became founding Artistic Director of the Tron theatre in Glasgow, becoming equally acclaimed for staging new writing and innovative productions of the classics. He was Drama Director of the *New Beginnings Festival of Soviet Arts* in Glasgow in 1999. He joined the RSC as an Associate Director in 1996 and has since directed numerous productions of Shakespeare's plays. He won the Laurence Olivier Award for Best Director for his version of the *Henry VI* plays in the RSC's *This England: The Histories* in 2001. He took over as Artistic Director of the RSC in 2003 and oversaw the extraordinarily successful Complete Works Festival in 2006–07. His own contribution to this was a cycle of all eight history plays, from *Richard II* through to *Richard III*, with the same company of actors. This transferred to London's Roundhouse Theatre in 2008 and won multiple awards. He talks here about his production of *Henry V* in that cycle.

Some productions explicitly signal later wars, such as the Falklands or the first Iraq war. Did yours? What are the gains and losses of doing so?

KB: Although I was aware of bringing a particular set of post-war sensibilities to bear on my reading, I sensed that a 1980s film version of such a piece would make for a profoundly different experience from that of Olivier's wartime version. People spoke of the film in connection with the Falklands war, but I'm glad we didn't consciously go with that contemporary emphasis.

EH: It was a contemporary setting so I did want people to think about contemporary conflicts. I don't think you lose anything by that. I think we gained lots by just aesthetically jogging people into the present.

NH: Full disclosure: I chose during the summer of 2002 to schedule *Henry V* to open in April 2003. The country had just fought the beginnings of a war in Afghanistan, and it seemed likely that we would soon be fighting another in Iraq. The play has often been a barometer of public opinion during times of war. Olivier's 1944 film found in it an unforced heroic patriotism; Kenneth Branagh's film (and Adrian Noble's RSC production) reflected ambivalence about the consequences of armed conflict in the Falklands.

As it turned out, the Iraq war started during rehearsals, and it would have been perverse not to play *Henry V* as a contemporary text. The enthusiasm for historical reconstruction is a recent development in theatrical history, and would have made no sense to Shakespeare's own company. None of his history plays were given period productions at the Globe: the entire cycle feels like a dialogue between fifteenth-century English history and the Elizabethan present. A three-way dialogue that includes our own present is nowadays inevitable, however the plays are presented.

This doesn't mean that the National Theatre production was *about* the Iraq war. It remained a play about Henry V, the victor of Agincourt; but in performance, it seemed constantly to throw light on current preoccupations. A striking example from the very start of the play: Henry needs rock-solid justification in law for the invasion of France – an action recommended by his dying father 'to busy giddy minds / With foreign quarrels'. The Archbishop obliges him, before the Council, at extraordinary length. In our production, he handed copies of an elaborately produced dossier round the cabinet table, and he referred to it repeatedly as he explained England's right under Salic law to take military action.

The scene made concrete a sense of historical continuity: war leaders have always gone to great trouble to massage the case for war. Maybe the same point could have been made had the scene been staged as an Elizabethan or medieval council of war, but the big gain was in immediacy and clarity. The audience, force-fed by news media on UN resolutions and dodgy dossiers, caught on instantly and were riveted by the sinuous substance of the archbishop's argument. The questions begged by its bizarre contortions seemed both rooted in history and utterly of the moment. Is this true? Is this relevant? Is this right?

A large portion of the play turned out to be about presentation: the king's rhetoric always in the service of spinning first the build-up to the war, then the initially perilous progress of the campaign, then its aftermath. We gained a vivid impression that Shakespeare was writing for us, now. We lost, of course, its corollary: the indisputable truth that Shakespeare was writing for his own audience, then – a truth that has animated much of the most interesting Shakespeare criticism in the last decade. A serious loss, but not a permanent one – there's always next time.

In retrospect, I think there was a more interesting loss. Such was the widespread mistrust of our own war leader's rhetoric, and even of his motives, that Henry was tainted by his association with Tony Blair. The resemblance between the two is only superficial. There is a characteristically Shakespearean ambiguity about Henry: ruthless and out for himself he may be, but he's also the heroic embodiment of the kind of nation-builder that has only recently fallen from public favour. It would have been an achievement in 2003 to give a theatrical presence to his heroism, and Adrian Lester came close partly through raw charisma, partly through a wonderfully persuasive aura of sincerity. But the audience may have wanted too badly to discuss the kind of leader it thought Blair was, and I suppose the production encouraged them. History may be kinder to Blair, at least with regard to his purity of motive, than we were in 2003. But at the National, although Henry was brave, resolute and inspiring, nobody in the audience trusted him an inch.

6. Adrian Lester as King Harry on the bonnet of an army vehicle in Nicholas Hytner's Iraq war production of 2003.

MB: We were rooted in the early Renaissance which helped us retain Shakespeare's moral ambiguity over the war with France, but the Chorus on Henry's return post-Agincourt, to London, openly speculated with the audience on the reception 'our generals' would receive on returning from war, without mentioning Iraq or Afghanistan by name.

Why does the Chorus so explicitly make us aware that we're an audience watching a play in a theatre? What decisions did you make regarding your Chorus?

KB: At Stratford Ian McDiarmid was playing both the Chorus in *Henry V* and Shylock in *The Merchant of Venice*. He remained onstage throughout as a sort of modern commentator on the action of the play and a reminder to the audience of the play's theatricality. This created a dissonance between the Chorus' reports and the reality of what they saw.

In the opening speech, the Chorus refers to Shakespeare's theatre. I wanted to place our Chorus in a disused theatre, and have the character deliver the speech while walking through an empty auditorium, eventually throwing open scenery doors to allow the camera to travel outside and into the 'real' world of our film. Early script discussions suggested the idea of starting in an empty film studio, and since much of the opening scene can be interpreted as alluding to the mystery and imagination employed in the medium of film, it seemed the proper and honest way to start. After that, much of the Chorus's contribution was broken up, with some speeches in voice over, to aid clarity and to maximise the eerie effect of his presence.

EH: I split the Chorus amongst the company of actors. I split it so it became a sort of mythological storytelling experience about a hero. The way I did it was to have the Chorus cast as soldiers in an imaginary battalion, telling the story (in the past tense) of their great leader. They came onstage at the beginning of the evening and started to tell the audience the story of a great hero, who they knew and fought with, who is now dead.

I think the Chorus is written and constructed in the way it is in order to say to the audience that these events are so extraordinary and enormous we can't possibly pay them justice on the stage, so you're going to have to imagine things that we can't possibly show you. That does two things: firstly, it invites the audiences' imagination to be engaged with the play beyond the stage, which is something you're always trying to do in theatre; and secondly, it instantly adds a mythological mystique to the whole tale. I love that. The play has several moments like that, for example the moment when Henry, talking about Saint Crispin's day, says people will talk about us on this day... 'From this day to the ending of the world, / But we in it shall be rememberèd'. The fact that it has been written in a play and that you are listening to it being performed at that moment is living proof. It gives a wonderful tingle up the back of your spine each time you hear it.

NH: Others have written more persuasively than I can about Shakespeare's career-long preoccupation with the purpose of playing and the relationship between theatre and truth. I suspect with the Chorus he was as much as anything turning the absurdities of the old chronicle plays on their heads and using his theatrical get-out-of-jail-free card: it's only a play, get over it.

One of the most striking things about the Chorus is how often the action we are promised fails to materialise. It's as if we're given first the approved, spin-doctored version of history, and then the messy reality. A little touch of Harry in the night? Not, in the event, a remotely inspirational touch: he skulks round the camp in disguise, and gets right up his soldiers' noses.

Penny Downie played the Chorus at the National Theatre as a passionate chronicler of the present, committed to her version of history. Act by act, she became more and more aware of the limitations of her vision, because the play itself was in argument with her. In a play that's so concerned with presentation, she – like Henry, like the French leadership, like Fluellen – struggled to impose her version of the truth. At the end, foreseeing the disaster to come, you felt she'd lost faith in her whole story.

MB: The Chorus is there to excite our imaginations, and to sharpen our wits in equal measure. To conspire with us in conjuring illusions while subtly inviting us to note how illusions may be achieved at our expense, through manipulative rhetoric.

The first speech is also an implied apology in a long line of charming self-deprecations on the Elizabethan stage designed to manage the expectations of the crowd, and calm the paranoia of the censors: 'We're merely players, you can't possibly have anything to fear from us.'

Forbes Masson, our Chorus, had an edge to him. Much of the audience were already familiar with him as Rumour from *Henry IV Part II*, who warned us not to believe a word that he or anyone said.

The Chorus is there partly because the Shakespearean theatre cannot accommodate a real battlefield, cavalry charges and thousands of arrows swishing through the air. But nowadays most Shakespeare lovers have seen Olivier and/or Branagh do Harfleur and Agincourt in full cinematic glory: do you just ignore that? How did you stage the war?

KB: For a modern audience, the abiding image of *Henry V* is provided by Laurence Olivier's famous film version, but the powerful Elizabethan pageantry and chivalric splendour of that extraordinary movie did not accord with the impression I received as I read the text afresh. To me, the play seemed darker, harsher, and the language more bloody and muscular than I remembered. I was very influenced by the military historian John Keegan's book *The Face of Battle*, in which he tried to describe Agincourt from the point of view of the soldier on the ground. Olivier's panoramic view looked at the battle from above and beyond, but if you were actually there on the ground you would have no idea what was going on except in the few yards around you. That was the sense we tried to convey, with the close-ups, the mud, the chaos, the uncertainty as to who was winning.

EH: The cinema and stage are very different places. The cinema fills in the dots in a very different way, so, no, the films didn't concern me at all. On stage you are doing something completely different. I had the

Chorus use lids of ammo boxes held up in front of them to become the front ramp of a landing craft, so that they were all behind this ramp delivering one of the choral speeches while they were going through the sea about to land on the beaches. That, I think, is as evocative an experience to watch as seeing the actual landing craft in the sea coming through the waves, because the imagination is a very powerful tool. I used bits and pieces of modern army paraphernalia for the Chorus to create the *mise en scène* for each part of the evening. And then occasionally one would lift beyond that and go into complete make-believe; I had a huge metal gunner's tower – a sort of post-industrialist construction – upstage, which the army would pull downstage like a siege tower when they attacked Harfleur. My memory of that is that it was quite a big moment: it always threatened to go off the end of the stage and land in the front row.

NH: Is full cinematic glory necessarily so real? Over the last hundred years, film has pulled a magnificent confidence trick, and persuaded us that a set of conventions (montage, moving camera, sound, music) every bit as artful as theatre conventions nevertheless approximate to reality. Strip Walton's music from Olivier's Agincourt, and you'd be left with something closer to what you're really watching: a lot of overdressed Irish extras struggling with prop broadswords in the fields of County Wicklow.

There's a much bigger problem in the staging of war than the apparent poverty of the stage. How many of us involved now in making or watching theatre or film have personal, or even second-hand, experience of battle? For many centuries, drama about war has been made by and for those who have lived through war. Shakespeare must have spoken to hundreds of soldiers, even if he wasn't himself involved in military action (as he might have been during the 1580s). Everyone in his audience must have known someone who had been to war, and the Chorus explicitly evokes the expected victorious return from Ireland of Essex's army (cut at the National, I'm afraid.) Olivier was himself a member of the Fleet Air Arm, and he made his film for a country at war: as he was shooting Henry V's invasion of France, British troops were invading

Nazi-occupied Normandy. We who know nothing are much better advised to find suggestive metaphors for conflict than to pretend we can involve an audience in full-scale reproduction. To me, the most convincing of recent war films was *Waltz with Bashir*, made by an Israeli director who had actually fought in the 1982 Lebanon war, but who nevertheless chose animation as his cinematic language. He decided that the reality of the massacre at Sabra and Shatila, which he had experienced, was beyond literal representation. The limitations of the theatre are therefore a release.

So how did we stage the war scenes? I'm now uneasy about reporting that we pillaged television news reports of the current conflict to create theatrical imagery that suggested battle. Television is, after all, the one form of access to the battlefield available to us that wasn't there for our battle-hardened forebears.

It was to our advantage (though not to the advantage of those who suffer the 'collateral damage') that recent wars have not been fought by huge armies, clashing on the battlefield. Small detachments of men, often no larger than a company of actors, fight it out on street corners. Cameramen crouch in nearby foxholes. So Agincourt was evoked by small groups of actors crawling on their bellies in murky pools of light on the vast empty stage of the (aptly named) Olivier Theatre. Officers sometimes play to the camera: as we were rehearsing, Colonel Tim Collins explicitly evoked the Saint Crispin's day speech in an address to his men in Iraq. Our Henry made his threats to the townspeople of Harfleur to the cameras; in the following scene, Katherine and Alice watched it on TV – a good reason to start learning English.

Video was a major tool in our armoury, though never as a substitute for stage action. Verbal rhetoric is Henry's weapon of choice in his propaganda campaign. In our linguistically impoverished age, spin is more often the province of the film-maker (at least it was until the advent of Barack Obama). Adrian Lester's Henry was often on television. He broadcast his declaration of war to the nation at the end of Act 1 scene 2: 'We'll chide this dauphin at his father's door'. Bardolph watched him briefly on the pub TV before switching over to the snooker.

MB: Our French court were proud, exotic birds suspended in the air, and at Agincourt they descended on the entrenched and earthbound English like golden eagles or the American air force.

We decided we would recognize the decisive role played by archers and our eagles became enmeshed in airborne tracers of white paper to the sound of volleys of arrows. These tracers then left a trail of destruction throughout the auditorium until the end of the

7. The dauphin (John Mackay) descends in Michael Boyd's 2007 production.

play. Fragments of torn silk, black and gold, floated seven metres from the grid to the stage as the French dead hung in the air and the dauphin descended upside down like Satan or Icarus. We few were happy to be free of the literalism that guides most TV and cinema.

What do you think Henry thinks about the Archbishop's argument at the start of the play?

KB: In rehearsal we'd played this scene in a very political way like a modern-day cabinet meeting. Brian Blessed, who played Exeter [in the RSC production and on film], let out a loud belly-laugh at the archbishop's 'bee metaphor' which underlined the difference between Henry and his 'war cabinet'. I wanted the first speech to Canterbury to put this man of God very explicitly on the spot with an injunction directed at the wily archbishops [see 1.2.11–34]. I wanted to produce a moral gravitas that would arrest the clerics and the court with its weight. When my Henry used words like 'sin' and 'baptism' and 'conscience', I wanted the audience to feel that these were real and practical concepts which were deeply felt. It seemed the only way to make the audience care, and thus to make them genuinely question this man's actions. It also created dramatic conflict: the archbishops are faced not with a warlord who simply wishes a plan for invasion to be given the Church's approval, but with someone who is asking real questions and underlining their own sense of responsibility.

EH: I think Henry knows exactly what Canterbury's up to. Hal's not stupid. It's a fantastic example of politicking: 'we need an excuse to go to war, give it to me'. There is a part of Henry that wants to be seen to be doing the right thing, and a part of him that actually *wants* to do the right thing, but he knows that Canterbury is talking everybody in circles. When Canterbury says 'as clear as is the summer's sun', after he's just reeled off the most extraordinarily complicated family tree, which *nobody* understands or is meant to understand, he's partly throwing down a smokescreen to show how clever he is – he's almost learnt it like a party piece – and it's partly Shakespeare's sense of irony: he's taking a little stand at politics. All of them in the room know exactly what Canterbury's up to, but they need to be *seen* to be doing it for the right reasons – and that's what matters most.

I've been, right from the word go, vehemently against the war in Iraq, and felt *so* clearly in the months leading up to it that we were being utterly bamboozled and lied to. It was so clear that it was terrifying for me. There was a lot of big business and a lot of money, and America wanted to go and Blair wanted to take us with them, so he said 'find me the reason'. I'm not suggesting, because it's not clearly in the text, that Henry has said that, but I certainly think that he wants it, he wants it to be true.

NH: I think he has briefed the archbishop to find him an excuse to do what his father told him to do. And I don't think you need to have seen *Henry IV Part II* to suspect this. He seems to me to be in icy control of the whole scene, determined to hear the Archbishop give him the right answer to the question that matters: 'May I with right and conscience make this claim?' I think he is gratified that the archbishop gives him the required advice, in much the same way that Tony Blair was gratified that the Attorney General delivered to him the notorious justification in international law for the invasion of Iraq. I think the scene is far more interested in the ways our war leaders use to take us to war than it is in the rights or wrongs of the cause (that comes later, on the eve of Agincourt). The scene seems to me to be neutral on the subject of the Salic law itself, though a dramatist as clever as Shakespeare must have meant something by writing for the archbishop a speech so preposterously long and hard to follow.

Plays, particularly Shakespeare's plays, change all the time. When Olivier made his film, who was interested in the justification of the cause? The cause spoke for itself, so Olivier cut the archbishop to the bone, and sent up what was left. And he was right to do so.

MB: The first scene makes it clear that Henry is already considering war and has been discussing deals with the Church to secure their support, before the ambassador gets near him. That's why Shakespeare is free to allow the speech to sound absurd. What really concerns Henry is the Church committing itself to public support for his actions. Shakespeare cleverly manages to destroy the French legal objections to an English succession at the same time as comically questioning the sincerity and morality of the Archbishop's show-stopping speech.

Is it necessary to have an understanding of Hal's background in the previous plays to fully appreciate what kind of a king he is in *Henry V*?

KB: It was important for an audience that might have no previous knowledge of the *Henry IV* plays to have an idea of the background to *Henry V*, and I wanted to achieve the greatest possible impact from Mistress Quickly's speech reporting the death of Falstaff, a character that the audience would not otherwise have encountered. I constructed this brief flashback from three separate scenes in the *Henry IV* plays. My intention was to give, in miniature, a sense of Falstaff's place among the surviving members of the Boar's Head crew, and to make clear his former relationship and estrangement from the young monarch. Both this scene and the flashback during Bardolph's on-screen execution help to illustrate the young king's intense isolation and his difficulty in rejecting his former tavern life.

EH: No. That's one the brilliant things about the play: it's a sequel or a prequel that can be seen out-of-joint without any problems whatsoever. I've done the play without *Henry IV*s and also as part of the Histories cycle. I think if you've seen *Henry IV* you get a lovely extra rich layer to it. The audience really enjoy the through-lines and the characters from *Henry IV*, the Pistols, the Nims, the Bardolphs, and seeing how Hal changes – and Shakespeare so successfully changes him that you're essentially watching a new person in *Henry V*. But if you see *Henry V* on its own you don't sit there thinking 'It feels like there are bits missing'. Because you don't know: in itself it's a really good piece.

NH: No. It's a great experience to see *Henry V* as the concluding play of a tetralogy that starts with *Richard II*, and if you played Prince Hal last night, your performance of King Henry is going to be very different from the one you'd give if you didn't. But *Henry V* is a stand-alone play, and there's clear evidence it isn't the play Shakespeare thought he was going to write when he finished *Henry IV Part II*. We're promised more of Falstaff in the Epilogue to *Part II*, but he's killed off before he gets a chance to appear. Maybe Shakespeare thought that a broken-hearted Falstaff would have been an unwanted downer; more likely, he realized that he was dealing with a completely different Henry, involved in a completely new narrative, and that Falstaff would have been theatrically irrelevant.

I directed the two *Henry IV* plays at the National a couple of years after we did *Henry V*. I'm glad we did them that way round: I didn't think there was much in the *Henry IV* plays that would benefit from the kind of production we gave *Henry V*. Different plays, different agenda, different Henry. I'd go so far as to put the question the other way round: you need to know what Hal became to appreciate fully what he's up to in *Henry IV*, and Shakespeare lets you know exactly that in his first soliloquy.

MB: For the actor (Geoffrey Streatfeild in our case) and those around him it is crucial to carry the detailed memory of Hal's dissolution and rebellion into his newly disciplined court as Henry V. It is then their job to pass their sense of surprise, danger and misgiving which surrounds the new Henry across to the audience.

Shakespeare more or less assumes a pre-existing knowledge and affection on the part of the audience for the world and characters of Eastcheap, and without that the early Pistol, Quickly and Bardolph scenes could be difficult. We flirted with the option of pulling David Warner's Falstaff out of the gloom the night before Agincourt, but found that by then the scene had no room for him. And in any case, Nick Asbury's Pistol represented Eastcheap perfectly well.

Who gets the best of the argument in the 'little touch of Harry in the night' scene when the disguised king debates with the common soldiers?

EH: I think Henry wins the philosophical and the moral side of the argument but the soldiers win the human side of the argument, which is, 'Well you come and put yourself in our shoes'. I don't think it's resolved in the end. What's interesting is that the idea would have been much more alien to an Elizabethan audience than it is to us, to whom in fact it is not alien at all. Whose responsibility is it? Do you have personal responsibility for the women and children you murder in the town that you've just laid siege to? Do you have personal responsibility in your jet when you press a button and drop a bomb and kill 700 people? Or is it the responsibility of the person who sends you there? And what happens on Judgement Day? What does God think? I think Harry articulates the argument fantastically well, says 'We've got to take responsibility for our actions', but at the same time they wouldn't be there if it wasn't for him. I think that would have held a strong currency for common people watching it. If you put that scene in front of a bunch of soldiers nowadays who've done a tour of duty in Iraq or Afghanistan or wherever, they'd probably have a very different opinion to the academic who comes out in favour of that speech. So to a degree it depends who's watching it.

NH: In 2003, the soldiers. It wasn't even close.

The then editor of the *Daily Telegraph* came to see our production, shortly after he'd been to Iraq and spent time talking to members of the army. He was a supporter of the war, but told me that he'd been particularly moved by the dialogue of the common soldiers as it reflected exactly what he'd heard in Iraq. The king's overlong response to Michael Williams feels like so much special pleading; but to be fair, it's a long time since anyone believed that war is God's beadle.

The business with Williams' glove seems to me to be very uncomfortable. Here's a king who has just won one of the most famous victories in British history, and in its aftermath his chief concern appears to be a mean-minded practical joke at the expense of an ordinary soldier who has unwittingly offended him. He sets up Fluellen to beat Williams, at considerable peril to them both: no sane general would manoeuvre two pumped-up squaddies, fresh from battle, into a fight with each other. In our production, when Fluellen went for Williams, the result was a beer-fuelled brawl that soon involved the entire division. It was maybe the most convincing bout of violence in the show, and it felt right that the undignified consequence of Henry's petty vendetta threatened to undermine the numbering of the dead. It didn't, of course: the naming of the dead never fails to bring a lump to the throat whatever the ceremony. But it must have been part of Shakespeare's plan, in a play where the most of the dead English are (in context, accurately) dismissed as 'None else of name', to bring so vividly and sympathetically to life some of the nameless. And, indeed, to name them with such touching precision.

MB: Williams has the easier task and by far the most vivid language, but Hal's doctrine of personal responsibility is at least robust enough for the scene not to be deemed treasonous. Williams wins, but that could be denied by the author.

If the text is to be trusted, Henry orders the killing of the French prisoners *before* hearing of the French attack on the boys and the baggage-carriers, so Fluellen is wrong in giving that as a justification. Is that a problem?

KB: The pace of the battle scenes was very important, so I wanted to move rapidly from Henry's anger to Montjoy's entrance. That meant that some of the business about the reasons for killing the French prisoners was cut. To balance that, we did earlier see Henry witnessing the execution of Bardolph face to face. I decided on including some significant scenes that Olivier's film, for obvious reasons, had left out. The violence and extremism of Henry's behaviour and its effect on a volatile war cabinet were elements that the Olivier version was not likely to spotlight.

EH: I did it, as I remember, that they killed the boys and the baggage so he killed all the prisoners. It's vicious, it's very brutal, and I showed that as well. There's a danger that it makes Harry seem justified in his murder, but on the other hand it's war, and we like to pretend there are rules in war, but actually there aren't. The Geneva Convention is great for us to have, it's like a comfort blanket, but the bottom line is it doesn't make a difference when you unleash that anarchy and then use the army to try and control it.

I did two things. Firstly, in the scene with Pistol and the French prisoner; Pistol beat the French prisoner to within an inch of his life. I wanted to show very clearly that the English were very violent against the French in the middle of the battle. And when Henry gave the order to kill the prisoners, we lined them up against the back wall of the RST and machine-gunned them all to death, very physically, very loudly. I didn't want it to feel like Henry was doing this with kid gloves. I wanted it to feel like he was brutal, decisive and violent. If you talk to people who have actually been in the theatre of operations, there is no time to mess around and ask these questions and worry about these things. You've got a responsibility to your men and you've got to win and, essentially, you've got to do it in any way that you can. That's the bottom line, and I think what Henry does is kill the prisoners in order to free up his men to fight. You can't keep soldiers busy looking after prisoners when they're supposed to be on the battlefield. I think with the changing around of the text there is a danger of softening what Henry does, and I know that historically he was particularly brutal on French campaigns. What I tried to do was embrace that in all its awfulness.

NH: It's only a problem if your production wants to whitewash Henry, as both Olivier and Branagh did in reordering events to make the slaughter of the French prisoners the consequence of the attack on the boys. There's no need to do this: the point is surely that war is an appalling business and that war crimes happen. Henry V is both hero and war criminal, and he isn't the first to be both.

2003 seemed to me to present a different issue, extra-textual but real nevertheless. I knew that the audience would be seeking out contemporary parallels, and I was sensitive less to the slurring of the reputation of Henry V, who can look after himself, than to the possibility of damning the soldiers who carry out his orders, and by association the soldiers who were carrying out orders on our behalf in Iraq. In our production when Henry gave the order 'Then every soldier kill his prisoners', the soldiers refused to follow it. They couldn't stomach it. So it was left to Fluellen to gun the prisoners down on his own.

MB: No. It's a joy. Shakespeare's understanding of the dynamic, aesthetics and morality of propaganda is unrivalled. Nor does he blench at the evils of war. Prisoners can rise up against you and keeping prisoners secure takes men away from your battle line, and Henry is in any case flawed. Fluellen's loyalty need not be seen as negative. The play has let us see the truth.

So then, King Henry V: ideal monarch or ruthless hypocrite? How much do you think we are supposed to admire him in the play?

KB: It is a more complex play than is traditionally acknowledged and Adrian's production strongly resisted the concept of a two-dimensional *Boy's Own* adventure. In my own performance, I tried to realize the qualities of introspection, fear, doubt and anger which I believed the text indicated: an especially young Henry with more than a little of the Hamlet in him. It was conveying these elements of the king's personality that gave me the initial idea for a new screen version – the idea of abandoning large-theatre projection and allowing close-ups and low-level dialogue to draw the audience deep into the human side of this distant medieval world.

Henry is a man with a close understanding of what war involves, and an intense, visionary appreciation of its consequences. He is a killer, a brilliant politician, but much of this is in embryo and is subject to change during the course of the play. Above all, he is a complicated, doubting, dangerous young professional – neither straightforwardly good nor consciously evil. Adrian and I both agreed that we should not try to explain this man but rather explore all these paradoxes and contradictions, with an awareness of his historical and social context. We wanted to be faithful to the complex inner debate that Shakespeare conducts on the subject of war, and as we discussed the play it seemed less like a historical pageant and more like a highly complicated and ambiguous discourse on the nature of leadership.

EH: I think the play releases the spirit of nationalism in us all if it works well, which is both exciting and bloody dangerous. Nationalism is a good thing in many respects; we should be proud to be who we are, proud of our culture, and proud of our roots and our identity. God knows England is a tribal enough place and has enough of that. But at the same time, that energy can release a violence in people that tips into 'Well I'm not going to let anyone else be different to me, that's a bad thing'. And it becomes very violent and nasty. I think the play deals in both those things. So at different times you feel proud to be British and also disgusted at the same moment. I think it's a good mix of those themes, which is an accurate reflection of the issues that Shakespeare is writing about.

NH: As always in Shakespeare, it's a bit of both, isn't it? (And your question begs the question: 'Who said that ideal monarchs can't also be ruthless hypocrites?')

I think Shakespeare set out to write a big hit *Henry V* play for his company. Agincourt was box-office gold – his was the fourth play on the subject to open in London in ten years; and he certainly borrowed wholesale from the only one of those to survive. The company and the audience presumably wanted hagiography, and I suppose you can read Shakespeare's play as uncomplicated hero-worship if you want to, and if you're prepared to ignore everything that tells you not to. Everything about Henry is questioned in the play. Was he justified in going to war? Was he politically wise to go to war? How good a strategist was he? How much did he care about his subjects? Were his show trials and show executions right, or worthwhile? The point is always the question itself; the answer is rarely unambiguous.

Henry does not have the saving grace of self-consciousness. His only soliloquy is marred by self-pity. He is no Hamlet. But his dazzling eloquence has such power that it seems almost to make irrelevant the question of his sincerity. Gentlemen in England now a-bed, who nowadays include nearly all of us, can still be galvanized by Olivier or Adrian Lester; or by those with graver responsibilities than theirs – like Colonel Collins or Winston Churchill – who still reach back for inspiration to Henry V.

MB: Henry is ruthless and expedient to the point where his actions are manipulative, and morally dubious. But he is vulnerable too, and utterly honest with us the audience. He has the appeal of the underdog at Agincourt, and shows real personal courage in overcoming his own grave misgivings to inspire his tattered army to victory. And then he's given one hell of a charmer of a last scene.

Gower, Fluellen, Jamy and MacMorris all have national characteristics that sometimes make one think of those jokes that begin an Englishman, a Welshman, a Scotsman and an Irishman ... Then we have the ridiculing of the affected French. How did you deal with what might now be perceived as the play's stereotyping and xenophobia?

KB: In the theatre, the last RSC production played for over three hours, even with significant cuts, and there was no choice writing the screenplay but to be even more savage. In any case the cuts dictated themselves. The more tortuous aspects of the Fluellen/Pistol antagonism, culminating in the resoundingly unfunny leek scene, were the first to go. The double-edged exchanges between Henry and Burgundy in Act 5 also, for my purposes, failed to advance the plot, and added little to the aspects of the play that we wanted to explore.

EH: With Fluellen, MacMorris, Jamy and Gower, we just played them as very passionate, proud Welshmen, Irishmen, Scotsmen and Englishmen, and audiences love that and adore that. As long as your characters are ferociously proud and strong in their arguments and perspectives and you're not sending them up, and if you get a good actor, then I think you're fine. What you've got is a wonderful portrayal of the United Kingdom attempting to be united. It's still a complete anomaly that we have an English rugby team and an English football team, yet we also have the British Lions – explain that to me. You try to explain to a child the idea of geography and country and nation and it's very hard, because they say 'Well, is Wales another country?' And you say, 'Well yes, but no, we're all united'. So we still argue about it and delight in it today, and when you put that on a stage the audience recognise it instantly and they adore it. I think it's passionate, funny and very contemporary. I think the ridiculing of the French is just a national pastime on our front, and likewise from the French to the English, and Shakespeare's tapping into that. I don't think much has changed. Those French jokes still hold a lot of currency in an auditorium, but essentially you're showing a group of people at war taking the piss out of the enemy, and then you're showing the enemy almost living up to that press and more, particularly with all the chat about the dauphin talking about his horse. But in the end Shakespeare counters it with a tremendously moving scene where Henry reads out the list of the dead, which is extraordinary. He gives them a roll call, honours them all, and I think there's a huge sense of shock at the size of the French loss. I did that with great pathos and seriousness, and as Henry was reading out the dead the soldiers slowly became aware of how many were gone, and I asked the actors to start to react in a deeper way at the loss, how extraordinary that was, and start to let it sink in and affect them. Every single name Henry reads out was from a great family, and they're all gone. So I think there is a payoff in the end; the soldiers and Henry really feel that God has supported them and the French have had a great loss, and that's something to be respected.

NH: The jokes aren't a problem if they are funny. Stereotypes aren't a problem in themselves: they become a problem if they are untrue, uncharitable and unfunny. It may be that Shakespeare would have been done for apostasy by the modern academy, but theatre audiences tend to be less censorious.

In any event, with his English, Welsh, Scottish and Irish captains, I think Shakespeare was saying something about the English army and the British nation – then, as now, multi-racial. (And then, as now, particularly dependent on Scottish, Welsh and Irish soldiers. The best play so far about the Iraq war on the ground is Gregory Burke's *Black Watch*: a Scottish regiment betrayed by Westminster.)

Some of the French are affected, some aren't. The dauphin is pretty intolerable, and ineffectual; but Burgundy's speech in Act 5 is an overwhelming lament for a war-torn land, and a dignified rebuke for the warmongering English king. Reading recently Anthony Beevor's account of the devastation of Normandy after the D-Day landings, I was constantly put in mind of Shakespeare's evocation of the consequences of a previous, and more hostile, English invasion.

MB: Gower was played by Paul Hamilton, also Talbot's Captain of Orléans in *Henry VI Part I* who later as Alexander Iden killed Jack Cade in *Henry VI Part II*, and fought alongside Richmond to destroy Richard III at Bosworth. A true, quiet, English hero.

Fluellen in Jonathan Slinger's hands was no fool, just single-minded, and so funny and palpable that you forgave national stereotyping. His 'Welsh correction' of Pistol was so vicious that you almost felt sorry for Pistol.

Jamy the Scotsman was a tricky task that several cast members tried their hand at, including one Scot. In the end we cut him down to one line, slapped a bonnet on his head and put him in Geoff Freshwater's capable hands.

MacMorris was played by a passionate Aussie, Rob Carroll, who managed to bring danger and violence to the National question while catching the laughs as well.

Shakespeare has disappointingly little light to shed on the issue of England in a new 'Britain' beyond a rather generalized rerun of his *Henry VI* themes of disunity at home reappearing on foreign battlefields.

Throughout his entire History cycle, the French are there to serve Shakespeare's moral, cosmic, and mostly comic purpose. His grossly unfair treatment of them united the crowd (in a way that the Spanish could not have), and mollified the censors. Like Satan, and the Vice before the Hellmouth of the Corpus Christi Mystery Plays, they get many of the best lines and most definitely the best costumes, and the subversion of the unquestionable xenophobia lies in the theatrical fact that we love them for being so venal and vivid.

And the wooing of the French princess: charming coda or more political manipulation?

EH: I think it is definitely political manipulation, although of course Shakespeare makes Katherine rather beautiful. He writes a scene which starts off as a scene the audience would all recognize, which is a contract, because people then largely didn't get married for love, they got married as part of a deal. It starts as a political deal and ends up as something rather beautiful, and I wanted that one kiss between Henry and Kate to symbolize the beginning of the repairing of the gulf between the two countries. So what began as something slightly cynical and dubious ended up as the beginning of a détente. Which of course doesn't come to pass: it gets tripped up and soon we're seeing Henry's coffin coming onstage in *Henry VI Part I*.

NH: Adrian Lester is inescapably charming, but none of us were persuaded of the scene's charm. You only have to see it from Katherine's point of view, and its charm completely evaporates.

8. William Houston as Henry wooing Catherine Walker as Katherine in a union that 'starts as a political deal' but 'ends up as something rather beautiful' in Ed Hall's production, 2000.

Maybe it's another of those scenes whose meaning has changed. Henry can be played with wit, seductive allure, the whole works; but you can't escape the fact that the victor is insisting not just that the daughter of the vanquished marries him, but that she tells him she loves him. 'It is not possible you should love the enemy of France', admits Henry, before trying to sell Katherine some stinking fish in the guise of heavy humour. 'In loving me you should love the friend of France, for I love France so well that I will not part with a village of it; I will have it all mine.' Please.

So we played it as honestly as we could: Adrian oozed charm; but Félicité du Jeu as Katherine didn't give an inch. She accepted him only on compulsion.

MB: This is a brilliantly achieved, intelligent and sexy scene bursting with wit and charm and character revelation. And Henry is an imperialist, and he has just been responsible for the massacre of fourteen thousand French.

Imperialism doesn't become a major issue for Shakespeare until *The Tempest*. Neither he nor his audience carried our luggage of the legacy of Empire. On the contrary; they had bright hopes for the Indies and the New World.

Shakespeare is never blind to the cruelty of war, but probably felt he had 'earthed' the issue of the French dead with his long and dignified acknowledgement of their passing after Agincourt.

The Iraq war did, however, come into play with this scene. We took a considerable risk: in order to be able to play the wooing scene for all it was worth and celebrate its joys, we played it on a stage constructed by the English on the coffins of the French dead. Having our cake and standing on it if you like. The risk paid off. The audience roared with laughter and felt very uneasy afterwards.

SHAKESPEARE'S CAREER IN THE THEATRE

BEGINNINGS

William Shakespeare was an extraordinarily intelligent man who was born and died in an ordinary market town in the English Midlands. He lived an uneventful life in an eventful age. Born in April 1564, he was the eldest son of John Shakespeare, a glove-maker who was prominent on the town council until he fell into financial difficulties. Young William was educated at the local grammar in Stratford-upon-Avon, Warwickshire, where he gained a thorough grounding in the Latin language, the art of rhetoric and classical poetry. He married Ann Hathaway and had three children (Susanna, then the twins Hamnet and Judith) before his twenty-first birthday: an exceptionally young age for the period. We do not know how he supported his family in the mid-1580s.

Like many clever country boys, he moved to the city in order to make his way in the world. Like many creative people, he found a career in the entertainment business. Public playhouses and professional full-time acting companies reliant on the market for their income were born in Shakespeare's childhood. When he arrived in London as a man, sometime in the late 1580s, a new phenomenon was in the making: the actor who is so successful that he becomes a 'star'. The word did not exist in its modern sense, but the pattern is recognizable: audiences went to the theatre not so much to see a particular show as to witness the comedian Richard Tarlton or the dramatic actor Edward Alleyn.

Shakespeare was an actor before he was a writer. It appears not to have been long before he realized that he was never going to grow into a great comedian like Tarlton or a great tragedian like Alleyn. Instead, he found a role within his company as the man who patched up old plays, breathing new life, new dramatic twists, into tired repertory pieces. He paid close attention to the work of the university-educated dramatists who were writing history plays and tragedies for the public stage in a style more ambitious, sweeping and poetically grand than anything which had been seen before. But he may also have noted that what his friend and rival Ben Jonson would call 'Marlowe's mighty line' sometimes faltered in the mode of comedy. Going to university, as Christopher Marlowe did, was all well and good for honing the arts of rhetorical elaboration and classical allusion, but it could lead to a loss of the common touch. To stay close to a large segment of the potential audience for public theatre, it was necessary to write for clowns as well as kings and to intersperse the flights of poetry with the humour of the tavern, the privy and the brothel: Shakespeare was the first to establish himself early in his career as an equal master of tragedy, comedy and history. He realized that theatre could be the medium to make the national past available to a wider audience than the elite who could afford to read large history books: his signature early works include not only the classical tragedy *Titus Andronicus* but also the sequence of English historical plays on the Wars of the Roses.

He also invented a new role for himself, that of in-house company dramatist. Where his peers and predecessors had to sell their plays to the theatre managers on a poorly-paid piecework basis, Shakespeare took a percentage of the box-office income. The Lord Chamberlain's Men constituted themselves in 1594 as a joint stock company, with the profits being distributed among the core actors who had invested as sharers. Shakespeare acted himself – he appears in the cast lists of some of Ben Jonson's plays as well as the list of actors' names at the beginning of his own collected works – but his principal duty was to write two or three plays a year for the company. By holding shares, he was effectively earning himself a royalty on his work, something no author had ever done before in England. When the Lord Chamberlain's Men collected their fee for performance at court in the Christmas season of 1594, three of them went along to the Treasurer of the Chamber: not just Richard Burbage the tragedian and Will Kempe the clown, but also Shakespeare the scriptwriter. That was something new.

The next four years were the golden period in Shakespeare's career, though overshadowed by the death of his only son Hamnet, aged eleven, in 1596. In his early thirties and in full command of both his poetic and his theatrical medium, he perfected his art of comedy, while also developing his tragic and historical writing in new ways. In 1598, Francis Meres, a Cambridge University graduate with his finger on the pulse of the London literary world, praised Shakespeare for his excellence across the genres:

> As Plautus and Seneca are accounted the best for comedy and tragedy among the Latins, so Shakespeare among the English is the most excellent in both kinds for the stage; for comedy, witness his *Gentlemen of Verona*, his *Errors*, his *Love Labours Lost*, his *Love Labours Won*, his *Midsummer Night Dream* and his *Merchant of Venice*: for tragedy his *Richard the 2*, *Richard the 3*, *Henry the 4*, *King John*, *Titus Andronicus* and his *Romeo and Juliet*.

For Meres, as for the many writers who praised the 'honey-flowing vein' of *Venus and Adonis* and *Lucrece*, narrative poems written when the theatres were closed due to plague in 1593–94, Shakespeare was marked above all by his linguistic skill, by the gift of turning elegant poetic phrases.

PLAYHOUSES

Elizabethan playhouses were 'thrust' or 'one-room' theatres. To understand Shakespeare's original theatrical life, we have to forget about the indoor theatre of later times, with its proscenium arch and curtain that would be opened at the beginning and closed at the end of each act. In the proscenium arch theatre, stage and auditorium are effectively two separate rooms: the audience looks from one world into another as if through the imaginary 'fourth wall' framed by the proscenium. The picture-frame stage, together with the elaborate scenic effects and backdrops beyond it, created the illusion of a self-contained world – especially once nineteenth-century developments in the control of artificial lighting meant that the auditorium could be darkened and the spectators made to focus on the lighted stage. Shakespeare, by contrast, wrote for a bare platform stage with a standing audience gathered around it in a courtyard in full daylight. The audience were always conscious of themselves and their fellow-spectators, and they shared the same 'room' as the actors. A sense of immediate presence and the creation of rapport with the audience were all-important. The actor could not afford to imagine he was in a closed world, with silent witnesses dutifully observing him from the darkness.

Shakespeare's theatrical career began at the Rose Theatre in Southwark. The stage was wide and shallow, trapezoid in shape, like a lozenge. This design had a great deal of potential for the theatrical equivalent of cinematic split-screen effects, whereby one group of characters would enter at the door at one end of the tiring-house wall at the back of the stage and another group through the door at the other end, thus creating two rival tableaux. Many of the battle-heavy and faction-filled plays that premiered at the Rose have scenes of just this sort.

At the rear of the Rose stage, there were three capacious exits, each over ten feet wide. Unfortunately, the very limited excavation of a fragmentary portion of the original Globe site, in 1989, revealed nothing about the stage. The first Globe was built in 1599 with similar proportions to those of another theatre, the Fortune, albeit that the former was polygonal and looked circular, whereas the latter was rectangular. The building contract for the Fortune survives and allows us to infer that the stage of the Globe was probably substantially wider than it was deep (perhaps forty-three feet wide and twenty-seven feet deep). It may well have been tapered at the front, like that of the Rose.

The capacity of the Globe was said to have been enormous, perhaps in excess of three thousand. It has been conjectured that about eight hundred people may have stood in the yard, with two thousand or more in the three layers of covered galleries. The other 'public' playhouses were also of large capacity, whereas the indoor Blackfriars theatre that Shakespeare's company began using in 1608 – the former refectory of a monastery – had overall internal dimensions of a mere forty-six by sixty feet. It would have made for a much more intimate theatrical experience and had a much smaller capacity, probably of about six hundred people. Since they paid at least sixpence a head, the Blackfriars attracted a more select or 'private' audience. The atmosphere would have been closer to that of an indoor performance before the court in the Whitehall Palace or at Richmond. That Shakespeare always wrote for indoor production at court as well as outdoor performance in the public theatre should make us cautious about inferring, as some scholars have, that the opportunity provided by the intimacy of the Blackfriars led to a significant change towards a 'chamber' style in his last plays – which, besides, were performed at both the Globe and the Blackfriars. After the occupation of the Blackfriars a five-act structure seems to have become more important to Shakespeare. That was because of artificial lighting: there were musical interludes between the acts, while the candles were trimmed and replaced. Again, though, something similar must have been necessary for indoor court performances throughout his career.

Front of house there were the 'gatherers' who collected the money from audience members: a penny to stand in the open-air yard, another penny for a place in the covered galleries, sixpence for the prominent 'lord's rooms' to the side of the stage. In the indoor 'private' theatres, gallants from the audience who fancied making themselves part of the spectacle sat on stools on the edge of the stage itself. Scholars debate as to how widespread this practice was in the public theatres such as the Globe. Once the audience were in place and the money counted, the gatherers were available to be extras on stage. That is one reason why battles and crowd scenes often come later rather than early in Shakespeare's plays. There was no formal prohibition upon performance by women, and there certainly were women among the gatherers, so it is not beyond the bounds of possibility that female crowd members were played by females.

The play began at two o'clock in the afternoon and the theatre had to be cleared by five. After the main show, there would be a jig – which consisted not only of dancing, but also of knockabout comedy (it is the origin of the farcical 'afterpiece' in the eighteenth-century theatre). So the time available for a Shakespeare play was about two and a half hours, somewhere between the 'two hours' traffic' mentioned in the prologue to *Romeo and Juliet* and the 'three hours' spectacle' referred to in the preface to the 1647 Folio of Beaumont and Fletcher's plays. The prologue to a play by Thomas Middleton refers to a thousand lines as 'one hour's words', so the likelihood is that about two and a half thousand, or a maximum of three thousand lines made up the performed text. This is indeed the length of most of Shakespeare's comedies, whereas many of his tragedies and histories are much longer, raising the possibility that he wrote full scripts, possibly with eventual publication in mind, in the full knowledge that the stage version would be heavily cut. The short Quarto texts published in his lifetime – they used to be called 'Bad' Quartos – provide fascinating evidence as to the kind of cutting that probably took place. So, for instance, the First Quarto of *Hamlet* neatly merges two occasions when Hamlet is overheard, the 'Fishmonger' and the 'nunnery' scenes.

The social composition of the audience was mixed. The poet Sir John Davies wrote of 'A thousand townsmen, gentlemen and whores, / Porters and servingmen' who would 'together throng' at the public playhouses. Though moralists associated female play-going with adultery and the sex trade, many perfectly respectable citizens' wives were regular attendees. Some, no doubt, resembled the modern groupie: a story attested in two different sources has one citizen's wife making a post-show assignation with Richard Burbage and ending up in bed with Shakespeare – supposedly eliciting from the latter the quip that William the Conqueror was before Richard III. Defenders of theatre liked to say that by witnessing the comeuppance of villains on the stage, audience members would repent of their own wrongdoings, but the reality is that most people went to the theatre then, as they do now, for entertainment more than moral edification. Besides, it would be foolish to suppose that audiences behaved in a homogeneous way: a pamphlet of the 1630s tells of how two men went to see *Pericles* and one of them laughed while the other wept. Bishop John Hall complained that people went to church for the same reasons that they went to the theatre: 'for company, for custom, for recreation . . . to feed his eyes or his ears . . . or perhaps for sleep'.

Men-about-town and clever young lawyers went to be seen as much as to see. In the modern popular imagination, shaped not least by *Shakespeare in Love* and the opening sequence of Laurence Olivier's

Henry V film, the penny-paying groundlings stand in the yard hurling abuse or encouragement and hazelnuts or orange peel at the actors, while the sophisticates in the covered galleries appreciate Shakespeare's soaring poetry. The reality was probably the other way round. A 'groundling' was a kind of fish, so the nickname suggests the penny audience standing below the level of the stage and gazing in silent open-mouthed wonder at the spectacle unfolding above them. The more difficult audience members, who kept up a running commentary of clever remarks on the performance and who occasionally got into quarrels with players, were the gallants. Like Hollywood movies in modern times, Elizabethan and Jacobean plays exercised a powerful influence on the fashion and behaviour of the young. John Marston mocks the lawyers who would open their lips, perhaps to court a girl, and out would 'flow / Naught but pure Juliet and Romeo'.

THE ENSEMBLE AT WORK

In the absence of typewriters and photocopying machines, reading aloud would have been the means by which the company got to know a new play. The tradition of the playwright reading his complete script to the assembled company endured for generations. A copy would then have been taken to the Master of the Revels for licensing. The theatre book-holder or prompter would then have copied the parts for distribution to the actors. A partbook consisted of the character's lines, with each speech preceded by the last three or four words of the speech before, the so-called 'cue'. These would have been taken away and studied or 'conned'. During this period of learning the parts, an actor might have had some one-to-one instruction, perhaps from the dramatist, perhaps from a senior actor who had played the same part before, and, in the case of an apprentice, from his master. A high percentage of Desdemona's lines occur in dialogue with Othello, of Lady Macbeth's with Macbeth, Cleopatra's with Antony and Volumnia's with Coriolanus. The roles would almost certainly have been taken by the apprentice of the lead actor, usually Burbage, who delivers the majority of the cues. Given that apprentices lodged with their masters, there would have been

9. Hypothetical reconstruction of the interior of an Elizabethan playhouse during a performance.

ample opportunity for personal instruction, which may be what made it possible for young men to play such demanding parts.

After the parts were learned, there may have been no more than a single rehearsal before the first performance. With six different plays to be put on every week, there was no time for more. Actors, then, would go into a show with a very limited sense of the whole. The notion of a collective rehearsal process that is itself a process of discovery for the actors is wholly modern and would have been incomprehensible to Shakespeare and his original ensemble. Given the number of parts an actor had to hold in his memory, the forgetting of lines was probably more frequent than in the modern theatre. The book-holder was on hand to prompt.

Backstage personnel included the property man, the tire-man who oversaw the costumes, call-boys, attendants and the musicians, who might play at various times from the main stage, the rooms above and within the tiring-house. Scriptwriters sometimes made a nuisance of themselves backstage. There was often tension between the acting companies and the freelance playwrights from whom they purchased scripts: it was a smart move on the part of Shakespeare and the Lord Chamberlain's Men to bring the writing process in-house.

Scenery was limited, though sometimes set-pieces were brought on (a bank of flowers, a bed, the mouth of hell). The trapdoor from below, the gallery stage above and the curtained discovery-space at the back allowed for an array of special effects: the rising of ghosts and apparitions, the descent of gods, dialogue between a character at a window and another at ground level, the revelation of a statue or a pair of lovers playing at chess. Ingenious use could be made of props, as with the ass's head in *A Midsummer Night's Dream*. In a theatre that does not clutter the stage with the material paraphernalia of everyday life, those objects that are deployed may take on powerful symbolic weight, as when Shylock bears his weighing scales in one hand and knife in the other, thus becoming a parody of the figure of Justice who traditionally bears a sword and a balance. Among the more significant items in the property cupboard of Shakespeare's company, there would have been a throne (the 'chair of state'), joint stools, books, bottles, coins, purses, letters (which are brought on stage, read or referred to on about eighty occasions in the complete works), maps, gloves, a set of stocks (in which Kent is put in *King Lear*), rings, rapiers, daggers, broadswords, staves, pistols, masks and vizards, heads and skulls, torches and tapers and lanterns which served to signal night scenes on the daylit stage, a buck's head, an ass's head, animal costumes. Live animals also put in appearances, most notably the dog Crab in *The Two Gentlemen of Verona* and possibly a young polar bear in *The Winter's Tale*.

The costumes were the most important visual dimension of the play. Playwrights were paid between £2 and £6 per script, whereas Alleyn was not averse to paying £20 for 'a black velvet cloak with sleeves embroidered all with silver and gold'. No matter the period of the play, actors always wore contemporary costume. The excitement for the audience came not from any impression of historical accuracy, but from the richness of the attire and perhaps the transgressive thrill of the knowledge that here were commoners like themselves strutting in the costumes of courtiers in effective defiance of the strict sumptuary laws whereby in real life people had to wear the clothes that befitted their social station.

To an even greater degree than props, costumes could carry symbolic importance. Racial characteristics could be suggested: a breastplate and helmet for a Roman soldier, a turban for a Turk, long robes for exotic characters such as Moors, a gabardine for a Jew. The figure of Time, as in *The Winter's Tale*, would be equipped with hourglass, scythe and wings; Rumour, who speaks the prologue of *2 Henry IV*, wore a costume adorned with a thousand tongues. The wardrobe in the tiring-house of the Globe would have contained much of the same stock as that of rival manager Philip Henslowe at the Rose: green gowns for outlaws and foresters, black for melancholy men such as Jaques and people in mourning such as the Countess in *All's Well that Ends Well* (at the beginning of *Hamlet*, the prince is still in mourning black when everyone else is in festive garb for the wedding of the new king), a gown and hood for a friar (or a feigned friar like the duke in *Measure for Measure*), blue coats and tawny to distinguish the followers of rival factions, a leather apron and ruler for a carpenter (as in the opening scene of *Julius Caesar* – and in *A Midsummer Night's Dream*, where this is the only sign that Peter Quince is a carpenter), a cockle hat with staff and a pair of sandals for a pilgrim or palmer (the disguise assumed by Helen in *All's Well*), bodices and kirtles with farthingales beneath for the boys who are to be dressed as girls. A gender switch such as that of Rosalind or Jessica seems to have taken between fifty and eighty lines of dialogue – Viola does not resume her 'maiden weeds', but remains in her boy's costume to the end of *Twelfth Night* because a change would have slowed down the action at just the moment it was speeding to a climax. Henslowe's inventory also included 'a robe for to go invisible': Oberon, Puck and Ariel must have had something similar.

As the costumes appealed to the eyes, so there was music for the ears. Comedies included many songs. Desdemona's willow song, perhaps a late addition to the text, is a rare and thus exceptionally poignant example from tragedy. Trumpets and tuckets sounded for ceremonial entrances, drums denoted an army on the march. Background music could create atmosphere, as at the beginning of *Twelfth Night*, during the lovers' dialogue near the end of *The Merchant of Venice*, when the statue seemingly comes to life in

The Winter's Tale, and for the revival of Pericles and of Lear (in the Quarto text, but not the Folio). The haunting sound of the hautboy suggested a realm beyond the human, as when the god Hercules is imagined deserting Mark Antony. Dances symbolized the harmony of the end of a comedy – though in Shakespeare's world of mingled joy and sorrow, someone is usually left out of the circle.

The most important resource was, of course, the actors themselves. They needed many skills: in the words of one contemporary commentator, 'dancing, activity, music, song, elocution, ability of body, memory, skill of weapon, pregnancy of wit'. Their bodies were as significant as their voices. Hamlet tells the player to 'suit the action to the word, the word to the action': moments of strong emotion, known as 'passions', relied on a repertoire of dramatic gestures as well as a modulation of the voice. When Titus Andronicus has had his hand chopped off, he asks 'How can I grace my talk, / Wanting a hand to give it action?' A pen portrait of 'The Character of an Excellent Actor' by the dramatist John Webster is almost certainly based on his impression of Shakespeare's leading man, Richard Burbage: 'By a full and significant action of body, he charms our attention: sit in a full theatre, and you will think you see so many lines drawn from the circumference of so many ears, whiles the actor is the centre . . . .'

Though Burbage was admired above all others, praise was also heaped upon the apprentice players whose alto voices fitted them for the parts of women. A spectator at Oxford in 1610 records how the audience were reduced to tears by the pathos of Desdemona's death. The puritans who fumed about the biblical prohibition upon cross-dressing and the encouragement to sodomy constituted by the sight of an adult male kissing a teenage boy on stage were a small minority. Little is known, however, about the characteristics of the leading apprentices in Shakespeare's company. It may perhaps be inferred that one was a lot taller than the other, since Shakespeare often wrote for a pair of female friends, one tall and fair, the other short and dark (Helena and Hermia, Rosalind and Celia, Beatrice and Hero).

We know little about Shakespeare's own acting roles – an early allusion indicates that he often took royal parts, and a venerable tradition gives him old Adam in *As You Like It* and the ghost of old

King Hamlet. Save for Burbage's lead roles and the generic part of the clown, all such castings are mere speculation. We do not even know for sure whether the original Falstaff was Will Kempe or another actor who specialized in comic roles, Thomas Pope.

Kempe left the company in early 1599. Tradition has it that he fell out with Shakespeare over the matter of excessive improvisation. He was replaced by Robert Armin, who was less of a clown and more of a cerebral wit: this explains the difference between such parts as Lancelet Gobbo and Dogberry, which were written for Kempe, and the more verbally sophisticated Feste and Lear's Fool, which were written for Armin.

One thing that is clear from surviving 'plots' or story-boards of plays from the period is that a degree of doubling was necessary. *2 Henry VI* has over sixty speaking parts, but more than half of the characters only appear in a single scene and most scenes have only six to eight speakers. At a stretch, the play could be performed by thirteen actors. When Thomas Platter saw *Julius Caesar* at the Globe in 1599, he noted that there were about fifteen. Why doesn't Paris go to the Capulet ball in *Romeo and Juliet*? Perhaps because he was doubled with Mercutio, who does. In *The Winter's Tale*, Mamillius might have come back as Perdita and Antigonus been doubled by Camillo, making the partnership with Paulina at the end a very neat touch. Titania and Oberon are often played by the same pair as Hippolyta and Theseus, suggesting a symbolic matching of the rulers of the worlds of night and day, but it is questionable whether there would have been time for the necessary costume changes. As so often, one is left in a realm of tantalizing speculation.

THE KING'S MAN

On Queen Elizabeth's death in 1603, the new king, James I, who had held the Scottish throne as James VI since he had been an infant, immediately took the Lord Chamberlain's Men under his direct patronage. Henceforth they would be the King's Men, and for the rest of Shakespeare's career they were favoured with far more court performances than any of their rivals. There even seem to have been rumours early in the reign that Shakespeare and Burbage were being considered for knighthoods, an unprecedented honour for mere actors – and one that in the event was not accorded to a member of the profession for nearly three hundred years, when the title was bestowed upon Henry Irving, the leading Shakespearean actor of Queen Victoria's reign.

Shakespeare's productivity rate slowed in the Jacobean years, not because of age or some personal trauma, but because there were frequent outbreaks of plague, causing the theatres to be closed for long periods. The King's Men were forced to spend many months on the road. Between November 1603 and 1608, they were to be found at various towns in the south and Midlands, though Shakespeare probably did not tour with them by this time. He had bought a large house back home in Stratford and was accumulating other property. He may indeed have stopped acting soon after the new king took the throne. With the London theatres closed so much of the time and a large repertoire on the stocks, Shakespeare seems to have focused his energies on writing a few long and complex tragedies that could have been played on demand at court: *Othello*, *King Lear*, *Antony and Cleopatra*, *Coriolanus* and *Cymbeline* are among his longest and poetically grandest plays. *Macbeth* only survives in a shorter text, which shows signs of adaptation after Shakespeare's death. The bitterly satirical *Timon of Athens*, apparently a collaboration with Thomas Middleton that may have failed on the stage, also belongs to this period. In comedy, too, he wrote longer and morally darker works than in the Elizabethan period, pushing at the very bounds of the form in *Measure for Measure* and *All's Well that Ends Well*.

From 1608 onwards, when the King's Men began occupying the indoor Blackfriars playhouse (as a winter house, meaning that they only used the outdoor Globe in summer?), Shakespeare turned to a more romantic style. His company had a great success with a revived and altered version of an old pastoral play called *Mucedorus*. It even featured a bear. The younger dramatist John Fletcher, meanwhile, sometimes working in collaboration with Francis Beaumont, was pioneering a new style of tragicomedy, a mix of romance and royalism laced with intrigue and pastoral excursions. Shakespeare experimented with this idiom in *Cymbeline* and it was presumably with his blessing that Fletcher eventually took over as the King's Men's company dramatist. The two writers apparently collaborated on three plays in the years 1612–14: a lost romance called *Cardenio* (based on the love-madness of a character in Cervantes' *Don Quixote*), *Henry VIII* (originally staged with the title 'All is True'), and *The Two Noble Kinsmen*, a dramatization of Chaucer's 'Knight's Tale'. These were written after Shakespeare's two final solo-authored plays, *The Winter's Tale*, a self-consciously old-fashioned work dramatizing the pastoral romance of his old enemy Robert Greene, and *The Tempest*, which at one and the same time drew together multiple theatrical traditions, diverse reading and contemporary interest in the fate of a ship that had been wrecked on the way to the New World.

The collaborations with Fletcher suggest that Shakespeare's career ended with a slow fade rather than the sudden retirement supposed by the nineteenth-century Romantic critics who read Prospero's epilogue to *The Tempest* as Shakespeare's personal farewell to his art. In the last few years of his life Shakespeare certainly spent more of his time in Stratford-upon-Avon, where he became further involved in property dealing and litigation. But his London life also continued. In 1613 he made his first major London property purchase: a freehold house in the Blackfriars district, close to his company's indoor theatre. *The Two Noble Kinsmen* may have been written as late as 1614, and Shakespeare was in London on business a little over a year before he died of an unknown cause at home in Stratford-upon-Avon in 1616, probably on his fifty-second birthday.

About half the sum of his works were published in his lifetime, in texts of variable quality. A few years after his death, his fellow-actors began putting together an authorized edition of his complete *Comedies, Histories and Tragedies*. It appeared in 1623, in large 'Folio' format. This collection of thirty-six plays gave Shakespeare his immortality. In the words of his fellow-dramatist Ben Jonson, who contributed two poems of praise at the start of the Folio, the body of his work made him 'a monument without a tomb':

And art alive still while thy book doth live
And we have wits to read and praise to give ...
He was not of an age, but for all time!

SHAKESPEARE'S WORKS:
A Chronology

1589–91	*? Arden of Faversham* (possible part authorship)
1589–92	*The Taming of the Shrew*
1589–92	*? Edward the Third* (possible part authorship)
1591	*The Second Part of Henry the Sixth*, originally called *The First Part of the Contention betwixt the Two Famous Houses of York and Lancaster* (element of co-authorship possible)
1591	*The Third Part of Henry the Sixth*, originally called *The True Tragedy of Richard Duke of York* (element of co-authorship probable)
1591–92	*The Two Gentlemen of Verona*
1591–92 perhaps revised 1594	*The Lamentable Tragedy of Titus Andronicus* (probably co-written with, or revising an earlier version by, George Peele)
1592	*The First Part of Henry the Sixth*, probably with Thomas Nashe and others
1592/94	*King Richard the Third*
1593	*Venus and Adonis* (poem)
1593–94	*The Rape of Lucrece* (poem)
1593–1608	*Sonnets* (154 poems, published 1609 with *A Lover's Complaint*, a poem of disputed authorship)
1592–94/ 1600–03	*Sir Thomas More* (a single scene for a play originally by Anthony Munday, with other revisions by Henry Chettle, Thomas Dekker and Thomas Heywood)
1594	*The Comedy of Errors*
1595	*Love's Labour's Lost*

1595–97	*Love's Labour's Won* (a lost play, unless the original title for another comedy)
1595–96	*A Midsummer Night's Dream*
1595–96	*The Tragedy of Romeo and Juliet*
1595–96	*King Richard the Second*
1595–97	*The Life and Death of King John* (possibly earlier)
1596–97	*The Merchant of Venice*
1596–97	*The First Part of Henry the Fourth*
1597–98	*The Second Part of Henry the Fourth*
1598	*Much Ado about Nothing*
1598–99	*The Passionate Pilgrim* (20 poems, some not by Shakespeare)
1599	*The Life of Henry the Fifth*
1599	'To the Queen' (epilogue for a court performance)
1599	*As You Like It*
1599	*The Tragedy of Julius Caesar*
1600–01	*The Tragedy of Hamlet, Prince of Denmark* (perhaps revising an earlier version)
1600–01	*The Merry Wives of Windsor* (perhaps revising version of 1597–99)
1601	'Let the Bird of Loudest Lay' (poem, known since 1807 as 'The Phoenix and Turtle' (turtle-dove))
1601	*Twelfth Night, or What You Will*
1601–02	*The Tragedy of Troilus and Cressida*
1604	*The Tragedy of Othello, the Moor of Venice*
1604	*Measure for Measure*
1605	*All's Well that Ends Well*
1605	*The Life of Timon of Athens*, with Thomas Middleton
1605–06	*The Tragedy of King Lear*
1605–08	? contribution to *The Four Plays in One* (lost, except for *A Yorkshire Tragedy*, mostly by Thomas Middleton)
1606	*The Tragedy of Macbeth* (surviving text has additional scenes by Thomas Middleton)
1606–07	*The Tragedy of Antony and Cleopatra*
1608	*The Tragedy of Coriolanus*

1608	*Pericles, Prince of Tyre*, with George Wilkins
1610	*The Tragedy of Cymbeline*
1611	*The Winter's Tale*
1611	*The Tempest*
1612–13	*Cardenio*, with John Fletcher (survives only in later adaptation called *Double Falsehood* by Lewis Theobald)
1613	*Henry VIII (All is True)*, with John Fletcher
1613–14	*The Two Noble Kinsmen*, with John Fletcher

KINGS AND QUEENS OF ENGLAND: From the History Plays to Shakespeare's Lifetime

	Lifespan	*Reign*
Angevins:		
Henry II	1133–1189	1154–1189
Richard I	1157–1199	1189–1199
John	1166–1216	1199–1216
Henry III	1207–1272	1216–1272
Edward I	1239–1307	1272–1307
Edward II	1284–1327	1307–1327 deposed
Edward III	1312–1377	1327–1377
Richard II	1367–1400	1377–1399 deposed
Lancastrians:		
Henry IV	1367–1413	1399–1413
Henry V	1387–1422	1413–1422
Henry VI	1421–1471	1422–1461 and 1470–1471
Yorkists:		
Edward IV	1442–1483	1461–1470 and 1471–1483
Edward V	1470–1483	1483 not crowned: deposed and assassinated
Richard III	1452–1485	1483–1485
Tudors:		
Henry VII	1457–1509	1485–1509
Henry VIII	1491–1547	1509–1547
Edward VI	1537–1553	1547–1553

	Lifespan	*Reign*
Jane	1537–1554	1553 not crowned: deposed and executed
Mary I	1516–1558	1553–1558
Philip of Spain	1527–1598	1554–1558 co-regent with Mary
Elizabeth I	1533–1603	1558–1603
Stuart:		
James I	1566–1625	1603–1625 James VI of Scotland (1567–1625)

THE HISTORY BEHIND THE HISTORIES: A Chronology

Square brackets indicate events that happen just outside a play's timescale but are mentioned in the play.

Date	Event	Location	Play
22 May 1200	Truce between King John and Philip Augustus	Le Goulet, Normandy	*King John*
Apr 1203	Death of Arthur	Rouen	*King John*
1209	Pope Innocent III excommunicates King John		*King John*
18/19 Oct 1216	Death of King John	Swineshead, Lincolnshire	*King John*
Apr–Sep 1398	Quarrel, duel and exile of Bullingbrook and Mowbray	Coventry	*Richard II*
3 Feb 1399	Death of John of Gaunt	Leicester	*Richard II*
Jul 1399	Bullingbrook lands in England	Ravenspur, Yorkshire	*Richard II*
Aug 1399	Richard II captured by Bullingbrook	Wales	*Richard II*
30 Sep 1399	Richard II abdicates	London	*Richard II*
13 Oct 1399	Coronation of Henry IV	London	*Richard II*
Jan–Feb 1400	Death of Richard II	Pontefract Castle	*Richard II*
22 Jun 1402	Owen Glendower captures Edmund Mortimer	Bryn Glas, Wales	*1 Henry IV*
14 Sep 1402	Henry Percy defeats Scottish army	Homildon Hill, Yorkshire	*1 Henry IV*

Date	Event	Location	Play
21 Jul 1403	Battle of Shrewsbury; death of Henry Percy (Hotspur)	Battlefield, near Shrewsbury, Shropshire	*1 & 2 Henry IV*
Feb 1405	Tripartite Indenture between Owen Glendower, Edmund Mortimer and Northumberland (Henry Percy)	Bangor	*1 Henry IV*
May–Jun 1405	Rebellion of Archbishop of York (Richard Scroop), Earl of Norfolk (Thomas Mowbray) and Lord Bardolph	Yorkshire	*2 Henry IV*
8 Jun 1405	Trial and execution of Archbishop of York and Earl of Norfolk	York	*2 Henry IV*
20 Mar 1413	Death of Henry IV	Westminster Abbey	*2 Henry IV*
9 Apr 1413	Coronation of Henry V	Westminster Abbey	*2 Henry IV*
c.1415–16?	Death of Owen Glendower	Wales?	*2 Henry IV*
Early Aug 1415	Execution of Earl of Cambridge, Lord Scroop and Sir Thomas Grey	Southampton	*Henry V*
14 Aug–22 Sep 1415	Siege of Harfleur	Harfleur, Normandy	*Henry V*
25 Oct 1415	Battle of Agincourt	Agincourt, Pas de Calais	*Henry V*
31 Aug 1422	Death of Henry V	Bois de Vincennes, near Paris	*1 Henry VI*
18 Jan 1425	Death of Edmund Mortimer	Ireland	*1 Henry VI*
Oct 1428–May 1429	Siege of Orléans	Orléans	*1 Henry VI*
17 Oct 1428	Death of Lord Salisbury	Orléans	*1 Henry VI*
18 Jun 1429	Capture of Lord Talbot at battle of Patay	Patay, near Orléans	*1 Henry VI*
18 Jul 1429	Coronation of Charles VII	Rheims Cathedral	*1 Henry VI*

Date	Event	Location	Play
6 Nov 1429	Coronation of Henry VI as King of England	Westminster Abbey	[1 Henry VI]
23 May 1430	Capture of Joan of Arc	Compiègne, near Soissons	1 Henry VI
30 May 1431	Execution of Joan of Arc	Saint-Ouen, near Paris	1 Henry VI
16 Dec 1431	Coronation of Henry VI as King of France	Notre Dame Cathedral, Paris	1 Henry VI
14 Sep 1435	Death of Duke of Bedford	Rouen	1 Henry VI
Summer–Autumn 1441	Arrest and trial of Eleanor Cobham and accomplices	London	2 Henry VI
20 May 1442	Lord Talbot created Earl of Shrewsbury	Paris	1 Henry VI
23 Apr 1445	Marriage of Henry VI and Margaret of Anjou	Titchfield, Hampshire	2 Henry VI
23 Feb 1447	Death of Humphrey, Duke of Gloucester	Bury St Edmunds	2 Henry VI
11 Apr 1447	Death of Cardinal Beaufort	Winchester	2 Henry VI
2 May 1450	Death of Earl of Suffolk	English Channel	2 Henry VI
Jun–Jul 1450	Rebellion of Jack Cade	Kent and London	2 Henry VI
Spring 1452	Richard, Duke of York, marches on London	London	2 Henry VI
17 Jul 1453	Death of Lord Talbot at battle of Cantillon	Cantillon, Gascony	1 Henry VI
22 May 1455	First battle of St Albans	St Albans, Hertfordshire	2 Henry VI
10 Jul 1460	Battle of Northampton	Northampton	[3 Henry VI]
Oct 1460	Richard, Duke of York, holds Parliament	London	3 Henry VI
30 Dec 1460	Battle of Wakefield	Wakefield, Yorkshire	3 Henry VI
2 Feb 1461	Battle of Mortimer's Cross	Near Wigmore, Herefordshire	3 Henry VI
29 Mar 1461	Battle of Towton	Near Tadcaster, Yorkshire	3 Henry VI

Date	Event	Location	Play
28 Jun 1461	Coronation of Edward IV	Westminster Abbey	*3 Henry VI*
1 May 1464	Marriage of Edward IV and Elizabeth Woodville	Northamptonshire	*3 Henry VI*
Jul 1465	Henry VI captured	Lancashire	*3 Henry VI*
26 Jul 1469	Battle of Edgecote Moor	Near Banbury, Oxfordshire	*3 Henry VI*
Oct 1470–Apr/May 1471	Readeption (restoration) of Henry VI	London	*3 Henry VI*
14 Apr 1471	Battle of Barnet; death of Warwick	Barnet, near London	*3 Henry VI*
4 May 1471	Battle of Tewkesbury; death of Edward, Prince of Wales	Tewkesbury, Gloucestershire	*3 Henry VI*
21 May 1471	Death of Henry VI	Tower of London	*3 Henry VI*
12 Jul 1472	Marriage of Richard, Duke of Gloucester, to Anne	Westminster Abbey	*Richard III*
18 Feb 1478	Death of Duke of Clarence	Tower of London	*Richard III*
9 Apr 1483	Death of Edward IV	Westminster	*Richard III*
Jun 1483	Death of Lord Hastings	Tower of London	*Richard III*
6 Jul 1483	Coronation of Richard III	Westminster Abbey	*Richard III*
2 Nov 1483	Death of Duke of Buckingham	Salisbury	*Richard III*
16 Mar 1485	Death of Queen Anne	Westminster	*Richard III*
22 Aug 1485	Battle of Bosworth Field	Leicestershire	*Richard III*
30 Oct 1485	Coronation of Henry VII	Westminster Abbey	[*Richard III*]
18 Jan 1486	Marriage of Henry VII and Elizabeth of York	Westminster Abbey	[*Richard III*]
Jun 1520	Meeting of Henry VIII and Francis I	'Field of the Cloth of Gold', near Calais, France	[*Henry VIII*]

Date	Event	Location	Play
17 May 1521	Death of Duke of Buckingham	Tower Hill, London	*Henry VIII*
29 Nov 1530	Death of Wolsey	Leicester	*Henry VIII*
25 Jan 1533	Marriage of Henry VIII and Anne Bullen (Boleyn)	Whitehall	*Henry VIII*
1 Jun 1533	Coronation of Anne Bullen (Boleyn)	Westminster Abbey	*Henry VIII*
7 Sep 1533	Birth of Princess Elizabeth	Greenwich Palace	*Henry VIII*
10 Sep 1533	Christening of Princess Elizabeth	Greenwich Palace	*Henry VIII*

FURTHER READING AND VIEWING

CRITICAL APPROACHES

Berman, Ronald, ed., *Twentieth Century Interpretations of Henry V* (1968). Useful collection of early twentieth-century studies.

Berry, Ralph, *Changing Styles in Shakespeare* (1981). Chapter on *Henry V*, pp. 67–83, argues that views of the play changed from being a 'nationalist epic' after the First World War.

Bloom, Harold, ed., *William Shakespeare's Henry V* (1988). Interestingly varied collection of critical essays.

Brennan, Anthony, *Henry V*, Harvester New Critical Introductions to Shakespeare (1992). Well-balanced introduction covering text and performance.

Hall, Joan Lord, *Henry V: A Guide to the Play* (1997). Useful broad introduction covering history, themes, structure and performance.

Hattaway, Michael, ed., *The Cambridge Companion to Shakespeare's History Plays* (2002). Another good starting point.

McEachern, Claire, *The Poetics of English Nationhood, 1590–1612* (1996). Strong 'new historicist' reading of several relevant works, with emphasis on Reformation context.

Meron, Theodor, *Henry's Wars and Shakespeare's Laws: Perspectives on the Law of War in the Later Middle Ages* (1993). Detailed historical account.

Quinn, Michael, ed., *Shakespeare: Henry V*, Casebook Series (1969). Useful compilation of early criticism and significant early twentieth-century studies.

Rabkin, Norman, *Shakespeare and the Problem of Meaning* (1981). Excellent reading of the play's ambivalence.

Rackin, Phyllis, *Stages of History: Shakespeare's English Chronicles* (1990). Particularly strong on the women in the history plays.

Rossiter, A. P., *Angel with Horns and other Shakespeare Lectures* (1961). Sane, balanced essays on the history plays.

Saccio, Peter, *Shakespeare's English Kings: History, Chronicle, and Drama* (1977). Handy comparison with sources and actual history.

Woodcock, Matthew, *Shakespeare: Henry V* (2008). Detailed discussion of play's critical history from early modern period to present day.

THE PLAY IN PERFORMANCE

Beauman, Sally, ed., *The Royal Shakespeare Company Centenary Production of Henry V* (1976). Detailed account of production with annotated text.

Branagh, Kenneth, *Henry V by William Shakespeare: A Screen Adaptation* (1989). Screenplay of Branagh's film plus introduction.

Brooke, Michael, 'Henry V on Screen', www.screenonline.org.uk/tv/ id/1048671/index.html. Valuable overview of film and TV versions.

Ewert, Kevin, *Henry V: Guide to the Text and its Theatrical Life*, Shakespeare Handbooks Series (2006). Useful introduction with detailed commentary and discussion of key productions.

Hoenselaars, Ton, ed., *Shakespeare's History Plays: Performance, Translation and Adaptation in Britain and Abroad* (2004). Chapter 3, 'A French History of Henry V' by Jean-Michel Déprats, plus numerous passing references.

Holland, Peter, *English Shakespeares: Shakespeare on the English Stage in the 1990s* (1997). Perceptive, readable overview.

Jackson, Russell and Smallwood, Robert, eds, *Players of Shakespeare 2* (1988). Includes Kenneth Branagh discussing playing Henry, pp. 93–106.

Loehlin, James N., *Henry V*, Shakespeare in Performance (1996). Detailed account of performances including Olivier and Branagh

films, BBC version, English Shakespeare Company and RSC 1975/
1984.

O'Connor, John, *Shakespearean Afterlives: Ten Characters with a Life of Their Own* (2003). Chapter 2 is on *Henry V* with the focus on film representations.

Parsons, Keith and Pamela Mason, eds, *Shakespeare in Performance* (1995). *Henry V*, pp. 83–8 with useful introduction by Niky Rathbone, lavishly illustrated.

Smith, Emma, ed., *King Henry V*, Shakespeare in Production (2002). Detailed stage history and text of play annotated with stage directions of important productions.

AVAILABLE ON DVD

Henry V, directed by Laurence Olivier (1944, DVD 2003). Starring Olivier as Henry, magnificent pageant dedicated to the Commandos and Airborne Troops who spearheaded the D-Day landings, with brilliant score by William Walton.

Chimes at Midnight, directed by Orson Welles (1965, DVD 2000). Condenses all the Falstaff material from both parts of *Henry IV* plus *Henry V* and *The Merry Wives of Windsor*. Multi-award nominated, with a star-studded cast, the whole thing as eccentric and brilliant as Welles' own performance in the part of Falstaff.

The Wars of the Roses, directed by Michael Bogdanov (1989, DVD 2005). Recording of English Shakespeare Company's eclectic stage production.

Henry V, directed by Kenneth Branagh (1989, DVD 2002). Multi-award winning: starring Branagh as Henry, grittier and darker than Olivier version but equally impressive.

REFERENCES

1 *The Times*, London, 26 November 1803.
2 *The Times*, London, 26 November 1803.
3 Anthony Brennan, *Harvester New Critical Introductions to Shakespeare: Henry V* (1992), p. xvii.
4 Brennan, *Henry V*, p. xviii.
5 *The Athenaeum*, No. 1640, 2 April 1859, pp. 459–60.
6 Brennan, *Henry V*, p. xix.
7 *Illustrated London News*, XXXIV, 967, 2 April 1859, p. 331.
8 Richard Foulkes, p. 28, quoted in James N. Loehlin, *Shakespeare in Performance: Henry V* (1996), p. 21.
9 Loehlin, *Henry V*, p. 21.
10 George C. D. Odell, *Annals of the New York Stage, 1875–1879*, Vol. X (1938), pp. 118–69.
11 Henry James, *The Scenic Art: Notes on Acting & the Drama, 1872–1901*, ed. Allan Wade (1948, reprinted 1957), pp. 22–7.
12 Norman Hapgood, *The Stage in America 1897–1900* (1901), pp. 174–205.
13 Brennan, *Henry V*, p. xxi, quotes the *Stratford Herald* review for 1902 which relates the spirit of Henry's troops with that of 'Baden-Powell and the defenders of Mafeking'.
14 Brennan, *Henry V*, p. xx.
15 Brennan, *Henry V*, p. xxi.
16 Brennan, *Henry V*, p. xxiii.
17 James Agate, *Brief Chronicles: A Survey of the Plays of Shakespeare and the Elizabethans in Actual Performance* (1943), p. 113.
18 Laurence Olivier, *Confessions of an Actor* (1982), pp. 79–80.
19 Gordon Crosse, *Shakespearean Playgoing, 1890–1952* (1953), p. 105.
20 Brennan, *Henry V*, pp. xxiii–xxiv.
21 Brennan, *Henry V*, p. xxv.
22 T. C. Worsley, *New Statesman and Nation*, XLII, 1078, 3 November 1951, pp. 489–90.
23 Richard David, 'Shakespeare's History Plays Epic or Drama?', *Shakespeare Survey*, 6 (1953), pp. 129–39.
24 Brennan, *Henry V*, p. xxvi.
25 Robertson Davies, *Saturday Night*, 71, 9, 7 July 1956, pp. 7–8.
26 J. G. Weightman, *The Twentieth Century*, CLX, 956, October 1956, pp. 344–5.
27 Weightman, *The Twentieth Century*.
28 Robertson Davies, *Saturday Night*, 71, 9, 7 July 1956, p. 8.
29 Brennan, *Henry V*, p. xxvii.
30 Bernard Levin, *Daily Express*, 26 February 1960.
31 Brennan, *Henry V*, pp. xxvii–xxviii, citing Tynan (1967), p. 154.
32 Brennan, *Henry V*, p. xxviii.
33 Brennan, *Henry V*, p. xxix.

34 Julius Novick, *Village Voice*, XXI, 28, 12 July 1976, p. 111.
35 Novick, *Village Voice*, p. 111.
36 Brennan, *Henry V*, p. xxxi.
37 Ruth Morse, *Times Literary Supplement*, 5055 (18 February 2000), p. 19.
38 Morse, *Times Literary Supplement*, p. 19.
39 Susannah Clapp, *Observer*, 18 May 2003.
40 Alistair Macaulay, *Financial Times*, 14 May 2003.
41 Ben Brantley, *New York Times*, 16 July 2003.
42 James, *The Scenic Art*, pp. 22–7.
43 Edgar Anstey, *Spectator*, 173, 6075, 1 December 1944, p. 503.
44 Robert Shaunessy, 'The Last Post: Henry V, War Culture and the Postmodern Shakespeare', *Theatre Survey*, 39, 1 (May 1998): pp. 41–61.
45 Philip French, *Observer*, 8 October 1989.
46 French, *Observer*, 8 October 1989.
47 Kenneth S. Rothwell, 'Kenneth Branagh's "Henry V": The Gilt in the Crown Re-Examined', *Comparative Drama*, 24, 2, Summer 1990, pp. 173–8.
48 John Ramsden, 'This story shall the good man tell his son . . .', *Henry V*, RSC programme, 1994.
49 Loehlin, *Henry V*.
50 Benedict Nightingale, *The Times*, London, 12 May 1994.
51 Michael Billington, *Guardian*, 12 May 1994.
52 'War is Sown from War', condensed from Erasmus' Essay on 'Beginning War' (1540), *Henry V*, RSC programme, 1965.
53 Brennan, *Henry V*, p.34.
54 Loehlin, *Henry V*.
55 Rhoda Koenig, *Independent*, 4 September 2000.
56 Charles Spencer, *Daily Telegraph*, 4 September 2000.
57 Catherine Bates, *Times Literary Supplement*, 15 September 2000.
58 Robert Speaight, *Shakespeare Quarterly*, XV, 4, Autumn 1964.
59 Gareth Lloyd Evans, 'Shakespeare, the Twentieth Century and "Behaviourism"', *Shakespeare Survey*, 20 (1967).
60 Michael Billington, *Guardian*, 29 March 1984.
61 Benedict Nightingale, *The Times*, London, 13 September 1997.
62 Rex Gibson, *Times Educational Supplement*, 19 September 1997.
63 Peter Holland, *English Shakespeares: Shakespeare on the English Stage in the 1990s* (1997).
64 Holland, *English Shakespeares*.
65 Jan Kott, *Shakespeare our Contemporary* (1964).
66 Ron Daniels in interview with Heather Neill, *Times Educational Supplement*, 19 September 1997.
67 Edward Hall talks to Terry Grimley About Henry V, *Birmingham Post*, 19 September 2000.
68 Bates, *Times Literary Supplement*.
69 Charles Peachment, *Sunday Telegraph*, 15 September 1994.
70 Paul Taylor, *Independent*, 13 September 1997.
71 Irving Wardle, *The Times*, London, 30 March 1984.
72 Ralph Berry, *Changing Styles in Shakespeare* (1981).
73 Holland, *English Shakespeares*.
74 Nightingale, *The Times*, 12 May 1994.
75 Michael Coveney, *Financial Times*, 29 March 1984.
76 Wardle, *The Times*, 30 March 1984.
77 Peter Hall, 'The Empirical Empire', *Henry V*, RSC programme, 1965.

78 Sally Beauman, ed., *The Royal Shakespeare Company Centenary Production of Henry V* (1976).

79 Ralph Berry, *Changing Styles in Shakespeare*, 1981.

80 Peter Hall, 'The Empirical Empire', in *Henry V*, RSC programme, 1964.

81 Carole Woddis, *London Theatre News*, 1 September 2000.

82 Alan Howard on Henry V from 'The Player King', in Judith Cook, *Shakespeare's Players* (1983).

83 Berry, *Changing Styles in Shakespeare* (1981), pp. 79–80.

84 Irving Wardle, *The Times*, London, 22 January 1976.

85 Benedict Nightingale, *New Statesman*, 89, 2300, 18 April 1975.

86 Spencer, *Daily Telegraph*, 4 September 2000.

87 John Gross, *Sunday Telegraph*, 3 September 2000.

88 Ron Daniels in interview with Heather Neill, *Times Educational Supplement*, 19 September 1997.

89 Taylor, *Independent*, 13 September 1997.

90 James Treadwell, *Spectator*, 27 September 1997.

91 Taylor, *Independent*, 13 September 1997.

92 *Plays and Players*, October 1997.

93 Nightingale, *The Times*, London, 12 May 1994.

94 Peter Holland, *English Shakespeares: Shakespeare on the English Stage in the 1990s* (1997).

95 Michael Billington, *Guardian*, 29 September 1984.

96 Wardle, *Times*, London, 30 March 1984.

97 Alan Howard on playing Henry V.

98 Irving Wardle, *The Times*, London, 13 July 1977.

ACKNOWLEDGEMENTS AND PICTURE CREDITS

Preparation of '*Henry V* in Performance' was assisted by a generous grant from the CAPITAL Centre (Creativity and Performance in Teaching and Learning) of the University of Warwick for research in the RSC archive at the Shakespeare Birthplace Trust. The Arts and Humanities Research Council (AHRC) funded a term's research leave that enabled Jonathan Bate to work on 'The Director's Cut'. Kenneth Branagh's interview is based, with his kind permission, on earlier interviews he has given about his stage performance and film (thanks to Jan Sewell for editing the material).

Picture research by Michelle Morton. Grateful acknowledgement is made to the Shakespeare Birthplace Trust for assistance with picture research (special thanks to Helen Hargest) and reproduction fees.

Images of RSC productions are supplied by the Shakespeare Centre Library and Archive, Stratford-upon-Avon. This Library, maintained by the Shakespeare Birthplace Trust, holds the most important collection of Shakespeare material in the UK, including the Royal Shakespeare Company's official archive. It is open to the public free of charge.

For more information see www.shakespeare.org.uk.

1. Directed by Dorothy Green (1946) Angus McBean © Royal Shakespeare Company
2. Directed by John Barton and Trevor Nunn (1964) Reg Wilson © Royal Shakespeare Company
3. Directed by Adrian Noble (1984) Joe Cocks Studio Collection © Shakespeare Birthplace Trust

4. Directed by Terry Hands (1975) Joe Cocks Studio Collection © Shakespeare Birthplace Trust
5. Directed by Adrian Noble (1984) Joe Cocks Studio Collection © Shakespeare Birthplace Trust
6. Directed by Nicholas Hytner (2003) © Donald Cooper/photostage. co.uk
7. Directed by Michael Boyd (2007) Ellie Kurttz © Royal Shakespeare Company
8. Directed by Ed Hall (2000) © Donald Cooper/photostage.co.uk
9. Reconstructed Elizabethan Playhouse © Charcoalblue

FROM THE ROYAL SHAKESPEARE COMPANY AND MACMILLAN

PB: 9780230243804   PB: 9780230243828   PB: 9780230243866   PB: 9780230243842

MORE HIGHLIGHTS IN THE RSC SHAKESPEARE SERIES

PB: 9780230576223   PB: 9780230232105   PB: 9780230232136   PB: 9780230232150   PB: 9780230232082

PB: 9780230576148   PB: 9780230576209   PB: 9780230576162   PB: 9780230576186   PB: 9780230576247

PB: 9780230217850   PB: 9780230217874   PB: 9780230217898   PB: 9780230217911   PB: 9780230221116   PB: 9780230200951

AVAILABLE IN ALL GOOD BOOKSHOPS OR TO ORDER ONLINE VISIT:
www.rscshakespeare.co.uk